CO

SPIRITS

Frontispiece: 'I borrowed from a local taxidermist every bird and beast that he possessed. These I piled upon the table, and the audience, concluding that I had shot them all, looked upon me with great respect.' (*City of Westminster: Sherlock Holmes Collection, Marylebone Library*)

CONAN DOYLE

and the

SPIRITS

The spiritualist career
of Sir Arthur Conan Doyle

KELVIN I. JONES

THE AQUARIAN PRESS

First published 1989

© KELVIN I. JONES 1989

British Library Cataloguing in Publication Data

Jones, Kelvin I.
Conan Doyle and the spirits: the spiritualist career of Sir Arthur
Conan Doyle.
1. Fiction in English. Doyle, Sir, Arthur Conan, 1859-1930.
Biographies
I. Title
823'.912

ISBN 0-85030-837-2

*The Aquarian Press is part of the Thorsons Publishing Group,
Wellingborough, Northamptonshire, NN8 2RQ, England*

Typeset by Trintype, Wellingborough, Northants
Printed in Great Britain by Mackays of Chatham, Kent

1 3 5 7 9 10 8 6 4 2

Contents

Acknowledgements

My thanks are due to the Society for Psychical Research, whose assistance has been invaluable and from whose archives I have quoted. I should also like to thank Owen Dudley Edwards, Geoffrey Stavert and Richard Lancelyn Green, all of whom have been of invaluable assistance to me in their various ways.

CHAPTER 1

An Unusual Childhood

> If we could conceive a race of beings which were constructed
> in material which threw out shorter or longer vibrations, they
> would be invisible unless we could tune ourselves up or tone
> them down. It is exactly that power of tuning up and
> adapting itself to other vibrations which constitutes a clair-
> voyant, and there is nothing scientifically impossible, so far
> as I can see, in some people seeing that which is invisible to
> others.[1]

Sir Arthur Conan Doyle wrote these words in 1922 in *The
Coming of the Fairies*, a book which provoked a storm of
controversy and which was to mar his credibility as a
popular writer. The very notion that the creator of the
perfect reasoning machine, Sherlock Holmes, should sustain
a belief in 'invisible beings' seemed utterly incomprehensible to the man in the street. Yet the ancestors of this
remarkable and complex man would probably not have
raised an eyebrow. Throughout his life the twin worlds of
the real and the unseen did battle in the mind of Arthur
Ignatius Conan Doyle. The roots of this conflict lay in the
Celtic-Catholic past which he inherited from both sides of
his family. In 1907 he told a reporter:

> My real love for letters, my instinct for story-telling, springs,
> I believe, from my mother, who is of Anglo-Celtic stock, with
> the glamour and romance of the Celt very strongly marked
> . . . In my early childhood, as far back as I can remember
> anything at all, the vivid stories which she would tell me
> stand out so clearly that they obscure the real facts of my life.
> It is not only that she was–is still–a wonderful story teller, but
> she had, I remember, an art of sinking her voice to a

horror-stricken whisper when she came to a crisis in her narrative, which makes me goosefleshy when I think of it. I am sure, looking back, that it was in attempting to emulate these stories of my childhood that I first began weaving dreams myself.[2]

The dreams that Arthur Conan Doyle wove throughout his life as writer, campaigner, and public figure in the cause of spiritualism were forged in a childhood unlike any other. Mary Doyle, his mother, had created for her young son a mythological landscape based upon her own illustrious antecedents. Young Conan Doyle's paternal side was equally rich in historical romance, and the resulting family tradition laid claim to his consciousness well before his emergence as a storyteller.

On the maternal side, Conan Doyle was descended from the Percy family of Northumberland. Through her cousins, the Scotts of Nurley, Doyle's mother was distantly related to Sir Walter Scott, whose historical romances lightened the dark days young Arthur spent at Stonyhurst, the Jesuit school. Doyle's maternal grandmother was Catherine Pack, the niece of the soldier Sir Denis Pack, the commanding general of the Scottish forces at the Battle of Waterloo. Catherine Pack's grandmother was herself a granddaughter of Mary Percy of Ballintemple, heir to the Irish branch of the Northumberland house. In the mid-seventeenth century the Rev. Richard Pack, head of Kilkenny College, married Mary Percy and thus combined a unique historical tradition.

Despite this remarkable blend of ancestry Catherine Pack was by no means a rich woman when she came to live in Edinburgh with her granddaughter, Mary Foley, in the 1850s. It was therefore something of a relief to her to be able to rent out part of her flat to a paying guest, a fellow citizen of Ireland sent from London to pursue his career as an artist. It was here that Mary Foley met Charles Doyle, Arthur Conan Doyle's father-to-be.

Charles Doyle himself possessed a rich and illustrious ancestry. Like many Irish Catholic families of note, the Doyles' genealogical tree was complex, having been subjected to a share of social and political turmoil. The Doyle coat of arms was established at Arklow in County Wicklow as far back as 1618,[3] but it is not until the seventeenth century that one is able to see the line of descent clearly emerge. As Sir Arthur pointed out in his memoirs:

The Doyles, Anglo-Norman in origin, were strong Roman Catholics. The original Doyle, or D'Oil, was a cadet-branch of the Staffordshire Doyles, which has produced Sir Francis Hastings Doyle and many other distinguished men. This cadet shared in the invasion of Ireland and was granted estates in County Wexford where a great clan rose of dependants, illegitimate children and others, all taking the feudal lord's name, just as the de Burghs founded the clan of Burke. We can only claim to be the main stem by virtue of community of character and appearance with the English Doyles and the unbroken use of the same crest and coat-of-arms.[4]

In 1668 John Doyle was dispossessed of his estates by the Duke of York. Like many Irish families, the Doyles suffered under the penal laws issued at the time of the Reformation. Even the small estate at Barracurra was removed from their grasp, and in 1762 John's grandson Richard moved to Dublin, where he began a new life as a silk merchant.[5] Richard's son, James, had two sons, the elder being John, born in 1797.

In John Doyle we see the creative and artistic element in Arthur Conan Doyle's background begin to emerge. John was a talented artist who perfected his technique of drawing under the tutelage of the Italian landscape painter Gabrielli and subsequently John Comerford, the Irish miniaturist. Leaving Dublin in 1817, John was determined to sever the links with his immediate past and travelled to London with his wife, Marianna. The Doyles lived at 17 Cambridge Terrace, just off the Edgware Road. John Doyle soon established a reputation for himself as a political satirist, and by 1829 had begun producing a series of *Political Sketches* for the Haymarket publisher, Maclean. His talent for caricature and whimsy was particularly shared by Richard, his second son, who was never formarlly taught, and whose achievement is thus even more remarkable than his father's. The Doyle family was large and probably not well off. Adelaide, the youngest daughter, died of consumption in 1844, and Francis, the third son, also died a few years later. The other five (James, Richard, Henry, Charles, and Annette) survived, the boys sharing their father's aptitude for drawing. Although they led a somewhat insular existence, the family atmosphere was far from dull. Half a century later, Charles Doyle, the youngest son, still recalled the discussions on politics and religion that lasted far into the night. And from

Richard Doyle's own journal, published in 1840, it is clear that the children, along with their uncle Michael Conan, made frequent trips to the opera, concerts, exhibitions, and art galleries. The children did not go to school but had a tutor, a Mr Street, who called a few times a week. Thus the family links were kept close.

Although John Doyle died in 1868, the family tradition for artistic achievement and an obsession with the past was continued through the efforts of his four sons. The eldest, James, produced a work entitled *The Chronicles of England* illustrated with colour pictures; he also devoted thirteen years of his life to the production of *The Official Baronage of England* – a monumental contribution to genealogy. Henry Doyle later became the manager of the National Gallery in Dublin, whilst the third son, Richard Doyle, is best remembered for his famous cover design for *Punch*.

It is with Richard and his younger brother, Charles, that we observe the Celtic tradition of fantasy and the bizarre in its most acute form. Richard found that success came comparatively quickly, and it was not long before he was being instructed by *Punch's* engraver, Swain, in the technique of drawing on wood. His extraordinarily decorative and whorled initial letters, heads, and tail pieces recall some of the early illuminated manuscripts created by the Celtic monks. Such a talent soon led to several commissions, the most interesting of which were done for Grimm's *Fairy Ring* where Richard's obvious empathy with the creatures of the elf world leaps form the page. His contributions to two later works, *The King of the Golden River* (a fairy-tale written by Ruskin) and *In Fairyland*, show a similar preoccupation with the phantasmagoria of the Celtic past. Richard's own style may have been influenced to some extent by his study of the work of the Pre-Raphaelites, several of whom (Holman Hunt, Millais, and Rossetti) he had met as a much younger man in his father's house at Cambridge Terrace.

This dream-like world of the supernatural was shared by Richard's younger brother, Charles, the father of young Arthur Conan Doyle. There is no doubt that from Charles, Arthur inherited that side of his nature which possessed a keen awareness of the subliminal.

In his own memoirs Conan Doyle tells us little of his father's character and interests, for reasons which we shall later elaborate. However, he does provide us with some useful biographical material. In 1849, at the age of 17, Charles was sent from London to Edinburgh 'with a recommendation to the priests that they should guard his young morals and budding faith'. From an early age, therefore, (observes Conan Doyle), his father had been thrown into a Scottish society 'rough, hard-drinking and kindly'. We learn that 'he had some fine religious instincts, but his environment was a difficult one'.

Charles Doyle's new post was as assistant to the surveyor in the Scottish Office of Works. The job was a demanding one, comprising architectural and draughtsman's skills, and one gains the impression that it was not entered into with great enthusiasm by the young artist. However, he stayed in this position for the rest of his working life, designing among other things, the windows of Glasgow Cathedral and the fountain at Holyrood Palace in Edinburgh.[6]

In 1855 Charles married Mary Foley and the couple went to live with Catherine Pack. Eventually they had 10 children, of whom seven (five girls and two boys) survived. Of the other children, Annette was born in 1856, Arthur in 1859, Caroline (Lottie) in 1866, and Constance in 1867. A fixed income made subsequent family life very difficult. As Conan Doyle sadly recalled in his memoirs:

> In prosaic Scotland . . . he excited wonder rather than admiration, and he was only known in the larger world of London by pen and ink book-illustrations which were not his best mode of expression. The prosaic outcome was that including all his earnings my mother could never have averaged more than £300 a year on which to educate a large family. We lived in the hardy and bracing atmosphere of poverty and we each in turn did our best to help those who were younger than ourselves. My noble sister Annette, who died just as the sunshine of better days came into our lives, went out at a very early age as a governess to Portugal and sent all her salary home. My younger sisters, Lottie and Connie, both did the same thing; and I helped as I could. But it was still my dear mother who bore the long, sordid strain.[7]

The impoverished existence endured by the Doyle children was something young Arthur was never able to forget. However, it was not merely the material circumstances which alienated him from Charles Doyle. All his adult life Arthur created for himself a positive, uncompromising persona. He would never admit defeat, and in his later campaigning days we see this tough, dogged stance fully exemplified. An examination of his father's personality makes the reason for this stance abundantly clear.

Charles Doyle appears to have been a gentle and sensitive character, ill-suited to the society in which he found himself. Contemporaries have described him as 'anaemic', 'melancholy', 'dreamy and remote'. One of Sir Arthur's earliest biographers, John Dickson Carr, provides us with an interesting vignette of the artist as a married man:

> He loved fishing, because when you fished the nagging world let you alone. To his family he was becoming a dreamy, long-bearded stranger, with exquisite manners and an unbrushed top hat. Each day he trudged the long walk from home to his office at Holyrood Palace and back again to pat the children's heads absent-mindedly, as he might have stroked his pets.[8]

This picture of an other-worldly, rather shabby-genteel Edward Lear character is perhaps a little over-simplified. Arthur himself recognized a far more complex personality, yet he is prepared to be discreet about details:

> . . . he had a charm of manner and courtesy of bearing which I have seldom seen equalled. His wit was quick and playful. He possessed, also, a remarkable delicacy of mind which would give him moral courage enough to rise and leave any company which talked in a manner which was coarse . . . He was unworldly and unpractical and his family suffered for it, but even his faults were in some ways the result of his developed spirituality. He lived and died a fervent son of the Roman Catholic faith.[9]

It has taken a recent researcher to uncover the facts about Charles Doyle's unfortunate mental and physical decline – a secret which Arthur Conan Doyle kept from the outside world until his death. In 1978, Michael Bond published a hitherto unknown collection of drawings and watercolours which had been bought in a job lot of books at a house in the New Forest (probably Bignell House, Doyle's country retreat). The Doyle Diary, as it is now called, gives us a remarkable glimpse into the mind of Charles Doyle as he endured the years of incarceration at three Scottish asylums. The manuscript is invaluable to the student of Arthur Conan Doyle the spiritualist, for it gives us a fine insight into his father's 'developed spirituality'.

The facts of the matter can be briefly stated. In the late 1870s, when he was in his late forties, Charles Doyle left Edinburgh, having experienced a major upheaval in his domestic affairs. On 10 October 1893 he died in the Crighton Royal Institution, Dumfries. The cause of his death was given as 'epilepsy of many years' standing'.[10] Although Arthur Conan Doyle refers to his father's retirement in a 'Convalescent Home', in fact he spent his declining years as a patient at three lunatic asylums, the Montrose Royal (Sunnyside) 1885–9, Dumfries (where he died), and Edinburgh Royal Infirmary, where he had been admitted in January 1892 from Sunnyside. At the latter institution, Mr Bond uncovered the following information:

> Two points of great interest came to light here. The first was that Charles had been admitted to Montrose Royal in May 1885 from a nursing home called Fordoun House (some fifteen miles to the north), which specialized in the treatment of alcoholics. His admission had apparently been an abrupt one, following an incident at home in which he had managed to obtain drink, had become violent and broken a window, and had then tried to escape. He was accordingly committed to Sunnyside under a detention order, though he became a paying patient. The second point of interest was that Charles's epilepsy had appeared to develop only *after* his admission to Montrose Royal: it was normal practice for mental hospitals at this date to enquire if a new patient was epileptic, but no mention was made of the condition in Doyle's case.[11]

It seems fairly evident that Charles Doyle had, from the very outset of his career, been an unstable, sensitive, and highly-strung individual. Most probably he had begun drinking very early on in his life. After his marriage his incipient alcoholism had intensified until at last he was no longer able to sustain his family. From then onwards, he became a prisoner of circumstances and a family embarrassment. This entry in his diary conveys something of the pathos of his situation:

> I believe I am branded as Mad solely from the narrow Scotch misconception of Jokes – if Charles Lamb or Tom Hood / had been caught, they would have been treated as I am, and the latter would probably have written 'the Song of a Shirt' . . .

In compiling a book of this Sort, a great deal consists in the knack of not saying too much . . . Nor is it only in this Book / that such is the case – Many Cases are definitely Settled only by the Force of the Doubt expressed, as many things are best / expressed by stating what they are not – as for instance my claim for Sanity is not best made by Enlarging / on my common sence – as in the possession of a Certain Class of ability demonstrated in this Book / and proved by 30 years of Official Public Life, tho' unfortunately not seen by certain Members of my / own Family–I would have thought, however–er, that it would be the duty no less than the pleasure of refined / Professional Gentlemen to protect men like myself – than otherwise – and not endorse utterly false conceptions / of sanity or insanity to the detriment of the life and liberty of a harmless gentleman –[12]

The question has to be asked: to what extent did Charles Doyle influence his elder son's existence? Certainly we should expect mixed feelings in such a relationship. That there was a measure of guilt felt on Arthur's part goes without saying. Yet from examining his memoirs there is certainly a measure of respect – perhaps arising from an attempt to justify the family position. One significant fact does arise concerning the father's imaginative powers and 'spirituality'. In the 1920s, Arthur mounted an exhibition of his father's work in London. His comments are interesting:

> The critics were surprised to find what a great and original artist he was – far the greatest, in my opinion, of the family . . . His brush was concerned not only with fairies and delicate themes of the kind, but with wild and fearsome subjects so that his work had a very peculiar style of its own, mitigated by great natural humour. He was more terrible than Blake and less morbid that Wiertz.[13]

The drawings and paintings which comprise the text of the Doyle Diary are indeed bizarre. Elf-like creatures cavort among delicately drawn flowers; there are peculiar heraldic emblems posed in absurd attitudes. The distortion and dream-like quality of the work is striking. As Owen Dudley Edwards remarks, 'His mind soared and dipped among giant animals, strange sprites, confrontations of the grotesque and mundane.'[14]

Despite Arthur's remarks about his father's work lacking morbidity, this is certainly not true of the Doyle Diary.

Everywhere we look death stalks the slight figure of Charles the artist. One particular, rather terrifying sketch shows a gaunt Charles shaking the hand of a skeletal grim reaper, the latter crowned in the manner of Christ.

Like his father, Arthur Conan Doyle had an ability to disturb, though this revealed itself principally in his fiction and especially his horror stories. Several themes dominate here: revenge is a most powerful emotion and one that looms large throughout his work (including many of the Sherlock Holmes stories). In the earlier work of the author (as we shall see) sexual guilt and obsession in various forms predominate. But overriding these preoccupations is a single and universal fear: the terror of the unseen. What makes Conan Doyle's stories so powerful is the constant interplay between actuality and the bizarre. This is perhaps best seen in the later science-fiction novel *The Lost World*, where scientific theory is turned upon its head. Charles Doyle would have loved such a yarn with its gargantuan prehistoric creatures bursting through into the world of late nineteenth-century materialism.

Charles Doyle's world (a world that indirectly led to his own unfortunate severance from reality) was one of elaborate fantasy. It was a perpetual twilight in which the possible walked hand in hand with the wildly improbable. Arthur Conan Doyle's talent as a fiction writer was to convey such an illusory world under the guise of the average storyteller. Thus, put at ease by the urbane maner of the reporter Ed Malone (*The Lost World*), we are all the more ready to accept the unbelievable adventures of the larger-than-life George Edward Challenger. In the Sherlock Holmes stories we again have a fine balance between reason and irrationality. Holmes, the perfect calculating machine, an apotheosis of Victorian rationalism, does battle against the evil forces of mankind. It is an interesting and familiar scenario in Conan Doyle's work and therefore something of a surprise to find that much later in his life he largely renounced fiction to concentrate upon what he regarded as his ultimate quest: the final proof of an afterlife. Here he found willing and vociferous enemies amongst both the scientific community and the religious establishment, ready to belittle the proponents of spiritualism. To be a successful fiction writer was no longer sufficient in itself. Conan Doyle felt compelled to take on the mantle of the crusader in much the same way as the hero of his Napoleonic stories, Sir Nigel. As a youth he had immersed himself in the heroic mode in his reading of Sir Walter Scott's historical novels and Macaulay's work. In later life he found himself living out the myth. The struggle to maintain the spiritual integrity of his ancestors – even though he was regarded as 'cranky', 'easily duped', or lacking perception – was a natural consequence of the tradition which had produced him. His son Adrian understood this well when he wrote:

> With his school text books of very secondary importance, he was already steeped in the intricacies of his main pedigrees, the cadet branches of his house, the marital connections of six centuries and, fundamental to it all, as a veritable yardstick for the values of life, inoculated with the unswerving and implacable code of the ancient chivalry, with all that it implies to the personality and character of the man that was to be. His fairy stories were the pages of Froissart and De Monstrelet: his mental adventures shaped and coloured from the sources of his own ancestry. In short, we have a picture of a child living from his tenderest years in the chivalric sciences of the fifteenth century in the bosom of a family to whom pride of lineage was of infinitely greater importance than the discomforts of that comparative poverty that had come to surround them. These are facts that I learnt from my father's own lips.[15]

In Adrian's view of his father's childhood we sense Sir Arthur's own compensation for the implicit failings of Charles Doyle. To have seen his father's gradual decline into alcoholism and final incarceration in an asylum must have been traumatic. No wonder that he sought refuge in the romantic trappings of the Middle Ages, where the code of chivalry offered a framework for his own existence.

When Arthur Conan Doyle was eight he was sent to live with the sister of John Hill Burton, the historiographer-royal for Scotland. This came as a blessed relief to Arthur's mother, who feared the dire effects of her husband's increasingly difficult behaviour on her young family. Life at Liberton Bank was not all that happy for young Arthur. Years later he remembered attending Newington Academy, where he had to suffer under 'a tawse-brandishing schoolmaster of the old type . . . From the age of seven to nine I suffered under this pock-marked, one-eyed rascal who might have stepped from the pages of Dickens. In the

evenings, home and books were my sole consolation save
for week-end holidays.'

When the family moved to 3 Sciennes Hill Place in
Newington, Mary was faced with a difficult decision. If her
son remained at home he would continue to be the victim of
undesirable influences. The area was less desirable, the
children thereabouts rough and uncompromising. Conan
Doyle recalled:

> We lived in a *cul de sac* street with a very vivid life of its own
> and a fierce feud between the small boys on either side of it.
> Finally it was fought out between two champions, I repre-
> senting the poorer boys who lived in flats and my opponent
> the richer boys who lived in the opposite villas. We fought in
> the garden of one of the said villas and had an excellent
> contest of many rounds, not being strong enough to weaken
> each other.[16]

In 1868, close to despair, Mary enrolled young Arthur at
the Jesuit preparatory school, Hodder, close to Stonyhurst,
near Preston, Lancashire, making an arrangement with the
school that Arthur would only be allowed to return home in
the summer and not the customary Christmas and Easter
holidays. These were happy years for the young boy and a
relief from the grim streets of Edinburgh. Conan Doyle
wrote:

> I had two years at Hodder. The year was not broken up by the
> frequent holidays which illuminate the present educational
> period. Save for six weeks each summer, one never left the
> school. On the whole, those first two years were happy years. I
> could hold my own both in brain and strength with my
> comrades. I was fortunate enough to get under the care of a
> kindly principal, one Father Cassidy, who was more human
> than Jesuits usually are. I have always kept a warm remem-
> brance of this man and of his gentle ways to the little boys –
> young rascals many of us – who were committed to his care.[17]

The gentle affection felt by Arthur Conan Doyle for the
youthful Francis Cassidy did not extend to his subsequent
encounters at Stonyhurst. The small boy who had grown
fond of his mother and the subsequent parental surrogate
figure of Father Cassidy found the dark and rather intimidat-
ing towers of Stonyhurst difficult to adjust to, so that he was
thrown back upon his own resources and forced into the role
of storyteller. Recalling those days much later on in his
career, he wrote:

On a wet half-holiday I have been elevated on to a desk and with an audience of little boys squatting on the floor, with their chins upon their hands, I have talked myself husky over the misfortunes of my heroes. Week in and week out those unhappy men have battled and striven and groaned for the amusement of that little circle. I was bribed with pastry to continue these efforts, and I remember that I always stipulated for tarts down and strict business, which shows that I was born to be a member of the Authors' Society.[18]

It is distinctly possible that the young Conan Doyle established this considerable reputation for himself as a defence mechanism against those pupils who were only too ready to attack him on cultural grounds. He was, after all, an Irishman and a Catholic by tradition and origin whereas many of the other pupils and staff were converts to the faith. Doyle himself always showed respect to other religious creeds in his defence of spiritualism, yet the same cannot be claimed on behalf of the Stonyhurst Jesuits. The narrow intolerance exhibited by these zealous priests did not allow for the breadth of vision which the young Arthur had already drawn from his familial background. There is no doubt that Conan Doyle's subsequent shift to agnosticism in his twenties had a great deal to do with this abrupt change in his cultural background.

The routine at Stonyhurst was certainly no more nor less severe than that of the average public school of the period. Conan Doyle did not take issue with this: it was the blind dogma with which he was later to disagree so violently:

Corporal punishment was severe, and I can speak with feelings as I think few, if any, boys of my time endured more of it. It was of a peculiar nature . . . The instrument was a piece of india-rubber of the size and shape of a thick boot sole. This was called a 'Tolley' – Why, no one has explained, unless it is a Latin pun on what we had to bear. One blow of this instrument, delivered with intent, would cause the palm of the hand to swell up and change colour.[19]

How far he stepped out of line under this rigid regime is apparent from his later comment that 'I was more beaten than others (not because) . . . I was in any way vicious, but it was that I had a nature which responded eagerly to affectionate kindness (which I never received) but which rebelled against threats and took a perverted pride in showing that it would not be cowed by violence'. This early tendency towards rebellion and nonconformity was to remain with Conan Doyle throughout his adult life. At Stonyhurst he developed an inherent distrust of all forms of unreasoning bureaucracy which manifested itself in his championing of a number of causes: the reform of the divorce law, the Congo atrocities, and the cases of Oscar Slater and George Edalji, to name but a few.

Stonyhurst is an important milestone in the later career of Conan Doyle the spiritualist, for it was here, behind the grey mullioned windows in the company of the Jesuits, that he met the unacceptable face of Roman Catholicism. In his autobiography he wrote: 'I heard Father Murphy, a great fierce Irish priest, declare that there was sure damnation for everyone outside the Church. I looked upon him with horror, and to that moment I trace the first rift which has grown into such a chasm between me and those who were my guides.'

Something of the fear and apprehension engendered by the Jesuits has been graphically conveyed in James Joyce's *Portrait of the Artist as a Young Man*. Here Stephen Dedalus experiences the full rigour of a hell-fire sermon given by a Jesuit priest. The object of this baptism by fire is the salvation of the soul. Thus the unwitting disciple learns to excoriate from his consciousness all vestige of love and human affection.

> Help me, my dear little brothers in Christ. Help me by your pious attention, by your own devotion, by your outward demeanour. Banish from your minds all worldly thoughts and think only of the last things, death, judgement, hell and heaven.

An enormous sense of guilt for crimes real and imaginary (ultimately there is no distinction) replaces the rational view, and a universal fear of sin invades every recess of the supplicant's mind:

> Every sin would then come forth from its lurking place, the most rebellious against the divine will and the most degrading to our poor corrupt nature, the tiniest imperfection and the most heinous atrocity . . . All were as one before the judgement seat of God. He would reward the good and punish the wicked.[20]

This apocalyptic view of the 'divine plan' was typical of the kind of material thrust into the receptive minds of the pupils of the Jesuits. And like Joyce, Conan Doyle never forgot it. It was surely the dogma of the convert. If you had been converted then you were allowed a glimpse of paradise. If you were not of the faith (and that meant the exclusion of most of humankind) then you were damned for all eternity.

The power of such a view is simple to comprehend in a post-Freudian world, based as it is on the twin emotions of morbidity and sexual fears. Conan Doyle battled with such emotions throughout his life, as his fiction readily testifies. It is small wonder therefore that he embraced the cause of spiritualism. For him, sexuality remained a largely taboo subject (so much so that he felt compelled to remove an entire Sherlock Holmes story from the second volume of the series issued by George Newnes the publishers; the story, entitled 'The Cardboard Box', dealt with adultery and mutilation). As a Victorian, he was bound by the same strictures that prevented all contemporary novelists from discussing the 'underbelly' of their era. Personally he endured the anguish of a forbidden love for his second wife, Jean Leckie, a relationship which had by circumstances to remain a platonic one until the death of his first wife, Louise Hawkins.

The circumstances of death and guilt fascinated Conan Doyle, and it is no coincidence that his most successful stories often deal with this subject. The Sherlock Holmes stories offer a precise formula to the reader whereby the deeds perpetrated by the criminal are teased into perspective by Holmes. The detective, acting as both scientist and diagnostician, reveals the culprit in his true colours. The stories, seen at a deeper level, act as a means to confession. (Indeed, in the second Holmes novel this form is fully developed. The explanation offered by Jonathan Small offers the reader a justification of the crimes committed by himself and his accomplices.)

By the time Conan Doyle had come to embrace spiritualism the 'problem' of human sexuality had been dealt with by rationalization. 'Of the spirit world', he remarks in *The New Revelation* (1918), 'people live in communities, as one would expect if like attracts like, and the male spirit still finds his true mate though there is no sexuality in the grosser sense and no childbirth.' This anaesthetizing of the sexual impulse was for Conan Doyle a way of resolving the problem of sexual guilt – indeed, of sexuality itself – which had been presented to him in his days at Stonyhurst as a threat to spiritual salvation.

Similarly the notion of a universe divided into paradise and everlasting hell was swept into the recesses of Doyle's subconscious in latter years as he grappled with the cartography of the spirit world. 'The revelation', he claimed in *The Vital Message*, 'abolishes the idea of a grotesque hell and of a fantastic heaven, while it substitutes the conception of a gradual rise in the scale of existence without any monstrous change which would turn us in an instant from man to angel or devil . . .'

Sin, that all-pervading element in the Catholic mind, could be greatly reduced by the admission of hereditary and environmental factors. No longer could it be regarded as a burden upon the individual soul. 'When we view sin in the light of modern science, with the tenderness of the modern conscience and with a sense of justice and proportion, it ceases to be that monstrous cloud which darkened the whole vision of the medieval theologian. Man has been more harsh with himself than an all-merciful God will ever be.'

As he struggled to exorcize the ghost of the Jesuit creed from his soul, Conan Doyle naturally sought sanctuary in the scientific theory which had given him sustenance as a medical student. It is more than evident, looking at these later pronouncements, that he paid dearly as an unwilling victim of the Jesuits' condemnatory view of existence, and much of his later religious stance can be directly linked back to this period.

Although it was not until he had left Stonyhurst that the latent rejection of Roman Catholicism reached its full flower, there is not much doubt that the seeds of this rejection were sown at that grim establishment. As an established writer of later years he had much to say about his erstwhile faith:

> I have already in my account of the Jesuits shown how, even as a boy, all that was sanest and most generous in my nature rose up against a narrow theology and an uncharitable outlook upon the other great religions of the world. In the Catholic Church to doubt anything is to doubt everything, for since it is a vital axiom that doubt is a mortal sin when

once it has, unbidden and unappeasable, come upon you, everything is loosened and you look upon the whole wonderful interdependent scheme with other and more critical eyes. Thus viewed there was much to attract its traditions, its unbroken and solemn ritual, the beauty and truth of its many observances, its poetical appeal to the emotions, the sensual charm of music, light and incense, its power as an instrument of law and order. For the guidance of an unthinking and uneducated world it could in many ways hardly be surpassed . . . All this I could clearly see, but if I may claim any outstanding characteristic in my life, it is that I have never faltered or compromised with religious matters, that I have always weighed them very seriously, and that there was something in me which made it absolutely impossible . . . to say anything about them save that which I, in the depth of my being, really believed to be true. Judging it thus . . . I found that the foundations not only of Roman Catholicism but of the whole Christian faith, as presented to me in nineteenth century theology, were so weak that my mind could not build upon them.[21]

To a young man already steeped in the rich trappings of medievalism, and whose imagination had been captivated by the Pre-Raphaelite paintings adored by his errant father, the ritualistic side of Roman Catholicism must have offered him a strong temptation. Conan Doyle's religious sense remained with him throughout his long life. A man of deep convictions and immense will-power, he treated much of his work, literary and otherwise, as an act of worship, and this is nowhere more true than in his devotion to the cause of spiritualism. In Joyce's novel *A Portrait of the Artist* the young Stephen Dedalus is similarly entranced and almost succumbs to the mysteries of his faith:

The boys were all there, kneeling in their places. He knelt among them, happy and shy. The altar was heaped with fragrant masses of white flowers; and in the morning light the pale flames of the candles among the white flowers were clear and silent as his soul. He knelt before the altar with his classmates, holding the altar cloth with them over a living rail of hands. His hands were trembling and his soul trembled as he heard the priest pass with the ciborium from communicant to communicant.

– *Corpus Domini nostri.*

Could it be? He knelt there sinless and timid; and he would hold upon his tongue the host and God would enter his purified body.

Like Stephen Dedalus, Joyce's persona for his lost youth, Conan Doyle came to reject this cult of self-abnegation. He shared with Joyce an inability to surrender his intellect to the dogma of the Jesuits which led logically to a renunciation of the entire precepts of orthodox Christianity. Later in life he was to replace religion with his own brand of humanistic mysticism reinforced by what he regarded as the 'proofs' of spiritualism. Significantly, both writers seemed to have viewed the rituals of Catholicism as a form of seduction, threatening their own identities. It would be hard to make out some sort of case for an Oedipal conflict here, yet not absolutely impossible.

Two key figures loomed large at Stonyhurst. The Rev. George Renerden Kingdon S.J. was the Prefect of Lower Studies in Sir Arthur's day and responsible for the everyday running of the establishment. He was a man diametrically opposed to the mechanistic tendencies of nineteenth-century science – so much so that when he became seriously ill in 1893 he refused to accept medical help. It was Kingdon that Conan Doyle had in mind when he attacked the Jesuits' narrow philosophy of education, but ironically it was King-don who shared Conan Doyle's later opinion that, without conviction and a sense of belief, science was worthless.

The other key figure was Conan Doyle's former classmate Herbert Thurston, who, unlike Doyle, later became a Jesuit. In the 1920s Father Thurston entered into a bitter public controversy with Conan Doyle about the nature of spiritualism. He had published a book entitled *Modern Spiritualism*[22] which stated the official Jesuit position. The work was a scathing attack which represented spiritualism as a form of Antichrist, paying a back-handed compliment to the age of materialism. In passing, Father Thurston dealt out a great deal of criticism to his erstwhile companion. Doyle was quick to reply, issuing his own short booklet, *The Roman Catholic Church: A Rejoinder* and publishing the work under his own imprint of the Psychic Press. In the preface to this dissertation, Conan Doyle pointed out to his readers some plain truths about Roman Catholicism:

Father Thurston, of the Order of Jesuits, has written a small book against Spiritualism. As he has made very free with my own name and experiences in the course of it, it is a challenge which I can hardly help taking up. I was born in a Roman Catholic family and was brought up as a Roman Catholic until such time as the narrow intolerance shown to other creeds led me to broader and more charitable cults. It is therefore natural that I should have thought a great deal about the old faith. There is much that is sweet and beautiful in it, and there is much which is vile and detestable. If some second reformation inside the Church itself were to preserve the one and destroy the other, it might still be a great agent for good in the world. It is however hardly likely to be so so long as it is the unresisting servant of the little Junta of prelates in Italy.[23]

Conan Doyle's quarrel here is not with the beliefs themselves but with the very system of the pyramidal priesthood structure under whose constraints he suffered. In his eyes their dogma had suffocated the essential principles of Christianity. In fact when it came to the Jesuits as individuals he had a great respect for their keen devotion. As he observed in *Memories and Adventures*, 'They were keen, cleanminded earnest men . . . with a few black sheep among them, but not many . . . In all ways, save in their theology, they were admirable, though this same theology made them hard and inhuman upon the surface . . .'[24]

Always a tolerant man in both his public and private life, Conan Doyle detested the intolerance of the Catholic hierarchy. The very notion that an all-powerful God would select a small section of humanity and invest it with divine knowledge to the exclusion of the remainder of the race was anathema to him. This explains much about his belief in spiritualism as a universal creed, transcending religious divisions. In *The Roman Catholic Church – A Rejoinder*, he wrote:

> The Psychic Investigator . . . holds that the object of life is the improvement of the spiritual part of man, consisting largely in the cultivation of unselfishness. If this beneficent process is being wrought by any creed then he would entreat that person to continue in the creed which was accomplishing the object of life. He would not raise a finger to prevent a Catholic from continuing to be a Catholic or a Baptist a Baptist, so long as they were getting good from it. He would, however, add certain knowledge as to the nature of death and of the beyond, because he holds that this knowledge is not a matter of faith, but of proof, and has been sent to be helpful to mankind.

To have regarded spiritualism as a natural adjunct of orthodox religious systems was perhaps a little naïve of him, yet he was ever an optimist about the human race.

He remained a staunch admirer of the Jesuits. In his later novel *The Refugees*, he paid an especially warm tribute to their courage:

> If the Church of Rome should ever be wrecked it may come from her weakness in high places . . . or it may be because with what is very narrow she tries to explain that which is very broad, but assuredly it will never be through the fault of her rank-and-file, for never upon earth have men and women spent themselves more lavishly and more splendidly than in her service.

Coming as it did at the apex of his career as a spiritualist, Conan Doyle obviously found Thurston's attack upon him both disturbing and unsettling. The specific arguments posed by both men will be examined in Chapter 10. There are, however, two crucial points of dispute which help to throw light on Conan Doyle's experiences at Stonyhurst.

The first of these concerns the Jesuit vision of hell. Conan Doyle vividly recalled being made to study a particularly odious text entitled 'Hell open to Christians', 'which in crude pictures depicted the various tortures of the damned'.[25] This sado-masochistic text quite obviously made a deep impression on the young Conan Doyle and filled him with loathing and abhorrence at the potential cruelty of the faith. 'We spiritualists,' he proclaimed, 'who by actual personal contact know something of the real conditions of the next life, are aware that this vision of flame and torture is a horrible chimera. It does not exist.' By establishing what he regarded as the proof of a tangible, scientifically evidential afterlife, Doyle had at last been able to come to terms with this terrible vision of his childhood.

The second area which gained his disapproval in later years concerned the role of women in the Catholic Church. Despite his later intolerant utterances about the Suffragette movement, there is clear evidence from his writings to suggest that he was (for his time) somewhat unorthodox in his view of the social and economic role of womankind. (The Sherlock Holmes stories, for example, are full of independently minded women like Miss Violet Hunter in 'The Solitary Cyclist' who have minds and bodies of their own.) This attitude may be rooted in his own childhood when his mother and his elder sister, Annette, certainly took charge of the family after the incarceration of Charles Doyle and made a profound impression upon him.

Although Conan Doyle showed a reluctance to discuss sexual matters in public and was bound by the usual moral constraints under which other contemporary writers also laboured, in private he was realistic and frank about such matters as adultery, divorce, and venereal disease (he won his doctorate for a dissertation about syphilis). He had harsh words for the Jesuit brethren when it came to the business of auricular confessions:

> Did a mad devil in his wildest mood ever invent anything so insane, so obviously immoral and degrading to both sexes as auricular confession between a young woman and a celibate priest? In the *Evening Standard* of yesterday (July 22nd) I observed that Dr. C. Douglas, himself, I believe, a Catholic, says, 'If Freud had asked any Roman Catholic priest of the last thousand years he would have been told that in the confessional something like 90 per cent of all confessions made dealt with sexual subjects.'
>
> It is not necessary to enlarge upon it. It is impossible to believe that the discussion of such matters with a man has no coarsening effect upon the mind of a woman . . . In the name of decency and common sense if such a confession is advisable why should it not be made to some discreet matron?[26]

He was equally scathing about the recruitment of young women to convents and believed that many of them endured lives of sorrow and repression after the fading of their initial idealism. ('Does not the poor disillusioned creature, her dreams shattered, her ideals all fading before hard realities, her fortune irretrievably gone, find herself under the power of some harsh unsexed woman, a rigid disciplinarian, who takes a pride in her aloofness from human weakness and sympathy?')

Before he left the Jesuits and commenced his training as a medical student, Conan Doyle was sent to Feldkirch to study German language and literature. 'Here,' he recalled, 'in the Jesuit school in the Vorarlberg province of Austria . . . the conditions were more much humane and I met with far more human kindness than at Stonyhurst, with the immediate result that I ceased to be a resentful young rebel and became a pillar of law and order.'[27]

Once free of the rigid constraints of Stonyhurst, Conan

Doyle was able to let his imagination roam free. He read a great deal of German Romantic literature, including Schiller and Goethe (from whom he quotes liberally in *The Sign of Four*). More importantly, perhaps, his attention was drawn to the Protestant interpretation of history as portrayed in the works of Macaulay. Outwardly he may well have regarded himself as a reformed rebel: inwardly he had moved far from the religious and doctrinal beliefs of his ancestors.

Yet for all this Conan Doyle had absorbed much from his Jesuit instructors. From them he had acquired a profound belief in a universal order of nature: a sense of divine purpose. This concept of a metaphysical structure found confirmation in the German philosophers he studied at Feldkirch, and it was something which never deserted him despite the agnosticism of his student years. He had also come to believe in the power of faith as a form of personal conviction. This was crucial to his development both as a writer and as a leading spiritualist, enabling him to ward off the attacks of cynical rationalists. Most important of all, he had understood that to suffer patiently for one's beliefs only served to reinforce that sense of pride and identity which had been a hallmark of the Doyles for centuries.

CHAPTER 2

Dreamland and Ghostland

On his way back to England, young Conan Doyle found time to visit his illustrious grand-uncle, Michael Conan. In his memoirs, Conan Doyle described this paternal relation as 'an intellectual Irishman of the type which originally founded the Sinn Fein movement', and there is no doubt that he made a profound impression on the young student nephew. Uncle Conan (from whom Arthur derived his middle name) shared Mary Doyle's passion for chivalry and family lineage, having traced his own descent from the Dukes of Brittany.

No doubt Conan Doyle would have loved to spend longer with this larger-than-life figure with his 'volcanic' temperament and devoted 'dicky bird' wife, but he had to return to the real world of family strife in an Edinburgh tenement. The Doyle family remained at 3 Sciennes Hill Place until 1875, but by 1876 they had moved to 2 Argyle Park Terrace, a large bow-windowed residence in a much more salubrious neighbourhood. The rent here was much higher than at the previous address (in fact it was almost double),[1] but the increased burden on the diminishing family income was relieved by the taking in of a lodger, a young doctor called Bryan Charles Waller who was a recent graduate of the University of Edinburgh.

There seems every likelihood that Waller had a steadying influence on young Arthur Conan Doyle and possibly the entire family thanks to his financial contribution and his professional background. Waller was himself a poet who had recently published a collection of his work and we know from Conan Doyles's memoirs that in his later years at

Stonyhurst he too had developed a love for poetry, having written (as he modestly described it) 'a good deal of indifferent verse'. With the absence of a secure father figure at this stage of his adolescence, we might imagine that a relationship of some kind was struck up between the two.

Times had indeed been hard for the close-knit family to which Arthur returned. John Innes Hay Doyle, Arthur's beloved brother, had been born in 1872, Jane Adelaide Rose (Ida) in 1874, and Bryan Mary Julia Josephine ('Dodo') in 1876. Then on 2 March 1877 a tenth child had been added to the family who subsequently died. During these difficult years the Doyles seem always to have been shifting from residence to residence. After the short stay at Argyle Park Terrace we find them later occupying part of a large mansion at 23 George Square. Significantly, however, the exorbitant rent of £85 is recorded as having been paid by Waller, not Charles Doyle, who himself had suffered at the hands of the new Surveyor of Scotland and whose occupation was now described simply as 'artist'.[2]

The Doyle family remained with their lodger at this address until 1881, the year prior to Arthur's departure to Portsmouth, and we can only assume that Waller remained a friend of the family during these difficult years, for by the time they had made the move to 15 Lonsdale Terrace (whose nearby Lauriston Gardens provided Doyle with the setting of his first detective novel, *A Study in Scarlet*) Waller was still paying the rent. As Owen Dudley Edwards records in his study of this period of Conan Doyle's life:

> The older children were by this stage slowly moving away from the nest . . . Annette took up a post as governess in Portugal in 1879, and was followed within the next three years by her next surviving sisters Lottie and Connie. Connie was probably sent to school in Portugal at Annette's expense. The three youngest children Innes, Ida and 'Dodo' (Bryan Mary Julia Josephine) were all under ten by 1882. Innes was sent down to Arthur in the late summer. Bryan Charles Waller brought Mary and the two youngest to Masongill, and lodged them in Masongill Cottage, a sizeable house on his estate.[3]

Despite the steadying hand of Bryan Waller, Charles Doyle's increasing reliance on alcohol did much to injure and unsettle the family, and the dread of this disenabling disease figures prominently in much of Conan Doyle's

31

subsequent fiction. It appears highly likely that what began as an addiction finally unsettled the balance of this sensitive man's mind. In an early short story which Conan Doyle omitted to reprint, entitled 'The Surgeon of Gaster Fell', there is a detailed portrait of the type of insanity which probably afflicted his father:

> My poor father's disease rapidly assumed both a religious and a homicidal turn, the attacks coming on without warning after months of sanity. It would weary you were I to describe the terrible experiences which his family have undergone . . . He has an intense dread of madhouses; and in his sane intervals would beg and pray so piteously not to be condemned to one, that I could never find the heart to resist him. At last, however, his attacks became so acute and dangerous that I determined, for the sake of those about me, to remove him from the town to the loneliest neighbourhood that I could find . . . He, poor fellow, was as submissive as a child when in his right mind, and a better, kinder companion no man could wish for . . .

Although this is a fictional account, its autobiographical origins are only too evident, and it gives us some idea of the anguish Conan Doyle must have experienced at the time when he embarked on his career as a medical student at the University of Edinburgh. Moreover, the religious twist to his father's deluded state must merely have reinforced his conviction not to ally himself with any of the religious dogmas offered by Catholic and Protestant faiths alike. He had seen at close hand the effect of a repressive existence upon the sensitive mind and the excesses to which it might lead.

The prospect of medical training at Edinburgh University was an exciting one for Conan Doyle, and it must have come as something of a relief, given the family circumstances. By now he had developed into a brawny, somewhat rebellious youth, eager to test himself against the world's challenges and demands.

It was indeed fortunate for him that he lived in such close proximity to this particular seat of learning. There was a world of difference between the Scottish and English universities, the latter being hidebound by considerations of social class and primarily intended for the sons of gentlefolk. As an outsider, because he was of Irish extraction and a Catholic (if not a committed one), Conan Doyle would have fitted into this atmosphere most uneasily. On the other hand, the Scottish universities thrived upon an atmosphere of anarchy and pragmatism, and the students themselves came from a variety of cultural and social backgrounds. As Conan Doyle recalled in his semi-autobiographical novel *The Firm of Girdlestone*:

> A lad coming up to an English University finds himself in an enlarged and enlightened public school. If he has passed through Harrow and Eton there is no very abrupt transition between the life which he has led in the sixth form and that which he finds awaiting him on the banks of the Cam and the Isis. Certain rooms are found for him which have been inhabited by generations of students in the past, and will be by as many in the future. His religion is cared for, and he is expected to put in appearance at hall and at chapel. He must be within bounds at a fixed time. If he behaves indecorously he is liable to be pounced upon and reported by special officials, and a code of punishment is hung perpetually over his head. In return for all this his university takes a keen interest in him . . .
>
> There is nothing of this in a Scotch University. The young aspirant pays his pound, and finds himself a student. After that he may do absolutely what he will. There are certain classes going on at certain hours, which he may attend if he choose. If not, he may stay away without the slightest remonstrance from the college. As to religion, he may worship the sun, or have a private fetish of his own upon the mantelpiece of his lodgings for all that the University cares . . . Examinations are periodically held, at which he may appear or not, as he chooses. The University is a great unsympathetic machine, taking in a stream of raw-boned cartilaginous youths at one end, and turning them out at the other as learned divines, astute lawyers, and skilful medical men. Of every thousand of the raw material about six hundred emerge at the other side. The remainder are broken in the process.

Conan Doyle began his medical studies in October 1876. He soon discovered that, as at Stonyhurst, he was to be thrown back upon his own resources. Very little guidance was offered to the typical medical student of the period, and the unremitting grind of a course comprising chemistry, anatomy, physiology, and a list of other compulsory subjects offered little to the imagination of the budding writer. An amiable and genial young man, Conan Doyle found the atmosphere at the university rather austere. In his memoirs he recalls:

> There was no attempt at friendship, or even acquaintance, between professors and students at Edinburgh. It was a strictly business arrangement by which you paid, for example, four guineas for Anatomy lectures and received the winter course in exchange, never seeing your professor save behind his desk and never under any circumstances exchanging a word with him. They were remarkable men, however, some of these professors, and we managed to know them pretty well without any personal acquaintance.[4]

Although Conan Doyle found the more mundane aspects of scientific theory rather dull, he was certainly not disenchanted with the practical application of medicine. The illustrious masters under whom he served in those early days found a memorable niche in his later fiction. There was, for example, the gargantuan figure of Professor Rutherford with 'his enormous chest and his singular manner'. Rutherford's rather direct and rather overbearing manner fascinated Conan Doyle so much that he later based one of his two major fictional creations on the character of the professor. Professor Challenger loomed large in Conan Doyle's successful science-fiction novel *The Lost World*, as the omniscient man of science who would tolerate no opposition. Challenger, that adamant pioneer who cared not what the popular press or the public at large thought of his theories, was of course largely a projection of Conan Doyle himself, but what is most significant is Challenger's dogged determination to pursue his ideas to their logical conclusion. This personification of self-sacrifice in the cause of a cherished belief figures large in the public career of Arthur Conan Doyle. In later years, with the publication of the spiritualist novel *The Land of Mist*, we see Challenger's denial of an afterlife gradually eroded until the lifelong upholder of materialistic views is forced to accept the principles of spiritualism. In this early period of Conan Doyle's life, Professor Rutherford provided an interesting role-model for the young medical student.

Perhaps the most remarkable of all the senior staff at Edinburgh who crossed Conan Doyle's path at this time was Joseph Bell. A skilful surgeon of many years' experience,

Bell's strong point was diagnosis not just of disease but also of occupation and character. Much has been made of Bell's importance to the Sherlock Holmes saga, and there is no doubt much of Bell's personality in the early persona of Holmes himself. Although there is clear evidence that Conan Doyle drew from Bell the amusing diagnostic process which usually crops up in each of the Holmes tales, it is more relevant to consider the impact which this astute man with his angular face and penetrating eyes made on the aspiring student of medicine. What Conan Doyle learnt from Joseph Bell was an approach to scientific method which reinforced his own already humanistic beliefs. In Bell's hands science was no longer the province of mere cause and effect: it depended also on a series of inferences which took into account psychological factors. The idea that a doctor could consider the human being not merely as a lump of matter or a functioning machine but as a self-determined entity driven by motives both conscioius and subconscious appealed to Conan Doyle.

The worsening situation at home drove Conan Doyle to seek immediate experience as an assistant to a number of general practitioners. His first venture occurred in the summer of 1878 when he was employed as a medical assistant to a Dr Richardson in one of the more poverty-stricken areas of Sheffield. This employment lasted a mere three weeks, which would suggest a baptism by fire or perhaps a clash of personalities. Following a short period of residence with his relatives in Maida Vale, Conan Doyle placed an advertisement in the newspapers and was pleased to find a placement with a Dr Elliot in a small town in Shropshire. The small community and relatively unpressurized pace of life allowed him time to think and to formulate his ideas about those vexed questions which had bedevilled him since his renunciation of Roman Catholicism.

After four happy months with Elliot, Doyle was ready for the winter term at the university once more. Its close proximity to his home at this period may well have provided difficulties for him, and when the following summer arrived he was only too glad to find new employment with a doctor in Birmingham. It was not simply that Charles Doyle was becoming more erratic and unmanageable as his psychosis worsened, but that Conan Doyle's own meagre earnings did little to assist his mother's financial situation. As Owen

Dudley Edwards has observed in his biographical treatment of those early years:

> While with one part of him Arthur must have regretted being hurried into adult responsibility so brutally as his father's disintegration demanded, with another he must equally have resented that Waller's role prevented his meeting more of those unwelcome adult obligations. The role of absent bread-winner went some way to remove him from these strains, a role, as he may have realised, in which countless Irish labourers in Scotland had preceded him, although often without his sense of preserving his gains and placing the family foremost.[5]

Dr Hoare's 'five-horse City practice' in Birmingham provided Conan Doyle with just the sort of hard experience which a keen student required. He experienced long hours at the dispensary where he made countless potions, pills, and ointments, and his visiting list comprised the very poorest denizens of the city. Conan Doyle's appreciation of the lives of the Victorian working classes was probably sharpened at this time, and it is a tribute to his fiction (especially the Sherlock Holmes stories) that he was able to describe vividly and with great accuracy the highest and the lowest of the land. His ability to communicate effectively with vast numbers at spiritualist venues up and down the country must have depended to a great extent on this initial exploration into the twilight world of industrial England.

Despite the rigorous nature of his daily work, by night he satiated his immense appetite for literature. At a second-hand bookshop he spent his pennies on the works of Tacitus. However, he learned even more from Swift and the English satirists, thus gaining a considerable grounding in the art of the novel. As he recalled in his memoirs:

> Anyone observing my actions and tastes would have said that so strong a spring would certainly overflow, but for my own part I never dreamed I could myself produce decent prose, and the remark of my friend, who was by no means given to flattery, took me greatly by surprise. I sat down, however, and wrote a little adventure story which I call 'The Mystery of the Sasassa Valley.' To my great joy and surprise it was accepted by 'Chambers Journal' and I received three guineas.[6]

Flushed with this success, Conan Doyle wrote another two short pieces, the first of which, entitled 'The Haunted

Grange of Goresthorpe', may be regarded as his first contribution to the literature of the supernatural. The fate of this early effort was unfortunate, for Blackwoods subsequently lost it. We do know that it was subtitled 'A True Ghost Story' and that it described a night in the life of a young medical student who is the reluctant owner of a haunted grange.* According to the bibliographer Richard Lancelyn Green, 'He and a friend sit up through the night and after observing blood dripping from the ceiling, go to investigate, whereupon the ghost of a drowned sailor and of a woman with marks upon her neck flee past them.'[7]

Some time in the early part of 1880, whilst on his second visit to the Birmingham practice, Conan Doyle attended a lecture entitled 'Does Death End All?', probably given by a local spiritualist group. Whether or not this had a profound impact upon him is not recorded. However, it is interesting that his interest should have been aroused at a time in his life when his father's descent into insanity had begun to escalate. By now he had rejected the whole basis of Roman Catholicism as an unwelcome burden upon his own spiritual development, whilst his wider reading had led him to accept the scientific conclusions of Huxley, Tyndall, Darwin, Spencer, and John Stuart Mill. It was quite impossible for him to sustain a fundamentalist view of the Bible. And since the Bible was the very basis of Christian dogma, man's image of God as an anthropomorphic entity had to be seen as naïve in the extreme. Conan Doyle himself expressed this point of view thus:

> A gap had opened between our fathers and ourselves so suddenly and completely that when a Gladstone wrote to uphold the Gadarene swine, or the six days of Creation, the youngest student rightly tittered over his arguments, and it did not need a Huxley to demolish them. I can see now very clearly how deplorable it is that manifest absurdities should be allowed to continue without even a footnote to soften them in the sacred text . . . There are no worse enemies of true religion than those who clamour against all revision or modification of that strange mass of superbly good and questionable matter which we lump all together into a single volume as if there were the same value to all of it.[8]

If the Bible was now to be regarded as merely an interest-

*According to Owen Dudley Edwards, this piece has been rediscovered and is now in the archives of Edinburgh University.

ing collection of fables and segments of Hebraic race history, then man's conception of his own place in a seemingly ordered and structured universe must be looked at afresh in the light of scientific discoveries.

Thrust back into the limbo of agnosticism, Conan Doyle sought sanctuary in the belief that creation was far from resembling the mechanistic structure posited by certain eighteenth-century philosophers. Instead he perceived in the anatomical precision of the human body and in the synthesis of mind–body experiences an organic pattern which required an imaginative interpretation.

> It was, then, all Christianity, and no Roman Catholicism alone, which had alienated my mind and driven me to an agnosticism, which never for an instant degenerated into atheism, for I had a very keen perception of the wonderful poise of the universe and the tremendous power of conception and sustenance which it implied. I was reverent in all my doubts and never ceased to think upon the matter, but the more I thought the more confirmed became by non-conformity. In a broad sense I was a Unitarian, save that I regarded the Bible with more criticism than Unitarians usually show. This negative position was so firm that it seemed to me to be a terminus; whereas it proved only a junction on the road of life where I was destined to change from the old well-worn line on to a new one.[9]

On his return from Birmingham, Conan Doyle enlisted as one of the crew on a whaler bound for the Arctic seas. He was but 20 years old at the time, nevertheless he was more than ready for the adventure of a lifetime. A long, hard voyage ensued in the company of a 50-strong crew comprising Shetlanders and Scotsmen. Strong gales and pack ice had to be endured along with the awesome grandeur and loneliness of this desolate part of the world:

> The perpetual light, the glare of the white ice, the deep blue of the water, these are the things which one remembers most clearly, and the dry, crisp, exhilarating air, which makes mere life the keenest of pleasures.[10]

Here, at the far end of the world, man's petty ambitions shrank into a fresh perspective. The wild, untamed romance of the place struck a chord in him. This impressionable young man who had spent much of his youth incarcerated under the iron rule of a censorious priesthood was able to glimpse Nature 'red in tooth in claw', and if anything was destined to convince him of some higher order in the affairs of man then this was surely it.

This unforgettable experience was to form the basis of a short story, 'The Captain of the Polestar', which he published in *Temple Bar* in January 1883, some three years later. As the work of a young writer it is without doubt a literary masterpiece, rivalling in its intensity and vivid portrayal of psychological conflict Edgar Allan Poe's novella *The Narrative of Arthur Gordon Pym*.

The story, which is told in diary form, recounts the experiences of a young student of medicine, John M'Alister Ray, who joins the crew of a sealer sailing north from Greenland to the Arctic seas. From the outset he appears deeply disturbed by the behaviour of the captain of the ship, described as a 'tall and well-formed [man], with dark, handsome face, and a curious way of twitching his limbs, which may arise from nervousness, or be simply an outcome of his excessive energy'. The neurasthenic Captain Craigie is a tragic and doomed figure, haunted both psychologically and literally by the phantom of his departed fiancée who, we are told at the conclusion of the story, 'died under circumstances of peculiar horror'. There is a marked parallel between Craigie and some of the manic-depressives who stalk the pages of Poe's short stories:

> His jaw and whole cast of countenance is manly and resolute, but the eyes are the distinctive feature of his face. They are of the very darkest hazel, bright and eager, with a singular mixture of recklessness in their expression, and of something else which I have sometimes thought was more allied with horror than any other emotion. Generally the former predominated, but on occasions, and more particularly when he was thoughtfully inclined, the look of fear would spread and deepen until it imparted a new character to his whole countenance. It is at these times that he is most subject to tempestuous fits of anger . . .

As the story progresses we become increasingly aware that the captain is in the grip of an obsession which must lead ultimately to insanity or death. Several times a shrouded figure is seen in close proximity to the ship – an omen which only serves to reinforce the nightmare quality of the Captain's persistent vision.

The erratic behaviour of Craigie, coupled with his immense melancholy and suicidal tendencies, would suggest that Conan Doyle had his own father in mind to some extent, for the story was actually written in 1882, when Charles Doyle had succumbed to alcoholism and ultimate insanity. Ray seems to be in a state of permanent anxiety as he attempts to allay the Captain's fears: 'These spectral alarms have a very bad effect upon the Captain. I feared that it might excite his sensitive mind . . . Unfortunately he overheard one of the men making an allusion to it . . . As I had expected, it brought out all his latent lunacy in an exaggerated form. I can hardly believe that this is the same man who discoursed philosophy last night with the most critical acumen and coolest judgement.' Here, surely, is an echo of the growing unease with which Conan Doyle witnessed his father's decline.

Like the subject of Poe's novella and Captain Ahab in *Moby-Dick* (Doyle was a great admirer of Melville and paid him high praise in his literary study *Through the Magic Door*), Craigie dies, sacrificing himself to his unattainable ideal on the frozen wastes of the icefields. Here Conan Doyle blends into the narrative a truly masterly touch, as he describes the symbolic reunion of the captain's tormented soul with that of his lover:

> He was lying face downwards upon a frozen bank. Many little crystals of ice and feathers of snow had drifted on to him as he lay, and sparkled upon his dark seaman's jacket. As we came up some wandering puff of wind caught these tiny flakes in its vortex, and they whirled up into the air, partially descended again, and then, caught once more in the current, sped rapidly away in the direction of the sea. To my eyes, it seemed but a snow-drift, but many of my companions averred that it started up in the shape of a woman, stooped over the corpse and kissed it, and then hurried away across the floe.

Even at this early stage in Conan Doyle's literary career we see the major theme that was to preoccupy him later as a spiritualist: the conquest of death. In Craigie, of course, the achievement is brought about not through rational means but by the surrender of his own miserable life. That Conan Doyle perceived death in terms of fear and the relinquishment of consciousness at this stage reflects his relative immaturity as a writer. (It was a form of experience that was to repeat itself in several of his more extended early works including the novella *The Parasite* and *The Mystery of Cloomber*). There is also present in the story a latent sexual element, for the extinct lover has the appearance of a *femme fatale* when her picture is glimpsed by Ray in Craigie's cabin. So fear combined with sexual dread and morbidity produced a powerful and unnerving effect upon the reader.

One interesting passage in the narrative reveals to us the extent to which Conan Doyle had already immersed himself in the subject of spiritualism. Craigie and Ray enter into a conversation about the nature of the soul, a subject which had obviously preoccupied Conan Doyle since his emergence from his Jesuit school:

> When [the Captain] chooses he can be a most fascinating companion, being remarkably well-read, and having the power of expressing his opinion forcibly without appearing to be dogmatic. I hate to have my intellectual toes trod upon. He spoke about the nature of the soul, and sketched out the views of Aristotle and Plato upon the subject in a masterly manner. He seems to have a leaning for metempsychosis and the doctrines of Pythagoras. In discussing them we touched upon modern spiritualism, and I made some joking allusion to the impostures of Slade, upon which, to my surprise, he warned me most impressively against confusing the innocent with the guilty, and argued that it would be as logical to brand Christianity as an error because Judas, who professed that religion, was a villain.

The unwillingness of Craigie to condemn spiritualism outright gives us an insight into Conan Doyle's perception of the movement which in the late 1870s and early 1880s was a topic of great controversy in the popular press. Dr Henry Slade was an American medium best known for his slate-writing phenomena. Although he was the subject of much stormy discussion as to alleged trickery, there were many who vouched for his authenticity. He had arrived in London in July 1876 at the request of Madame Blavatsky, who had been asked by Grand Duke Constantine of Russia to make a scientific investigation of spiritualism. Having taken up temporary residence in Russell Square, he was immediately pronounced genuine by the leading spiritualist journals of the day. Interestingly, there is a curious resemblance between Craigie and Slade, which suggests that Conan Doyle may have used the latter as a model for the tormented captain of his story. Certainly Craigie possesses the hallmarks of a psychic, as can be seen from this contemporary description of Slade quoted many years later in Conan Doyle's *History of Spiritualism*:

> A highly-wrought, nervous temperament, a dreamy mystical face, regular features, eye luminous with expression, a rather sad smile, and a certain melancholy grace of manner, were the impressions conveyed by the tall, lithe figure introduced to me as Dr. Slade.[11]

In August 1881, Conan Doyle passed his final examination at Edinburgh University, emerging as a Bachelor of Medicine and Master of Surgery. Following an eventful and sometimes stressful voyage to West Africa on the steamer *Mayumba*, he endeavoured at last to establish himself in medical practice in order to establish his own longed for independence and further assist 'the Ma'am'.

His temperament at this time swung between two poles: a desire for experimentation and adventure and a tendency towards introspection. The former aspect had been gratified by the two remarkable voyages he had recently undergone; also his daring self-experimentation with the sedative gelsemium (the subject of his first medical publication). The latter had led him to draw upon a variety of experiences and gave rise to those few short stories which he had been lucky enough to place in such magazines as *Chambers* and *London Society*, which were always on the lookout for new talent. These early literary efforts frequently project the persona of a sensitive, rather depressive young man – a reflection in part, perhaps, of that more feminine side of his personality inherited from his father. In 'That Little Square Box', published in the winter of 1881,[12] for example, we encounter a young man who witnesses the covert dealings of two men whom he believes may be Fenians intent on planning a terrorist outrage on board a ship. He has, we are told, 'the misfortune to be a very nervous man' whose 'love of solitude, even in . . . boyhood, was one of my distinguishing characteristics'. The story has a humorous outcome for the two strangers, far from being Fenians, are in reality pigeon fanciers attempting to set a new world record in their own league. There is an element of self-censure expressed here, for it is the young narrator's innate suspicion and timidity which gives rise to his prolonged anguish. That he is psychically sensitive (something that Conan Doyle never actually claimed for himself) is clear when we learn that he is possessed of 'a peculiar temperament' and is liable to presentiments of danger:

> There is a theory that [this] arises from a species of second-sight, a subtle spiritual communication with the future. I well remember Herr Raumer, the eminent spiritualist, remarked on one occasion that I was the most sensitive subject as regards supernatural phenomena that he had ever encountered in the whole of his wide experience.

The medical opportunity greatly desired by Conan Doyle came as the result of a friendship he had struck up in his last year at Edinburgh University with a much older man. George Turnavine Budd came from an illustrious medical family, his father having been an authority on zymotic disease and a pioneer in the discovery of transmission of typhoid infection through excreta. A bull of a man with deep-set, bloodshot eyes, overhanging brows, and stiff yellowish hair, he had already established for himself a reputation for unorthodox methods and eccentric behaviour which at once set alarm bells ringing in Mary Doyle's brain. Since the age of 23 Budd had earned the disrespect and envy of the medical establishment by waging a series of controversial campaigns in the pages of certain journals, often using his father's name to add weight to his arguments. There is every reason to believe that Budd's flimsy, ill-reasoned polemics did not go unnoticed by the Doyle lodger, Bryan Waller, and one can well imagine that Conan Doyle was warned about the pernicious effects of such a friendship.

Before he left for Africa, Conan Doyle had already received a telegram from Budd imploring him to go to Bristol. When he arrived hot-foot from Birmingham, he discovered that Budd had run up debts after an unsuccessful attempt at continuing his father's practice. Unable to offer anything more than common-sense advice, Conan Doyle returned to Birmingham.

He had been back in England only a few months when he received another telegram from the indefatigable Budd, claiming that he had commenced a prosperous practice in Plymouth and offering him an income of £300 per year. With some initial hesitation, probably based in part on his mother's misgivings, Conan Doyle travelled down in the summer of 1882 and there endured what he later described as six weeks 'more fitted for some rollicking novel than for the sober pages of a veracious chronicle'. Budd's unortho-dox methods had proved an instant success, the main principle being that he offered free consultation but charged for medicines. In a short time this advertising gimmick had attracted people in their hundreds to the surgery where Conan Doyle dealt with simple surgical cases whilst the gargantuan Budd bullied, cajoled, and lectured his clients in the consulting-room.

Over the next few weeks Mary continued to write letters of warning to her errant son, several of which, it seems, were intercepted and read by Budd and his wife. Faced with increasing suspicion and hostility from the pair, Conan Doyle felt himself being pushed into an increasingly awk-ward position as the 'junior partner', especially since he had done his utmost to defend the man and his methods. As Conan Doyle later recalled:

> Apparently he imagined he was a man of strange suspicions and secret plottings – that I was a party to such sentiments, whereas they were actually called forth by my defence of him. His manner changed, and more than once I caught his fierce grey eyes looking furtively at me with a strange sullen expression, so much so that I asked him what was the matter. He was actually scheming my ruin, which would be nothing financially, since I had nothing to lose, but would be much both to my mother and me if it touched my honour.[13]

Matters finally came to a head and in July 1882 Budd insisted that the arrangement must be terminated. Conan Doyle must establish himself in another area whilst Budd would provide him with a pound a week in lieu of capital and as compensation. Thus it was that in the summer of 1882 Conan Doyle arrived in Portsmouth with 'one small trunk' containing his earthly possessions and a 'cash ba-lance' of under £10. After he had been settled in Southsea for some while, he received an acrimonious letter from Budd, claiming that a letter (which was actually in Conan Doyle's possession) had been discovered, written by Mary Doyle and referring to Budd as a bankrupt and unscrupulous swindler. So by a devious trick Budd was able to terminate his financial commitment.

Such was the impact made upon Conan Doyle in this

short, unhappy episode of his early career that in 1895 he felt compelled to publish a semi-autobiographical version of the events entitled *The Stark Munro Letters*. Subtitled 'a series of sixteen letters written by J. Stark Munro, M.B. to his friend and former fellow-student, Herbert Swanborough, of Lowell, Massachusetts, during the years 1881–1884', the work describes the struggles of a young doctor under the aegis of the 'Collingworths' and is a fascinating mixture of philosophy and amusing autobiography (Conan Doyle used the pseudonym in order to protect Budd's widow). Although, as Conan Doyle admitted, 'there are some few incidents there which are imaginary', he drew very closely upon the actual events which took place at Budd's riotous establishment. (Two major exceptions are the case of the lunatic and of Lord Saltire in Chapter 4.)

If it is true, as Owen Dudley Edwards suggests, that the work may well have been written as early as 1885,[14] then the philosophical and religious speculations contained in the letters cast an interesting light on the views of the author during this period. It is clear, for example, that his rejection of Catholicism, and subsequently Christianity (although not its humanistic teachings), was initially a most painful process:

> When first I came out of the faith in which I had been reared, I certainly did feel for a time as if my life-belt had burst. I won't exaggerate and say that I was miserable and plunged into utter spiritual darkness. Youth is too full of action for that. But I was conscious of a vague unrest, of a constant want of repose, of an emptiness and hardness which I had not noticed in life before. I had so identified religion with the Bible that I could not conceive them apart. When the foundation proved false, the whole structure came rattling about my ears. And then good old Carlyle came to the rescue; and from him, and partly from my own broodings, I made a little hut of my own, which has kept me snug ever since . . .[15]

Thomas Carlyle, whom Conan Doyle had discovered as the Scottish interpreter of the German Romantic movement, advocated, like Schiller and Goethe before him, a return to the mainspring of human endeavour: the worship and inspiration of Nature. Nature, Munro concludes, is the true revelation of the Deity to man. 'The nearest green field is the inspired page from which you may read all that it is needful for you to know.'

Bereft of religious absolutes, many nineteenth-century writers and intellectuals believed, like Carlyle, that the mechanistic vision of the universe offered by physicists was inadequate. There was a divine purpose in Nature which, although it could not yet be fully understood, was nevertheless discernible. Conan Doyle concurred with this view:

> Wisdom and power and means directed to an end run all through the scheme of Nature. What proof do we want, then, from a book? . . . Nor is it only in the large things that we see the ever present solicitude of some intelligent force. Nothing is too tiny for that fostering care. We see the minute proboscis of the insect carefully adjusted to fit into the calyx of the flower, the most microscopic hair and gland each with its definite purposeful function to perform. What matter whether these came by special creation or by evolution? We know as a matter of fact that they came by evolution, but that only defines the law. It does not explain it.[16]

Having accepted this post-Darwinian model of the universe, Conan Doyle found himself facing the age-old problem of evil. If, as he assumed, the Deity was some kind of omniscient engineer, then how could he allow imperfection and deviance to flourish? To Conan Doyle, the most pressing problems of drink and immorality were dissipated by a kind of hereditary determinism:

> It seems to me, then, that Nature, still working on the lines of evolution, strengthens the race in two ways. The one is by improving those who are morally strong, which is done by increasing knowledge and broadening religious views, the other, and hardly less important, is by the killing off and extinction of those who are morally weak. This is accomplished by drink and immorality. These are really two of the most important forces which work for the ultimate perfection of the race . . . Looked at in one's own day, one can only see that they produce degradation and misery. But at the end of a third generation from then, what has happened? The line of the drunkard and of the debauchee, physically as well as morally weakened, is either extinct or on the way towards it.[17]

It is interesting to speculate whether Conan Doyle let himself to be to some extent doomed by his father's alcoholism. 'A majority of drunkards', he claimed, 'never perpetuate their species at all,' which of course leaves the minority whose offspring carry the burden of guilt. This hereditary notion of evil applies equally well to Conan Doyle's preoccupation with syphilis – a subject to which he had devoted a considerable proportion of his time as a medical student.

The problem of the location of man's spiritual self remained a mystery. Medical science could not explain such a conundrum. The soul remained elusive:

> I ask myself, where is the man, the very, very inmost essence of the man? . . . It does not lie in the limbs which serve him as tools, nor in the apparatus by which he is to digest, nor in that by which he is to inhale oxygen. All these are mere accessories, the slaves of the lord within. Where, then, is he?[18]

Munro, like his creator, was convinced not only of the soul's reality (although science was unable to prove its existence) but also of the immortality of the body. Since matter could not be destroyed but merely transformed, the individuality of man would be preserved after death. Further, the souls of men and women were destined to indissolubility: '. . . every male soul will have a female one attached to or combined with it, to round it off and give it symmetry.'

Clearly Conan Doyle regarded the Darwinian legacy as a movement which could embrace differing views. If evolutionary theory was to be accepted for what it was, then Christian ideas of reckoning and judgement were superfluous. The life in the hereafter – if indeed there was one – would be a continuation of present existence but also a refinement of it. Added to this was the distinct possibility that man's earthly progress would lead to a refinement of his spiritual status:

> . . . our civilisation will endure and grow more complex. Man will live in the air and below the water. Preventative medicine will develop . . . Education and a more socialistic scheme of society will do away with crime. The English-speaking races will unite . . . The forms of religion will be abandoned, but the essence will be maintained; so that one universal creed will embrace the whole civilised earth . . .[19]

The optimism shown here was a response to the Darwinian revolution and it was something Conan Doyle had encountered before, most powerfully in the writings of the nonconformist and explorer William Winwood Reade. Sherlock Holmes was later to pay tribute to Reade when he recommended Reade's book to Watson in *The Sign of Four* as

'one of the most remarkable books ever penned'. Remarkable it certainly was: well received it was not. Condemned
by critics as 'obscene', 'blasphemous', and 'a thoroughly
worthless book' when it first appeared in 1872, the book
offered both an interpretation of world history and a critique
of religious movements. Reade's message was clear and
without comfort to orthodox Christian believers: 'Supernatural Christianity is false. God-worship is idolatry. Prayer
is useless. The Soul is not immortal. There are no rewards
and there are no punishments in a future state.' Reade's
conception of human existence ran directly parallel to Conan
Doyle's. Far from being an atheist, as some had claimed,
Reade believed God to be incomprehensible and possessing
a nature which man could never ascertain. Neither was God
a Personal Creator for, as he pointed out on several occasions, if this were so, then the Creator cannot be at once
omnipotent *and* benevolent. From this central dilemma none
of the great monotheistic religions have ever been able to
release themselves (it is important to note that Herbert
Spencer, whom Conan Doyle refers to as one of his youthful
inspirations, held similar views on this subject):

> We teach that there is a God, but not a God of the anthropoid
> variety . . . God is so great that he cannot be defined by us.
> God is so great that he does not deign to have personal
> relations with us human atoms that are called men. Those
> who desire to worship their Creator must worship him
> through mankind. Such it is plain is the scheme of Nature.[20]

Despite Reade's injunction to humanity that it must give
up all notions regarding the immortality of the soul (something which Conan Doyle himself found he could not
accept) and pass through 'a season of mental anguish', he
too maintained an unquenchable optimism about the future,
believing that 'The world will become a heavenly commune
to which men will bring the inmost treasures of their hearts
. . . they will labour together in the Sacred Cause–the
extinction of disease, the extinction of sin, the perfection of
genius, the perfection of love, the invention of immortality,
the exploration of the infinite, the conquest of creation.'

Thus when Conan Doyle took up residence at 1 Bush
Villas, Southsea, in July 1882, he had renounced religion
altogether but not lost his belief in an omniscient God. He
had read Darwin, Spencer, and Reade and found there the

possibility of a system of belief. but instead of relying upon blind faith as the Jesuits had instructed him, he was to accept only what could be proved, for, as he himself put it, 'The evils of religion have all come from accepting things which cannot be proved.'

Fortunately for Conan Doyle, the move to Southsea was a gamble which eventually paid off, but in his first months there he experienced considerable financial difficulties. His rooms were unfurnished and the new doctor had nothing in the way of capital to enable him to present a polished professional image to his potential clientele. In his memoirs, Conan Doyle recalled how 'the back room was furnished with my trunk and a stool. Inside the trunk was my larder, and the top of it was my dining-room table.' At the outset business was disappointingly slow, and he had to pay for his food from the few bottles of medicine which he was able to sell. Nevertheless, for the first time in his busy life he had his independence and was no longer living under the constraints of church and home. It was indeed fortunate that the few short stories he had been able to place during this period augmented his diminished income.

Within less than a month of his arrival at Southsea, the Ma'am sent Conan Doyle's younger brother Innes to stay with him, possibly to relieve the situation at home, but perhaps also to induce an added sense of responsibility in her eldest son, following the near disaster of the Budd episode. As Geoffrey Stavert has revealed in his illuminating biography,[21] one of Inne's teachers was the Rev. E. Elliot. In July 1930, soon after Conan Doyle died, Elliot wrote a reminiscence of the Doyle brothers for a local paper. Regarding Conan Doyle's spiritual views, he had this to say:

> His religious views were nebulous and vague; he would speak reverently of the Bible, but with a smile, as if he had no serious convictions. He was sceptical and tolerant but never antagonistic to religious faith . . .

It seems likely, as Geoffrey Stavert suggests, that Elliot was the original of the 'High Church Curate of St. Joseph's' who is one of young Munro's first visitors at Oakley Villas in *The Stark Munro Letters*. Conan Doyle's account of this interview is both amusing and illuminating:

> 'I trust,' said he, 'that we shall see you at St. Joseph's?' I was

compelled to explain that it was not probable.

'A Roman Catholic?' he asked, in a not friendly voice.

'I shook my head, but nothing would discourage him.

'Not a dissenter!' he exclaimed, with a sudden hardening of his genial face.

I shook my head again.

'A, a little lax – a little remiss!' he said playfully, and with an expression of relief. 'Professional men get into these ways. They have much to distract them . . .'

The gentle satire of this passage reveals Conan Doyle's reluctance openly to declare his agnosticism. When pressed to declare his beliefs Munro replies that 'religion is a vital thing, still growing and working . . . there were many eternal truths spoken of old and handed down to us in a book . . . But there are others yet to be revealed . . .

Clearly Conan Doyle wished to keep his religious notions to himself and was not prepared to pay lip-service to the trappings of conventionality. It would have been only too easy for him to have made contact with the local Catholic community. As he pointed out in his memoirs, 'My Catholic relatives had sent me introductions to the Bishop and I was assured that there was no Catholic doctor in the town. My mind, however, was so perfectly clear and I had so entirely broken away from the old faith that I could not possibly use it for material ends. I therefore burnt the letter of introduction.'

That Conan Doyle chose to burn that letter suggests a ritual significance. Perhaps he was destroying the last link between himself and the overbearing faith which had imprisoned his identity. Certainly since Feldkirch he had struggled to establish his own pattern and a clear picture of how he could best fulfil his ambitions. He had exposed himself to a variety of unusual experiences, travelled widely, and proved to his ever-anxious mother that he could stand on his own two feet.

At Southsea he worked hard and played hard to prove his point. In the first year of practice there he made £154, in the second year £250 rising to £300. Neither was he lonely. When not examining patients he was writing; when not writing he enjoyed the cheerful company of his younger brother. For some while the two brothers lived completely alone until Conan Doyle decided that it would assist them both considerably if they were to rent out part of the house.

An advertisement was placed in an evening newspaper and two elderly sisters soon took up residence.

In an attempt to widen his clientele, Conan Doyle made himself known among members of the local community. As he recalled in *Memories and Adventures*:

> Above all, I learnt a fact which I could whisper in the ear of every other man who starts, as I have done, a stranger among strangers. Do not think that the practice will come to you. You must go to it. You may sit upon your consulting-room chair until it breaks under you, but without purchase or partnership you will make little or no progress. The way to do it is to go out, to mix everywhere with men, to let them know you . . .

His interests during this period were as fascinating as they were diffuse. By the middle of 1883, for example, Conan Doyle had written no fewer than eight articles for the *British Journal of Photography* about his various expeditions to places of interest, and development processes. (This fascination with photography was to re-emerge in later years in the great debate over William Hope of the Crewe circle.) He wrote numerous letters home to his mother and other relatives. But all the while he knew that a career as a general practitioner was not in itself sufficient to satisfy his ambition.

By the autumn of 1883, almost a year after the move to Southsea, the Portsmouth Literary and Scientific Society seemed an attractive prospect to Conan Doyle. Its members drawn from the upper echelons of middle-class society, were, like himself, professional men with an intellectual approach to topics that lay outside their daily sphere of interest. Most probably Conan Doyle had been introduced to the society through like-minded medical practitioners in the town, for there was a degree of mutual tolerance exercised by members of the local medical profession.

Records show[22] that Dr Doyle had been nominated to join the Society by November 1883, and by the 20th of that same month his membership had been confirmed. The president of this august if somewhat pretentious society was a most remarkable man whose name Conan Doyle would never forget. That he made a profound impact on Conan Doyle's religious and scientific views is certainly evident from the attention devoted to him in the author's autobiography. It is not just that Major-General Alfred W. Drayson, FRAS (to allow him his full, resounding title) had served in the far corners of the British Empire, nor that he was the author of several remarkable astronomical works, a book entitled *The Art of Practical Whist*, and dozens of articles published in *The Boys' Own Paper* (a magazine to which Conan Doyle had contributed) and *Every Boy's Magazine* – General Drayson, had chosen to retire in Southsea because it seemed an appropriate milieu which would best serve his eclectic interests. And, most important for Dr Doyle, Alfred Drayson was a committed and active spiritualist.

CHAPTER 3

The Survival of Bodily Death

Shortly after he opened his practice in the Portsmouth suburb of Southsea, Conan Doyle became deeply interested in the pseudo-science known as mesmerism. Having declared his intention of seeking a belief system which would be based upon verifiable fact rather than blind, unreasoning faith, the experiments of the mesmerists offered him a possible solution to his problem.

The term 'mesmerism', although little used today, originates from Friedrich Anton Mesmer (1734–1815) of Mersburg in Southwest Germany. Mesmer, who studied medicine in Vienna and obtained a degree there, held a theory that the planets exercised a strong influence upon human behaviour and the mechanisms of the body. Moreover, he believed the force involved was electrical and that the key to this electrical force lay in the power of the magnet. Mesmer imagined that if a diseased part of the human body were stroked with a magnet the invisible force it emanated would effect a cure.

It did not take long for Mesmer to achieve celebrity among the Viennese middle class. Neurotic Viennese ladies wore magnetized clothes, even ate their food from magnetized plates. Eventually Mesmer changed the basis of his interpretation, believing that magnetism was an innate human energy which could, under the correct circumstances, be tapped. He devised what he termed a 'baquet', a tub filled to the brim with bottles of powdered brass and iron filings. From under the lid protruded a number of flexible iron rods which his patients were invited to touch and stroke.

Flushed with success, Mesmer moved to Paris in 1778 and won the patronage of Marie Antoinette, whose physician,

Charles d'Eslon, was convinced of the therapeutic power of the new 'magnetic' treatment. Louis XVI appointed a special commission to investigate the truth of Mesmer's claims but its conclusions were negative. Any beneficial results were the result of patient suggestibility rather than scientific cause and effect. Moreover, the commission warned against any further use of the mesmeric method, since the sessions in which patients participated often involved the stroking and touching of the female genitalia. Respectable Parisian society could not accept such a perversion. Eventually Mesmer retired to Vienna, where he was found guilty of spying and sentenced to two months' imprisonment. Subsequently he moved to Switzerland, where he died in 1815.

Although Mesmer had himself been discredited, his disciples continued their investigations, but without the elaborate and somewhat suggestive trappings. The Marquis de Puységur inspired the modern hypnotic movement, whilst his associate, Deleuse, carried the use of hypnosis further and established the validity of post-hypnotic suggestion.

In Britain the ideas of Mesmer and his followers were interpreted in a more orthodox manner. One of the first to be persuaded was John Elliotson, a doctor and a founder member of University College Hospital. In 1843 he began a magazine *The Zoist*, which dealt with mesmerism and related subjects, and he was able to amputate a man's thigh after placing him under hypnosis.

It is probable that Conan Doyle first heard of mesmerism through the work of James Braid, an Edinburgh-trained doctor who lived in Manchester. At first Braid had been cynical about the mesmerists' claims, but when he took the trouble to investigate mesmerism he became convinced of its powers. Braid was heavily influenced by the writings of Baron von Reichenbach, who in 1845 had identified what he defined as the 'odylic force', a magnetic influence carried by certain crystals, magnets, and human beings. People who were sensitive to the 'od force' perceived a halo or aura surrounding others and they were referred to as 'sensitives'. The typical sensitive was a person of a nervous or melancholy temperament. Reichenbach also believed that since the od-force was generated by heat and certain types of chemical energy, the decomposing human body provided a powerful source. The luminescence which could be sensed or perceived near cemeteries thus supplied an explanation for ghosts.

Whilst many scientists of the period were ready to dismiss the claims of mesmerism, the possibilities offered by hypnotism were more widely accepted. In the year that Conan Doyle commenced work at Southsea, a French physician, Liébault, achieved international success when he was able to cure a case of severe sciatica using the hypnotic method. The patient had been under the care of the distinguished neurologist Bernheim, who was so taken with Liébault's undoubted success that he joined forces to found the Nancy school of hypnotism. Ultimately the work of these two pioneers came to the attention of Charcot, whose own dramatic methods inspired much of the early work of Sigmund Freud.

In April 1884 Conan Doyle published a short story in *Cassell's Saturday Journal* entitled 'John Barrington Cowles'.[1] Cowles is a young man who falls under the influence of a diabolical female mesmerist, Kate Northcott. The character of Cowles bears something of a resemblance to the younger Conan Doyle, being a sensitive individual who, as a medical student, has won a prize in physics at Edinburgh University. The woman in the piece, whose mesmeric abilities have already resulted in the death of her two previous fiancés, is essentially evil, described as 'a vampire soul behind a lovely face'. As a result of her attentions, Cowles meets a tragic end, the story being narrated by his friend Robert Armitage. The piece is a fascinating precursor of Conan Doyle's later novella *The Parasite*, where the theme of sexual exploration and domination is dealt with on a broader canvas.

A more tongue-in-cheek treatment of the mesmeric theme can be observed in 'The Great Keinplatz Experiment', which Conan Doyle published in July 1885,[2] a month before his marriage to Louise Hawkins. The story is about a disastrous experiment in mind transfer conducted by an eccentric anatomist, Professor von Baumgarten.

> By experiments which extended over twenty years, [the Professor] obtained a basis of facts upon which it was his ambition to build up a new, exact science which should embrace mesmerism, spiritualism and all cognate subjects. In this he was much helped by his intimate knowledge of the more intricate parts of animal physiology which treat of nerve currents and the working of the brain; for Alexis Von Baumgarten was Regius Professor of Physiology at the Uni-

versity of Keinplatz, and had all the resources of the laboratory to aid him in his profound researches.

Despite the humorous overtones implicit in the story, Conan Doyle uses the framework to air some of his own theories about the relationship between mind and body. Clairvoyance, telepathy, and astral projection could be explained if consciousness was regarded as an independent, self-regulating function. Professor von Baumgarten, Conan Doyle's mouthpiece, expresses this theory in the following terms:

> . . . it is evident that under certain conditions the soul or mind does separate itself from the body. In the case of a mesmerised person, the body lies in a cataleptic condition, but the spirit has left it. Perhaps you reply that the soul is there, but in a dormant condition. I answer that this is not so, otherwise how can one account for the condition of clairvoyance, which has fallen into disrepute through the knavery of certain scoundrels, but which can easily be shown to be an undoubted fact. I have been able myself, with a sensitive subject, to obtain an accurate description of what was going on in another room or another house. How can such knowledge be accounted for on any hypothesis save that the soul of the subject has left the body and is wandering through space? For a moment it is recalled by the voice of the operator and says what it has seen and then wings its way once more through the air. Since the spirit is by its very nature invisible, we cannot see these comings and goings, but we see their effect in the body of the subject, how rigid and inert, now struggling to narrate impressions which could never have come to it by natural means.

This extremely detailed account of mind/body separation remained essentially the same throughout Conan Doyle's subsequent career. It is of course a popularization of the many similar theories being propounded by psychic investigators of the period.

Chief among the investigators of hypnotism and clairvoyance at this time were two fellows of Trinity College, Cambridge. In 1882 Frederick Myers and Edmund Gurney had founded the Society for Psychical Research. They had done this as a response to an article published in the *Nineteenth Century* in June 1882, in which it had been initially suggested that thought-transference could be proved by repeatable scientific experiment. Over the next four years

Myers, Gurney, and Frank Podmore (an associate researcher) investigated literally hundreds of accounts of abnormal
experiences from the public domain. In reviewing the evidence they were struck with the great predominance of
alleged apparitions at or near the moment of death. Their
conclusions were subsequently published in a massive two-
volume work entitled *Phantasms of the Living* (1886).
Although Conan Doyle would not yet have read this at the
time of the story's composition, he would almost certainly
have studied an article by Gurney and Myers which
appeared in the *Fortnightly Review* for March 1883. In their
article, the authors argued that there was a strong analogy
between their experimental cases of thought-transference
and some of these spontaneous cases of telepathy, and they
believed that the transference of a shock or impulse from
one living person to another at such a distance as to negate
the possibility of normal communication could be demonstrated. Myers and Gurney believed that telepathy could
follow a provable causal law rather like the law of atomic
combination in chemistry.

In their introduction to *Phantasms of the Living* Myers and
Gurney reveal the inadequacy of scientific methodology.
Like Conan Doyle, they perceived that its concentration on
objective results concerning the properties of matter took no
account of *subjective* experience.

> . . . . I wish to point out that the *emotional* creed of educated
> men is becoming divorced from their *scientific* creed; that just
> as the old orthodoxy of religion was too narrow to contain
> their feelings and aspirations; and consequently that just as
> the fabric of religious orthodoxy used to be strained in order
> to admit the discoveries of geology or astronomy, so now
> also the obvious deductions of materialistic science are
> strained or overpassed in order to give sanction to feelings
> and aspirations which it is found impossible to ignore . . my
> argument is that . . . telepathy . . . would be the first
> indication of a possible scientific basis for much that now
> lacks not only experimental confirmation, but even plausible
> analogy . . .

Although Conan Doyle's story is really a gentle satire on
the somewhat over-academic approach of pioneers like
Myers and Gurney, on another level it reveals the extent to
which he had begun to take seriously the theoretical considerations which they had suggested. Since religion had been

tested and found wanting it was up to science to provide the answers. However, the question of the validity of spiritualist phenomena was an altogether more problematic one for him to consider.

In March 1885 a colleague of Conan Doyle's, Dr Pike (who, like Conan Doyle, was on the honorary staff of the Royal Portsmouth Hospital), came to him with a request. A young patient of his, Jack Hawkins, had been suffering a series of fits which lately had been getting worse. Would Conan Doyle offer a second opinion? Conan Doyle examined the youth and diagnosed cerebral meningitis. Since the condition was undoubtedly terminal, Conan Doyle suggested that the patient should be accommodated in one of the upper rooms at Bush Villas where he could be carefully attended. Hawkins had an older sister, Louise, who became a frequent visitor to Conan Doyle's house. A relationship was soon struck up between this attractive young woman and Conan Doyle, and by the autumn of that same year the Ma'am was delighted to hear that a marriage was in the offing.[3] The knot was subsequently tied on 6 August at Thornton-in-Lonsdale parish church (Westmorland) in the presence of relatives and Dr Bryan Charles Waller, Conan Doyle's mentor.

We know very little about Louise Hawkins. Her photograph suggests a pale, rather shy young woman. She was not without means, having an income from her late father's estate of £100 a year. Conan Doyle maintained an unfortunate reserve when writing about her in his memoirs, since he obviously had regard for his second wife's feelings. However, there is a distinct possibility that Conan Doyle's first experiences in spiritualism may have been inspired by her own involvement.

Prior to 1886, Conan Doyle's position about the issue of life after death was that of a sceptic. In *The New Revelation* he recalled:

> I did not, of course, believe in an anthropomorphic God, but I believed then as I believe now, in an intelligent Force behind all the operations of Nature – a force so infinitely complex and great that my finite brain could get no farther than its existence. Right and wrong I saw also as great obvious facts which needed no divine revelations. But when it came to a question of our little personalities surviving death, it seemed to me that the whole analogy of Nature was

against it. When the candle burns out the light disappears. When the electric cell is shattered the current stops. When the body dissolves there is an end of the matter. Each man in his egotism may feel that he ought to survive, but let him look, we will say, at the average loafer – of high or low degree – would anyone contend that there was any obvious reason why *that* personality should carry on? It seemed to be a delusion, and I was convinced that death did indeed end all . . .

He went on to say that he had always regarded spiritualism as 'the greatest nonsense upon earth', that he had read about 'the conviction of fraudulent mediums', and that, at about this time (1886), he had met some friends who 'were interested in the matter'. He participated in table-moving seances and got 'connected messages spelt out by tilts' which it would have been impossible to receive by chance. He became convinced that someone was moving the table and had 'puzzled and worried' over the matter.

The 'friends' referred to by Conan Doyle seem likely to have been acquaintances of Louise Hawkins. As Geoffrey Stavert adroitly pointed out in his biography,[4] Conan Doyle attended experimental seances with the wife and family of a solicitor, Douglas Morey Ford, whose elder brother, Arthur Vernon Ford, was an ophthalmic surgeon. (Conan Doyle himself specialized in this area of medicine.) Stavert quotes from an account of one of these seances which casts a rather humorous light on these experimental session:

> It would have been about 1885 that D (i.e. Douglas) and his family made the acquaintance of Arthur Conan Doyle. It is well known that Conan Doyle was extremely interested in psychic phenomena and a number of sessions of table turning took place at D's house, when his wife Honor and her family and friends participated with Doyle and his circle. D did not believe in spiritualism and indeed frowned on the practice. There is a family story that on one occasion when a session of 'table turning' was in progress, and the table was apparently of its own volition heading out of the door, D arrived home and was incensed to find what was going on, and did not mince his words. Presumably any interruption of the friendship between the two families was only short-lived, as the family still maintained contacts many years later . . .[5]

Conan Doyle's attitude to spiritualism prior to this period remained detached and tongue-in-cheek. In 'The Ghosts of

Goresthorpe Grange', published in *London Society* in 1883,
the main character, who describes himself as 'an earnest
student of the supernatural', becomes the owner of a feudal
mansion, Goresthorpe Grange. (The self-made grocer is in
fact a mocking self-portrait of Conan Doyle by the name of
'D'odd' whose family dates back 'to the prehistoric era'.)
Disappointed with the lack of occult presence, D'odd adver-
tises for a medium, with disastrous results. (The medium
turns out to be a confidence trickster who specializes in
burglary.) When he visits his London agent, help is provided from a red notebook which lists a number of (obviously fake) 'psychic investigators':

'What were we looking up, again?'
'Ghosts,' I suggested.
'Of course, page 41. Here we are. "J.H. Fowler & Son,
Dunkel Street, suppliers of mediums to the nobility and
gentry; charms sold – love philtres – mummies – horoscopes
cast." Nothing in your line there, I suppose.'
I shook my head despondently.
'Frederick Tabb,' continued my wife's cousin, 'sole chan-
nel of communication between the living and the dead.
Proprietor of the spirits of Byron, Kirke White, Grimaldi,
Tom Cribb, and Inigo Jones. That's about the figure!'
'Nothing romantic enough there,' I objected.
'Here is another,' said my companion. 'Christopher
McCarthy; bi-weekly seances – attended by all the eminent
spirits of ancient and modern times. Nativities – charms –
abracadabras, messages from the dead. He might be able to
help us . . .'

Conan Doyle's interest in spiritualism was intensified
through his friendship with the president of the Portsmouth
Literary and Scientific Society. What initially excited Doyle
about Alfred Drayson was his revolutionary approach to a
number of astronomical subjects. By the time the two met
through their joint membership of the Society, Drayson had
notched up an impressive record of publications in this area,
in addition to his other writings. He astounded the scientific
community by propounding the theory that the earth had a
second rotation – a theory which explained the procession of
the equinoxes, the changes in polar distance, and the
decrease in the obliquity. Initially scorned by geologists, his
conclusions were eventually accepted. He also pointed out
that the then accepted belief that the satellites of Uranus

moved from east to west was a delusion.

Throughout his career, Conan Doyle retained an immense respect for this eccentric genius. In an unpublished letter to Sir Oliver Lodge, he wrote asking whether the name of Drayson had ever meant anything to him, and comparing him in status to Copernicus. It is evident that Conan Doyle regarded Drayson as a genius.

Impressed by the scholarship and urbanity of the retired general, Conan Doyle was willing to listen to his advice in the field of psychic experimentation. Conan Doyle regarded the whole subject of spiritualism as a 'problem' and was only too glad to be able to ask Drayson's advice. In *Memories and Adventures* he comments:

> His opinion therefore was not negligible upon any subject, and when he told me his views and experiences upon Spiritualism I could not fail to be impressed, though my own philosophy was far too solid to be easily destroyed. I was too poor to employ professional mediums, and to work on such subjects without a medium is as if one worked at astronomy without a telescope.

As far as Conan Doyle was concerned, spiritualism lacked a clearly defined philosophy and was anarchic in structure. Theosophy, on the other hand, seemed eminently attractive to him, having a 'very-well-thought-out and reasonable scheme'.[7] Drayson appears to have had some influence on this brief flirtation with what was then a popular movement among middle-class intellectuals, introducing the occultist A.P. Sinnett (author of *Esoteric Buddhism* and *Occult World*) to the young doctor.

Conan Doyle was particularly taken with the concepts of karma and reincarnation.

The basis of Theosophy was simple enough, being a westernized interpretation of elements of Tibetan Buddhism. The inspiration for the movement was a controversial woman, Madame Blavatsky. She claimed to be a *chela*, or disciple of a brotherhood whose members, known as *mahatmas*, had the ability to summon up apparitions of themselves and to make astral journeys.

Theosophy received something of a setback when in 1884 Richard Hodgson of the Theosophical Society travelled to India to investigate accusations of fraud which had been levelled against Madame Blavatsky. Conan Doyle refers to this episode in his memoirs, and it would seem that his disenchantment with the movement originated from this investigation. Nevertheless, the basic idea of Theosophy still remained popular, with its seven principles, starting from the gross body and proceeding upwards, and the principle of nirvana. It was of course antipathetic to spiritualism, for reincarnation ran counter to the idea of the dead retaining their untarnished individuality.

Conan Doyle clearly experienced some regrets about the discrediting of Madame Blavatsky and took Sinnett's doubts seriously. While admitting that 'the woman undoubtedly had real psychic powers, whatever their source', he had to admit that the publication of her letters 'leaves an unpleasant impression', concluding that 'theosophy will be in a stronger position when it shakes off Madame Blavatsky altogether'.[8]

From what Conan Doyle tells us in *The New Revelation*, it was his own dissatisfaction with the seances organized at his own home with his wife and friends that led him to seek Drayson's advice:

> I have no psychical powers myself, and those who worked with me had little more. Among us we could just muster enough of the magnetic force, or whatever you will call it, to get the table movements with their suspicions and often stupid messages. I still have notes of those sittings and copies of some, at least, of the messages. They were not always absolutely stupid. For example, I find that on one occasion, on my asking some test question, such as how many coins I had in my pocket, the table spelt out: 'We are here to educate and to elevate, not to guess riddles.' And then: 'The religious frame of mind, not the critical, is what we wish to inculcate.' Now, no one could say that that was a puerile message. On the other hand, I was always haunted by the fear of involuntary pressure from the hands of the sitters.

One particular incident annoyed and disillusioned him. A long and detailed message came through to the 'home circle' which purported to be from a spirit who had been a commercial traveller. The man, who had been killed in a fire at a theatre in Exeter, asked the circle to write to his family at a village called Slattenmere, in Cumberland. Conan Doyle carried out this instruction only to have his letter returned through the dead letter office. He was so disgusted that for a while his interest in spiritualism waned. Drayson attempted to reassure Conan Doyle about the incident, telling him:

> This world is full of weak or foolish people. So is the next. You need not mix with them, any more than you do in this world. One chooses one's companions. But suppose a man in this world, who had lived in his house alone and never mixed with his fellows, was at last to put his head out of the window to see what sort of place it was, what would happen? Some naughty boy would probably say something rude. Anyhow, he would see nothing of the wisdom or greatness of the world. He would draw his head in thinking it was a very poor place. That is just what you have done. In a mixed seance, with no definite aim, you have thrust your head into the next world and you have met some naughty boys. Go forward and try to reach something better.[9]

Determined that some of his own enthusiasm should rub off on the young doctor, General Drayson invited him to attend some of his own family's seances. Conan Doyle dutifully obliged but still remained rather unimpressed.

> They sat round a dining-room table which after a time, their hands being upon it, began to sway and finally got sufficient motion to tap with one leg. They then asked questions and received answers, more or less wise and more or less to the point. They were got by the tedious process of reciting the alphabet and writing down the letter which the tap indicated. It seemed to me that we were collectively pushing the table and that our own wills were concerned in bringing down the leg at the right moment.[10]

He remained interested but quite sceptical about these clumsy attempts to invoke psychic phenomena. The messages obtained from the sessions were specific and from deceased members of the Drayson family – a fact which Conan Doyle did not find especially remarkable. Twenty such sessions occurred at the Drayson establishment, but nothing evidential was offered to Conan Doyle himself.

Somehow the table-rapping version of spiritualism seemed lamely inadequate to him. What was needed was a series of controlled experiments with definite results. The willing suspension of critical judgement displayed by his family would never convince someone like Conan Doyle whose training had been scientific and disciplined.

Fortunately another member of the Literary and Scientific

Society, an architect by the name of Henry Ball, was rather more structured in his approach to psychic experimentation. He and Conan Doyle shared a common interest in telepathy, an interest which for Conan Doyle's part had been greatly inspired by F.W.H. Myers's early experiments which were to be later recorded in his mammoth study, *Human Personality and its Survival of Bodily Death*. The two men therefore conducted an intensive series of experiments with a medium called Horstead which commenced on 24 January 1887 and continued with intervals until the beginning of July.[11] Sadly the detailed records kept by Conan Doyle at this time are not in the public domain, but we can gain some idea of their content by referring to his memoirs. 'Again and again,' he recalls, 'sitting behind [Ball], I have drawn diagrams, and he in turn has made approximately the same figure. I showed beyond any doubt whatever that I could convey my thought without words.'

The success of these telepathic studies in the spring of 1887 convinced Doyle that he should retain an open mind about the whole area of psychic phenomena. If the scientific method could be employed with modest success in these affairs, then the physical laws of the universe held by physicists must be modified:

> It was clear now that my position had been too rigid. I had compared the thought-excretion of the brain to the bile-excretion of the liver. Clearly this was untenable. If thought could go a thousand miles and produce a perceptible effect then it differed entirely not only in degree but in kind from any purely physical material. That seemed certain, and it must involve some modification of my old views.[12]

By July 1887 he had subtly shifted his position. At the end of June an 'elderly gentleman who was reputed to have considerable mediumistic power' impressed Ball and Conan Doyle by his telepathic capacity. Conan Doyle, amazed at the accuracy of the results obtained, wrote a detailed letter to the spiritualist journal *Light*, recounting the experiment:

> . . . for some days I had been debating in my mind whether I should get a copy of Leigh Hunt's *Comic Dramatists of the Restoration* . . . I had thought the matter over, but had dismissed it from my mind a day or two before the seance. On sitting, our medium came quickly under control, and delivered a trance address, containing much interesting and elevating matter. He then became clairvoyant, describing one

or two scenes which we had no opportunity of testing. So far, the meeting had been very interesting, but not above the possibility of deception. We then proposed writing. The medium took up a pencil, and after a few convulsive movements, he wrote a message to each of us. Mine ran: 'This gentleman is a healer. Tell him from me not to read Leigh Hunt's book.' Now, sir, I can swear that no one knew I had contemplated reading that book, and, moreover, it was no case of thought-reading, for I had never referred to the matter all day. I can only say that if I had had to devise a test message I could not have hit upon one which was so absolutely inexplicable on any hypothesis except that held by Spiritualists. The message of one of my friends, referring to his own private affairs, was as startingly correct as mine.[13]

What intrigued Conan Doyle so much about this particular experiment was that it went beyond the telepathic proofs obtained by Ball and himself. If the mind of a sensitive could actually probe into his own memory and respond to its contents, then human consciousness could most definitely exist independently of its bodily constraints. This was way above the mediocre dramatics of the seance room which he referred to in his letter as 'a mere idle resort for the indulgence of a foolish, purposeless curiosity'. The experiment had proved without doubt the reality of the spirit:

> Let a man realise that the human soul, as it emerges from its bodily cocoon, shapes its destiny in exact accordance with its condition; that the condition depends upon the sum result of his actions and thoughts in this life . . .

Since the soul had an integrity all its own, the individual could no longer find refuge in the confessional. The spiritual law implicit here was 'self-acting and inexorable'. Each act was engraved upon the consciousness of the soul and could not be removed; existence both before and after death was existential.

Despite the demands placed on him by a busy practice and his participation in psychic affairs, Conan Doyle found the time to write for the popular market. In November 1887 he found a publisher for his short detective novel, *A Study in Scarlet*. Today this slight work earns a high price among book collectors since it introduced perhaps the most famous of all fictional detectives, Sherlock Holmes. Yet when it appeared in *Beeton's Christmas Annual*, published by Ward Lock, it received little attention from the critics.

The central character of this murder story is an ascetic who occupies a suite of rooms in Baker Street. From the outset, Holmes, a consulting detective, intrigues the narrator, Dr Watson. He keeps odd hours, lives by a Bohemian code, is introverted and subject to fits of depression. In fact he conforms precisely to the neurasthenic type of individual already depicted by Conan Doyle in some of his earlier short stories. Although Holmes represents the supreme rationalist, his appearance suggests that of the medium, clairvoyant, or mystic:

> His eyes were sharp and piercing . . . and his thin, hawk-like nose gave his whole expression an air of alertness and decision. His chin, too, had the prominence and squareness which mark the man of determination . . .

The mesmeric impression conveyed by Conan Doyle's detective works powerfully upon his fellow-lodger at Baker Street, so that, throughout the narrative, we remain entranced by his every word and action and the mechanism of the plot seems quite unimportant.

The concept of the mesmeric individual had already figured prominently in Conan Doyle's short story 'John Barrington Cowles' which I have already mentioned. Here the central character is female and possesses, unlike Holmes, the ability to obsess and corrupt her victims. Kate Northcott, the seductress of the young medical student, inherits a diabolic strain from her father, who met his end in an attempt to steal the 'everlasting fire' from the temple of sun worshippers. Whereas Holmes represents the triumph of reason over fear and the unknown, Northcott, described variously as a 'fiend' and a 'ghoul', mesmerizes and destroys her victims through inexplicable means. It seems clear that at this period of his life Conan Doyle saw the relationship between the conscious and subconscious in terms of an inexorable battle for control between the male and female aspects of personality. How else can we explain his preoccupation with hypnotism and mind-control?

The penetrating eyes and air of determination shared by several of Conan Doyle's central characters in these early stories mark out a strong, dominant personality which is symbolic and therefore all the more powerful in its effect upon the reader. The features of what one could term here the 'id' prototype are clear-cut, almost unworldly. In describing Kate Northcott, the narrator is compelled to remark:

> In my whole life I have never seen such a classically perfect countenance. It was the real Greek type – the forehead broad, very low, and as white as marble, with a cloudlet of delicate locks wreathing round it, the nose straight and clean cut, the lips inclined to thinness, the chin and lower jaw beautifully rounded off, and yet sufficiently developed to promise unusual strength of character.
>
> But those eyes – those wonderful eyes! If I could but give some faint idea of their varying moods, their steely hardness, their feminine softness, their power of command . . .

In Conan Doyle's next novel, *The Mystery of Cloomber* (1888), the theme of the occult is developed in a more intricate manner, incorporating the Blavatskian idea of the *chelas* into a simple revenge story.

Set in the west of Scotland, the novel relates the experiences of one John Fothergill West, a law student and son of a renowned Oriental scholar, whose half-brother, William Farintosh, is the proprietor of a large estate at Branksome. When Farintosh decides to undertake a tour of Italy, the Wests take up residence at Branksome. Nearby lies the Gothic mansion of Cloomber Hall, whose new owner, General Heatherstone, presents something of a problem to West junior. Within days of his occupation, the General employs gangs of workmen in the construction of a high wooden fence, and victuals the house as if for a siege. Determined not to be put off by such misanthropic behaviour, John and his sister Esther strike up an acquaintance with the General's son and daughter, with whom they eventualy forge romantic attachments.

Eventually it becomes clear to West that the General's wish to remain secluded arises from the instinct for self-preservation and that he is to suffer terrible but inexplicable retribution.

Heatherstone's paranoia abates somewhat when a dilapidated stranger who appears in the vicinity of Cloomber Hall introduces himself to the General and makes it clear to West that he is an old acquaintance from the Indian military campaigns, eager to act as his unpaid bodyguard.

Despite the immense precautions taken by Heatherstone, his fears are realized when, during a heavy storm, a barque is shipwrecked in a nearby bay. On the disintegrating poop West spies three dark-skinned strangers who subsequently re-emerge, apparently unscathed, on the mainland. In conversation with the captain and mate of the sunken ship, West discovers that the crew had been made uneasy throughout the voyage by the supernatural aura which surrounded these three Buddhists, particularly their leader, Ram Singh, a man of tremendous psychic presence and in some ways curiously similar to the *femme fatale* in 'John Barrington Cowles':

> The stranger's broad, unruffled brow, his clear, searching gaze, firm-set yet sensitive mouth and clean-cut, resolute expression, all combined to form the most imposing and noble presence which I had ever known. I could not have imagined that such imperturbable calm and at the same time such a consciousness of latent strength could have been expressed by any human face.

The three men are members of a Theosophical sect derived from a Tibetan lamasery. Known under the various names of Sannasis, Yogis, Sevras, Qualanders, Hakims or Cufis, these adepts worship the God of Knowledge, and possess the secrets of Nature. Ram Singh himself turns out to be a *chela* of a lower grade to that of his companions. However, all have the power of astral projection, a fact which is demonstrated to West when he visits their primitive shelter:

> 'You have now an opportunity,' [said Ram Singh], in a subdued, reverential voice, 'of seeing a spectacle which few Europeans have had the privilege of beholding. Inside that cottage you will find two Yogis – men who are only one remove from the highest plane of adeptship. They are both wrapped in an ecstatic trance, otherwise I should not venture to obtrude your presence upon them. Their astral bodies have departed from them, to be present at the feast of lamps, in the holy Lamasery of Rudock in Tibet. Tread lightly, lest by stimulating their corporeal functions you recall them before their devotions are completed.'

Heatherstone's doom, which was predicted forty years before at the time of his offence (he had murdered the arch-adept, one Ghoolab Shah, whilst on a campaign in northern India), finally awaits him at the loathsome Hole of Cree, a kind of archetypal orifice which bears a remarkable resemblance to the great Grimpen Mire of Conan Doyle's later novel *The Hound of the Baskervilles*:

On each side lay shallow sheets of stagnant water overlying a treacherous bottom of semi-fluid mud, which rose above the surface here and there in moist, sweltering banks, mottled over with occasional patches of unhealthy vegetation. Great purple and yellow fungi had broken out in a dense eruption, as though Nature were afflicted with a foul disease, which manifested itself by this crop of plague spots.

Conan Doyle's ability to present disturbing images drawn from our subconscious sexual fears is only too apparent here as is his undoubted capacity to create a feeling of intense loathing and dread for the Buddhist assassins. At a deeper level the story deals with two powerful themes: the fascination for the occult and an obsession with racial hatred. (Conrad's *The Heart of Darkness* is an interesting parallel.)

That a spiritualistic philosophy held a very strong attraction for Conan Doyle at this time can be seen in Heatherstone's comments to his doctor. The General, who is recovering from a high fever and attacks of delirium, quizzes his GP about the 'odyllic force' (about which the latter knows nothing):

'Ah, you western scientific men are very much behind the day in some things,' (Heatherstone remarked). 'In all that is material and conducive to the comfort of the body you are pre-eminent, but in what concerns the subtle forces of Nature and the latent powers of the human spirit your best men are centuries behind the humblest coolies of India. Countless generations of beef-eating, comfort-loving ancestors have given our animal instincts the command over our spiritual ones. The body, which should have been a mere tool for the use of the soul, has now become a degrading prison in which it is confined. The Oriental soul and body are not so welded together as ours are, and there is far less wrench when they part in death.'

Oriental mysticism of this sort was very popular among psychic researchers of the period. The impetus had come from Madame Blavatsky, but she was not alone in focusing the public's attention on the wonders of the fakir and the Hindu magician. The American illusionist Harry Kellehar, for example, was typical of the large group of individuals who spent their time touring the villages of northern India and witnessing levitations, snake-charming tricks, and other apparently psychically inspired phenomena.[14] Frequently members of the Society for Psychical Research used hypnotic suggestion to explain these events.

Conan Doyle's persistent interest in mind–body experiences reached new heights when in February 1889 he participated in a demonstration of hypnotism at Southsea. Such mesmeric exhibitions were common at the time. Sadly for Conan Doyle, he showed some involuntary resistance to the exercise and the experiment failed.[15] The demonstration was given by Professor Milo de Meyer, a Frenchman whose theatrical approach to the subject bears a great similarity to that of Charcot (the latter's successful treatment of neurotic patients had attracted the attention of Sigmund Freud, who himself used hypnotism for a short while). For example, one man was asked, whilst in a trance, to simulate the murder of his father, and another had a pin pushed into his arm.

Whatever the conclusions he had come to regarding hypnotic suggestion, there is no doubt that by the summer of 1889 Conan Doyle had come to accept the 'proofs' of spiritualism. Nevertheless he retained a healthy scepticism regarding the subject, which clearly suffered from a lack of scientific method and which, in many respects, was far from offering him an adequate philosophy.

On 7 May 1889 a Mr John Beaumont of Bournemouth talked to an audience of approximately 150 people at the Yorke Rooms, St Paul's Road, close to Conan Doyle's own residence.[16] His subject was spiritualism, or rather the pernicious influence exerted on the public by this popular movement, which he described as 'an old snake of Satan's in a new dress'. Although the talk only lasted for an hour and a half, it produced a vigorous response from Dr Doyle, whose letter to the *Evening News* of 9 May was headed: 'Spiritualism. A Fraud or a Revelation?' (The letter was unsigned, but the style and content are undoubtedly Conan Doyle's.) In his long defence of spiritualism, Conan Doyle maintained that its critics were unreasonable since they were motivated either by religious bigotry or by scientific dogma. Spiritualism was a popular movement which provided an answer to the puzzle of death and which should be given the credit it deserved. He went on to point out:

> When any new form of knowledge arises above the mental horizon of the human race there are always a certain number of well-meaning but narrow-minded men who are ready to denounce it as being opposed to Scriptural teaching . . . Since all the lines of thought have had to encounter this

opposition, it is no wonder that Spiritualism should be no exception. It stands in the curious position . . . of being attacked by two different bodies of men upon diametrically opposite grounds . . . The effect of this double opposition has been that in forty years Spiritualism has spread from an obscure American village over the whole civilized world; that a recent computation has put the number of professed Spiritualists at 30,000,000 . . .

Conan Doyle sweeps away the religious objections to the movement as being short-sighted and largely irrelevant. In the Bible itself, he claims, there is clear evidence of spiritualistic gifts being shared by the disciples, and he goes on to pose the question: 'Is it reasonable to suppose that the all-powerful Creator had given man powers, and implanted in him possibilities of knowledge, which he is never under any circumstances to use? Had the omnipotent Deity designed that death should be an absolute barrier between this world and the next, would He not have made it so? . . . Far from being a termination of man's affairs, death is but a frail partition through which loving hands may meet. A Spiritualist cannot fear death – He knows that it only marks a fresh stage in his ascending course, and opens up for him a wider field of knowledge and usefulness . . .'

The idea of death as a physical mechanism which enables the soul to progress upwards in an evolutionary spiral bears some resemblance to the philosophy of the Tibetan Buddhists which Conan Doyle had referred to in *The Mystery of Cloomber*. Spiritualism was seen by him as a necessary component of a much wider religious experience in which the body played a very subservient role. Hence the *proofs* offered by practising spiritualists were of the utmost importance. Conan Doyle's view about this matter did not change radically until his death in 1930.

If proof were needed then he could quote the names of a dozen 'men of scientific attainments who have spent years in investigation under the most rigid test conditions'. (Among the dozen mentioned are Sir William Crookes, Alfred Russel Wallace, and J.G. Wood–many of whose works on spiritualism he must have been well acquainted with by this time.) Their testimony was proof in itself, but he could add to this his own testament, based as it was on the performances of unpaid mediums who were entirely above fraud. He concludes:

Spiritualism is no more to be judged by venal public mediums, than Christianity is to be condemned because in every Church there are a certain number of hypocrites and time-servers.

This letter (eight paragraphs, a column in length) stands as a clear condemnation of the hostility held by certain churchmen towards the new movement. It also shows us that, however limited his own experience of psychic phenomena and their scientific treatment, Conan Doyle had reached a point of certainty and was ready to accept the basic belief in the indestructability of the human soul. Spiritualism was indeed the new religion, and like all new religions what it lacked in track record could be compensated for in terms of its potential power to uplift and invigorate humanity.

The last years of the old decade had been busy ones for Dr Doyle of Southsea. Apart from his medical duties and family commitments, he had been hard at work on several new projects. His first historical novel, entitled *Micah Clarke*, which had been finished early in 1888, was published in 1889. Moreover, the limited success of *A Study in Scarlet* in the USA encouraged Lippincotts to sign him up for a second detective novel, which he later entitled *The Sign of Four*.[17] Sherlock Holmes, although not yet a household word, was becoming more widely known.

The welcome granted to *Micah Clarke* spurred Conan Doyle on to begin the research for a second, even more ambitious historical piece. This time the background was the reign of Edward III, which Doyle himself described as 'the greatest epoch in English history'. Although it is not well-remembered today, *The White Company* remains an impressive evocation of the age of chivalry, vulgarity, and romance and is extremely effective as a period piece.

March 1890 brought Conan Doyle further literary success when his publishers, Longman, brought out a collection of 10 of his short stories under the title of the lead piece, *The Captain of the Polestar*. Significantly the book was dedicated to his friend Major-General Alfred Drayson, 'as a token', Conan Doyle wrote, 'of my admiration for his great and as yet unrecognised serves to Astronomy'. Among the occult tales contained in this collection is an Egyptological yarn, entitled 'The Ring of Thoth'.

The story, although a slight apprentice piece, is of interest to us because of its concern with death and immortality. Briefly, the plot concerns the experiences of one John Vansittart Smith, a student of Egyptology, who is unfortunate enough to be locked in a section of the Egyptian rooms at the Louvre. A shadowy figure, whom he had presumed was employed as a cleaner, wakens the narrator and the latter then witnesses the bizarre unwrapping of a mummy. In his attempt to escape from this unwelcome scene, the scholar draws attention to himself and then has little choice but to hear the desecrator's story. It transpires that the nocturnal visitor, Sostra by name, has had to endure centuries of extended life, having self-administered a life-giving elixir which had also been intended for his long-deceased love, a daughter of the governor. This wandering Egyptian's quest to find everlasting peace provides the pathos of the story, and although the narrative seems unduly rambling at points, the central obsession with the life-in-death theme certainly provides interest. Only be securing the potion which lies around the neck of his deceased betrothed can the Egyptian terminate his own existence. This added twist to the story justifies the implied necrophilia.

Ever restless and seeking new causes, Conan Doyle's next excursion into the unknown occurred when he read of an announcement by a German physician named Koch that he would be giving a demonstration of a new and revolutionary cure for the dread disease consumption (the very disease which was later to afflict poor Louise Doyle). As Conan Doyle noted in his memoirs, 'since the simple things of life have always been the most pleasant to me, it is possible that I should have remained in Southsea permanently but for this new episode in my life'. Since the demonstration was to be held in Berlin, Conan Doyle saw the perfect opportunity to escape from the dull routine of domesticity and felt an 'irresistible impulse' to travel abroad. Unfortunately, Dr Koch refused to see Conan Doyle, so he had to rely on the notes of the lecture made by a friendly American. He came to the conclusion that the proposed cure was 'experimental and premature'.

On the journey back from Berlin Conan Doyle made the acquaintance of a skin specialist called Malcolm Morris who informed him that he would be much better suited to using his talents in London. Since Conan Doyle was particularly interested in ophthalmology, Morris suggested that he spend six months in Vienna acquiring the necessary skills. After consulting Louise and the Ma'am, Conan Doyle disposed of the Southsea practice and on 12 December 1890 was given a farewell dinner at the Grosvenor Hotel by his fellow members of the Portsmouth Literary and Scientific Society. Several days later he said farewell to Bush Villas and set out for pastures new.

The Conan Doyles reached Vienna on Monday 5 January 1891. Conan Doyle's forebodings about the Viennese jaunt were confirmed when he discovered that the lectures were exclusively in German and that he was unfamiliar with many of the technical terms used. He came to the conclusion that he could have learned far more in London, and spent most of the time in the hospital writing a short and unexceptional book entitled *The Doings of Raffles Haw*, which he himself described as 'not a notable achievement'. The story, which is about a chemist who discovers how to change other metals into gold and who then develops a charitable streak, leading to disastrous social consequences, appears to be a rather amusing if unconvincing parable.

The residence in Vienna lasted for two months rather than the predicted six, the family returning to London on 24 March. Conan Doyle immediately took on a suite of rooms in Montague Place and began to look for a place close to Harley Street where he could set up practice as an oculist. At last he secured the use of a front room at 2 Devonshire Place, near Wimpole Street, at a rent of £120 per year. On 9 April he made an entry in his diary which was later to assume great significance in his life as a writer: 'Sent "A Scandal in Bohemia" to A.P. Watt.' It was the first of the Sherlock Holmes short stories, and the beginning of fame and fortune.

CHAPTER 4

A Student of Psychic Phenomena

Every morning Conan Doyle walked from his lodgings at Montague Place, reached his consulting-room at ten and then sat there until three or four in the afternoon without seeing a single patient. Clearly the move to London and the hoped-for specialism in oculism was a disaster. However, during the long, silent hours, Conan Doyle was far from idle. Every day he returned home bearing sheaves of paper which represented his first attempts to break into the mass market for detective fiction in short-story form. Sherlock Holmes had been tried in novel format but had not met with much success. The short story, on the other hand, offered the possibility of a single character maintaining his popularity throughout the series, which could provide a variety of plots and bizarre incidents.

It turned out to be the perfect formula. A.P. Watt, whom Conan Doyle desribed as the 'king of agents', had impressed Greenhough Smith, the editor of the *Strand Magazine*, with 'A Scandal in Bohemia', in which the able detective spends his time trying to obtain a certain compromising photograph from Irene Adler, an adventuress of dubious repute. Greenhough Smith encouraged Conan Doyle to produce more of these amusing pieces, which then followed in quick succession. (On 10 April he finished 'A Case of Identity', on Monday the 20th he sent off 'The Red-Headed League', and on the 27th 'The Boscombe Valley Mystery.'

On 14 May this prolific output was interrupted by the onset of a severe attack of influenza. Conan Doyle collapsed and for a fortnight he remained in considerable danger. When he finally did recover, he found himself as weak as a

75

baby but possessed of a clear mind. He realized what folly it was to subsidize a non-productive practice with his now considerable earnings as a writer. The arrangement should be reversed:

> I determined with a wild rush of joy to cut the painter and trust for ever to my power of writing. I remember in my delight taking the handkerchief which lay upon the coverlet in my enfeebled hand, and tossing it up to the ceiling in my exultation. I should at last be my own master. No longer would I have to conform to professional dress or try to please anyone else. I would be free to live how I liked and where I liked. It was one of the great moments of exultation of my life . . .

Once recovered from his attack of influenza, Conan Doyle began to search for a suburban home for his family. He moved into 12 Tennison Road in the quiet suburb of South Norwood on 25 June. A month later 'A Scandal in Bohemia' appeared in the *Strand Magazine* and the public were clamouring for more Sherlock Holmes stories.

In the April of that same year Conan Doyle had received £57. 8s. 9d. for a short story entitled 'Lot No. 249'. The story, which represented yet another foray into the occult, concerns the activities of one Edward Bellingham, an Oxford student with an unhealthy interest in necromancy, who, along with two other students, Smith and Monkhouse Lee, occupies a set of rooms in a Gothic corner turret. In his study Bellingham keeps a mummy, 'a horrid, black, withered thing, like a charred head on a gnarled brush'. With the assistance of some ritual based on an ancient papyrus, the student is able to converse with the corpse and reanimate it, much to the horror and disbelief of his fellow lodgers. Having discovered the trick, Bellingham imparts his secret to Monkhouse Lee, who will have nothing to do with the affair. The two men quarrel and Lee vows that he will tell his sister (for whom Bellingham harbours a desire) of Bellingham's gruesome activities. Bellingham sets his creature on to Lee and the latter is hurled into the river, nearly drowning as a result of the attack. Aware of the threat posed by Bellingham, Smith takes matters into his own hands and confronts him with the evidence. Naturally Bellingham denies everything, and when Smith leaves his rooms to confide in his doctor, he is pursued by the mummy. Fortunately he reaches Dr Peterson's house in the nick of time, where he signs a written statement of all that has transpired and returns to Bellingham bearing with him a revolver and a large amputating knife.

The final scene of the story is truly grotesque, with Bellingham at gun point being made to cut up the mummy into sections:

> In frantic haste he caught up the knife and hacked at the figure . . . The creature crackled and snapped under every stab of the keen blade. A thick yellow dust rose up from it. Spices and dried essences rained down upon the floor. Suddenly, with a rending crack, its backbone snapped asunder, and it fell, a brown heap of sprawling limbs upon the floor.

The story's obsession with death and the concept of reanimimation reveals how Conan Doyle's interest in the principle of life after death had remained strongly rooted during this period of immense activity in his professional career.

For Conan Doyle the year 1891 had fulfilled his expectations. As his diary for that year shows, he had made about £1,500 from his writings – a considerable sum, much of it drawn from the payments made to him by the editor of the *Strand*. By autumn Greenhough Smith was asking Conan Doyle for more of the Sherlock Holmes stories, but Conan Doyle refused, partly because he considered his historical novels to be far more important. The *Strand* persisted. Conan Doyle wrote to his mother on 14 October: '[They] are simply imploring me to continue Holmes . . . And so I will write by this post to say that if they offer me £50 each, *irrespective of length* I may be induced to consider my refusal. Seems rather high-handed, does it not?' High-handed or not, the terms were agreed and another six stories began to make their appearance. Through a wet autumn the stories flowed from his pen: 'The Adventure of the Blue Carbuncle', 'The Adventure of the Speckled Band' (late October), 'The Adventure of the Noble Bachelor', 'The Adventure of the Engineer's Thumb', and 'The Adventure of the Beryl Coronet' (late November). Then he began to grow weary of his succubus. 'I think of slaying Holmes in the last [story],' he wrote to the Ma'am, 'and winding him up for good and all. He takes my mind from better things.' Outraged by this callous attitude, his mother protested. Conan Doyle relented, producing one of his finest Holmes stories yet, 'The Adventure of the Copper Beeches'.

Meanwhile the press reviews of *The White Company* had started to appear. On the whole they were very disappointing, accusing the work of unoriginality. Nevertheless it was seen as an exciting adventure yarn – hardly the praise for which Doyle had been prepared.

In December Conan Doyle commenced yet another historical novel, though this time the background and plot were utterly unlike *The White Company* and *Micah Clarke*, being concerned with the Huguenots and the court of Louis XIV. Although Conan Doyle himself remained somewhat noncommittal about *The Refugees*, it was praised by several critics and is certainly, even by today's standards, a remarkable, fast-moving narrative, rich in historical detail.

He wrote two more novels whilst at South Norwood: his autobiographical study, *The Stark Munro Letters*, which dealt with the Budd episode, and his religious feelings; and a Napoleonic story entitled *The Great Shadow*. The latter, although a slighter effort than his larger historical novels, contains a wonderfully detailed and vivid description of the Battle of Waterloo.

Conan Doyle's increasing success as a literary figure was of considerable assistance to his family. Although his elder sister, Annette, had died of influenza in Lisbon in 1889, Lottie and Connie could now enjoy financial independence and the latter moved in with her brother at Tennison Road. (She had made the acquaintance of a journalist, Ernest William Hornung, the author of the famous Raffles stories, whom she later married.) Conan Doyle's wife 'Touie', who had given birth to a daughter, Mary, in 1889, was expecting her second child in the autumn of 1892. Although not very strong, she enjoyed long cycling expeditions with her husband and in the August went on a holiday to Norway with him. In October sister Lottie (Conan Doyle's favourite) arrived back from Portugal to make her permanent home at South Norwood. Finally in November Touie gave birth to a son, who was named Alleyne Kingsley. The domestic bliss of the Conan Doyles left very little time for spiritualism.

Conan Doyle took his wife and children for two holidays in Switzerland in the following year. The first was in the spring, at the time when the new Sherlock Holmes stories which were appearing in the *Strnad* offered him unlimited success and prosperity. It was then that he visited the Reichenbach Falls at Meiringen and thus conceived the story in which he would terminate Holmes and (as he hoped) put him out of his mind for ever. 'All is very well done here,' he wrote to his mother. 'I am in the middle of the last Holmes story, after which the gentleman vanishes, never to return! I am weary of his name.' Thus, in 'The Adventure of the Final Problem', Holmes 'dies' in the clutches of his brilliant adversary, Professor James Moriarty, hurled into the dark ravine which Conan Doyle had thought a fitting memorial to his man of reason.

Things had been going too well for Conan Doyle, and in the autumn of 1893 the first of two blows struck him. In August the Conan Doyles had returned to Switzerland so that Conan Doyle could deliver a lecture at Lucerne on 'Fiction as a Part of Literature'. When the couple returned Touie began to complain of a pain in her side. She had also developed a cough which she could not get rid of. At first Conan Doyle thought that the journey had proved too much for her frail constitution. He sent for Dr Dalton, a general practitioner who lived nearby in Norwood. Dalton's diagnosis confirmed Conan Doyle's worst suspicions: Touie was suffering from what was then called 'galloping consumption' – tuberculosis.

Still stunned by the news, Conan Doyle acted quickly to allieviate matters. 'I then set all my energy to work to save the situation,' he wrote. 'The home was abandoned, the newly bought furniture was sold, and we made for Davos in the High Alps where there seemed the best chance of killing this accursed microbe which was rapidly eating out her vitals. And we succeeded . . . [postponing] the fatal issue from 1893 to 1906.'

Before the Conan Doyle menage transferred to Switzerland, another dark cloud passed across their lives. On 10 October Charles Doyle died at the Crighton Royal Institution, Dumfries, the cause of death being given as 'epilepsy of many years' standing'. Although Charles Doyle's death came as no surprise to his successful son (Charles had meticulously kept review copies of Arthur's books and held him in considerable admiration), the tragic circumstances of his life must have come flooding back, and with them a measure of justifiable resentment and guilt.

By the end of November the Conan Doyles were living at

the Kurhaus Hotel, Davos. Here Conan Doyle had the time and opportunity to return to the subject which, above all others, interested him most: the possibility of life after death. Ever since he had written that letter to *Light* in July 1887, he had carried on a correspondence with F.W.H. Myers, the great psychic investigator. Conan Doyle shared with Myers an approach to psychic phenomena which was historical rather than traditionally scientific. Examining the available evidence, both men tended to draw conclusions which would conform to their own spiritualistic theories. As Conan Doyle wrote in his second Southsea Notebook, 'The end and aim of spiritual intercourse is to give man the strongest of all reasons to believe in spiritual immortality of the soul, to break down the barrier of death, to found the grand religion of the future.'[1]

By this time Conan Doyle had read most of the studies of the occult which also formed the background to the research undertaken by Myers and Edmund Gurney. He had read Kardec and the visionary Swedenborg. He was also deeply fascinated by the followers of Charcot, whose work convinced him that cryptaesthesia and clairvoyance were in some way linked with an existence in the hereafter.

More importantly, Conan Doyle had begun to read the *Transactions of the Society for Psychical Research*, sent to him by one of its founder members, Oliver Lodge. Conan Doyle was impressed by one particular account of an entity Lodge had summoned up in a seance. On 30 December he had written an enthusiastic reply to Lodge regarding this incident, pressing him to accept the evidence of the spirit presence; he regarded Lodge's approach as far too cautious. He also showed a keen interest in eliciting from the spirits of the deceased information about the period of existence before birth.[2]

Conan Doyle, who had become a member of the Society for Psychical Research in November 1893, discovered that the majority of the work undertaken by the Cambridge researchers was concerned with an area which deeply fascinated him. Throughout 1893 Frank Podmore, Henry Sidgwick, and F.W.H. Myers had given addresses to their members on such subjects as 'Sensory Automatism and Induced Hallucinations', 'Motor Messages from the Subliminal Self', 'Telepathic Dreams', 'The Mechanism of Hysteria', and 'Mind-Healing, Faith-Healing and the Miracle of

Lourdes'. Myers, the godfather of the Society, held a theory that the various types of psychic phenomena witnessed at seances were each derived from a form of self-imposed hypnotic trance. Among these he listed automatic drawing and painting, automatic speech ('inspiration' or 'possession'), and telekinetic activities. In a long paper entitled 'The Subliminal Consciousness' published in 1894 (in which he acknowledged his debt to the researches of Breuer and Freud) Myers described the various stages of what he defined as 'motor automatism'.

> [These] messages . . . develop modifications of the percipient's general organic condition or coenesthesia; and the first dim telepathic sense apparently hesitates between several channels of expression. They then pass through various definitely specialised forms; and finally, as we shall see where automatic script is considered, they, too, merge into an unanalysable act of cognition in which the motor element of the message has disappeared.

The aims and objectives of the SPR were identical with those of Conan Doyle. When it was formed in January 1882 it had set out a specific programme of research which included an examination of the influence exerted on one mind by another; the study of hypnotism, clairvoyance, and allied phenomena; enquiry into hauntings and apparitions; investigation into the physical phenomena of spiritualism; and investigation into Reichenbach's discoveries of the odylic force.

Of course, membership of the SPR did not imply that one was automatically a spiritualist. In fact it tended to attract to its ranks physicists (William Barrett, a founder member, was one), clergymen, and men from different walks of life who shared a passion for psychic phenomena. Among those who represented the original council were the medium the Rev. Stainton Moses, Professor Balfour Stewart, Edmund Gurney, the co-author of *Phantasms of the Living*, and Arthur Balfour the MP. Of the members, Moses and Dawson Rogers were committed spiritualists, being the founders of the journal *Light* to which Conan Doyle had written his initial letter of enquiry. Above all else the Society aimed to approach problems in a spirit of scientific enquiry and without prejudice or prepossession of any kind. This approach conformed exactly to Conan Doyle's requirements at the time.

Conan Doyle shared Myers's view that the central issue as to the place of man in the universe could only be explained by answering questions regarding the nature of human personality. Like Conan Doyle, Myers became convinced very early on in his career as an investigator of the importance of the concepts of the subconscious or unconscious (Myers used the term 'subliminal'). Personality represented a momentary point of consciousness and was anchored to the more important 'subliminal self'. It was the subliminal self from which the paranormal processes derived.

Nordon[3] records how in 1888 Conan Doyle had written an unpublished essay which attempted to relate the various data from the fields of cryptaesthesia and intellectual phenomena. Having read Binet's *Animal Magnetism* he had this to say:

> A man is impelled to do some act by the irresistible action of a hypnotic suggestion which may have been made some months before. Yet to him the action appears to emanate from himself and however outré it may be he will always invent some plausible reason on why he has done it. He would scout the idea that the impulse came from without, and yet we know that it is so. How can we tell that all our acitons are not of this nature? What appears to us to be our own choice may prove really to have been as unalterable and inexorable a fate – the unavoidable result of the sum total of suggestions which are acting upon us.

Conan Doyle's problem here with the concept of free will depended largely on his acceptance of the views of the Nancy school. Unlike the mesmerists, who believed in a supposed 'magneto-therapy' and the concept of a sudden profound nervous change in the individual, scientists like Liébault and Bernheim affirmed that hypnotic trance was a form of sleep in which hypnotic suggestion was the sole cause of hypnotic responsiveness. According to Bernheim the human mind is extraordinarily suggestible – and suggestibility lay at the root of the hypnotic trance.

Myers defined suggestion as a 'successful appeal to the subliminal self' but was unable to explain exactly why the hypnotic process was so irregular and capricious. What fascinated Conan Doyle about Myers's theory of hypnosis was the importance he placed upon the spiritual integrity of man. The subliminal self exercised a much greater control over man's actions than had hitherto been assumed (here

Myers seems to have reached much the same conclusion as Breuer and Freud) and the organism controlled by that self was fed and revitalized by it in an organic way:

> The spirit's control is not uniform throughout the organism, nor in all phases of organic life. In waking life it controls mainly the centres of supraliminal thought and feeling, exercising little control over deeper centres . . . But in sub-liminal states – trance and the like – the supraliminal processes are inhibited, and the lower organic centres are retained more directly under the spirit's control. As you get into the profounder part of man's being, you get nearer to the source of his human vitality. You get thus into a region of essentially greater *responsiveness* to spiritual appeal than is offered by the superficial stratum which has been . . . hardened . . . into a definite adaptation to the earthly environments.'[4]

In January 1894, shortly after he received the *Transactions of the Society for Psychical Research* from London, Conan Doyle began work on a novella entitled *The Parasite*. His fascination with hypnotism had been freshly fired by a lengthy address about mesmerism given by Balfour and reprinted in the *Transactions*. Although he was extremely dismissive of this short work, *The Parasite* provides a fascinating insight into the twin areas of sexual obsession and mesmeric control.

The story concerns one Professor Austin Gilroy. An elderly academic who describes himself as a 'highly psychic man', Gilroy conforms precisely to the neurasthenic type of individual who makes his appearance elsewhere in Conan Doyle's fiction: dark eyes, a thin olive face, tapering fingers – in all essentials a dreamer, 'full of impressions and intuitions'.

Gilroy is a rationalist whom a departure from reason affects 'like an odd smell or a musical discord'. He scorns the efforts of his colleague, Wilson, a psychic researcher bearing an uncanny resemblance to Myers:

> His whole life and soul and energy works to one end. He drops to sleep collating his results of the past day, and he wakes to plan his researches for the coming one . . . he goes on, uncomplainingly, corresponding with a hundred semi-maniacs in the hope of finding one reliable witness . . . collating old books, devouring new ones, experimenting, lecturing, trying to light up in others the fiery interest which is consuming him . . .

Despite his scepticism, Gilroy accepts an invitation from Wilson to attend a private demonstration of mesmerism at his house. There he and his fiancée, Agatha, are introduced to a clairvoyant, Miss Penelosa, a crippled woman of West Indian origin with penetrating grey-green eyes. Agatha allows herself to be hypnotized and later appears at Gilroy's house and announces that their engagement is at an end. Perplexed and dismayed, Gilroy discovers that Agatha, who has retained no conscious knowledge of the refusal, carried out the action whilst under post-hypnotic suggestion.

Following this convincing demonstration, Gilroy becomes convinced of the power of hypnotism and is willing to concede that the human soul possesses its own individual identity. Previously his materialistic interpretation of the universe had led him to assume that consciousness was a mere by-product of the body's functions. At this point in the novella, Gilroy's views closely resemble those of the young Conan Doyle:

> The brain, I thought, secreted the mind, as the liver does the bile. But how can this be when I see mind working from a distance, and playing upon matter as a musician might upon a violin. The body does not give rise to the soul then, but is rather the rough instrument by which the spirit manifests itself. The windmill does not give rise to the wind, but only indicates it . . .

Eager to learn more about the powers of Miss Penelosa, Gilroy submits to hypnotic treatment. Conscious of her eyes (grey-green, deep, inscrutable) boring into his, Gilroy soon loses consciousness and afterwards realizes that he is a perfect subject for such mesmeric experiments.

Although he is warned by his colleague Charles Sadler (a young anatomist) about the baleful influence exercised by Miss Penelosa, Gilroy ascribes this to professional envy and continues to participate in the experiments. Slowly, his personality begins to change:

> Agatha says that I am thinner, and darker under the eyes. I am conscious of a nervous irritability which I had not observed in myself before. The least noise, for example, makes me start, and the stupidity of a student causes me exasperation instead of amusement.

Added to this complication is the unacceptable fact that Miss Penelosa has developed a strong attraction for the professor and, try as he may, he cannot now resist her summons. Gilroy, now conceiving her as 'a monstrous parasite' and himself as a puppet dancing to her every command, locks himself in his room. However, his feelings of success at this attempt to defend his free will are dashed when he discovers that the clairvoyant has fallen ill and has thus experienced a diminution of her powerful will.

Once Miss Penelosa has recovered, Gilroy breaks out his room and finds himself in her boudoir. A scene of implied sexual perversity follows in which Miss Penelosa passes her hand over Gilroy's hair 'as one caresses a dog'. Gilroy thrills to her touch ('I was her slave, body and soul, and for the moment I rejoiced in my slavery'). A few minutes later, as her power fades, Gilroy's revulsion comes flooding back and he abuses the clairvoyant in a blind fury.

Now a vendetta is launched against Gilroy by Miss Penelosa. His concentration lapses during lectures and his mind slowly deteriorates to such an extent that he is suspended by the university authorities. The picture looks even blacker when, following a reported raid on a branch of the Bank of England, Gilroy discovers his own coat, impregnated with the same green paint which had appeared on the bank window.

Gilroy decides to act. He confronts Miss Penelosa and threatens to murder her if she does not desist. The clairvoyant treats him with utter contempt, warning him that when his fiancée returns from holiday with her parents she will be the next object of her machinations.

Returning to his lodgings, Gilroy falls into a deep sleep. When he awakes, he finds himself in Agatha's boudoir, clutching a small phial of sulphuric acid. He realizes that he has been the intended perpetrator of a vitriol throwing but is unable to comprehend why Agatha has escaped her fate. Recognition dawns when, on hurrying to Miss Penelosa's home, he is given the news of her death that very afternoon.

Despite its light-weight form, *The Parasite* is a novella of extraordinary intensity. It was a book Conan Doyle was eager to discard in later years, probably because of the vivid portrayal of sexual domination which lies at the heart of the piece. It is interesting that Conan Doyle should have returned to a theme which had preoccupied him several years before. The natural alliance of hypnotism and sexual entrapment suggests a fear of subconscious processes. It also suggests that he had to a large extent repressed his own sexual feelings whilst maintaining the persona of the out-wardly active sportsman and public careerist.

In the late summer of 1894, whilst on a visit to England from Davos, Conan Doyle was asked by the Society for Psychical Research to accompany two of its leading members, Frank Podmore and Dr Sydney Scott, to the home of a Colonel Elmore at Charmouth in Dorset.[5] The house had become unbearable to its owners since it was plagued by unceasing poltergeist phenomena. On the second night of their vigil, Conan Doyle and the others were awoken by a sound 'like some one belabouring a resounding table with a heavy cudgel'. Although the deafening noise appeared to come from the kitchen, when the three men rushed in they were confronted with locked doors, barred windows, and unbroken threads. The phenomena did not repeat themselves, much to Conan Doyle's disappointment. However, he recalls in his memoirs that some 10 years later 'the skeleton of a child about 10 years old was dug up in the garden'. The suggestion was that the child had been murdered there some time in the past and that the phenomena were connected with this tragedy.

Having disposed of Sherlock Holmes for ever (as he then thought) and safely ensconced his ailing wife among the invigorating mountains, Conan Doyle continued to court the publicity which was offered him. In December 1894 he toured America with his impresario, Major Pond, and there gave 40 readings from Boston to Washington and from Chicago to New York. He was surprised (and somewhat appalled) to find that everyone he encountered wanted to hear about Sherlock Holmes but very little else. Nevertheless, the trip was a financial success, raising about £1,000 from audience receipts. (This he invested in a magazine edited by Sam McLure.) Much invigorated, he returned to Davos, where he introduced the local inhabitants to skiing (a sport limited to Norway at that time) and divided the rest of his time between playing golf and writing the series of Brigadier Gerard stories which later appeared in the *Strand Magazine*. He also persuaded the editor of the *Strand* to serialize his boxing epic, *Rodney Stone*, which was a vigorous homage to the age of prize-fighting.

In the autumn of 1895, whilst on a short return visit to England, Conan Doyle discovered from his friend Grant Allen that the area around Hindhead, Surrey, was beneficial to the victims of consumption. He went down to look for himself and, satisfied with what he saw, bought a large plot of land. Conan Doyle placed the architectural work in the hands of his old friend and fellow psychic researcher Mr Ball of Southsea before leaving with his wife and his sister Connie for a tour of Egypt.

The hot dry climate of Egypt proved very beneficial to Touie and she rapidly improved. Conan Doyle climbed the Great Pyramid, played golf on the links of the Mena Hotel and practised riding. As usual, new experiences proved invaluable to him as a writer. Early in 1896 he took his family up the River Nile to Wadi Halfa–an expedition which provided him with the inspiration for his semi-documentary novel *The Tragedy of the Korosko*, in which a group of Moslem fanatics hold captive a group of British tourists.

By the end of April the heat had become too oppressive for his wife, so they left Egypt and returned to England in May. Finding that the house at Hindhead would not be ready for some while, Conan Doyle took a furnished house at Haslemere for a year, finally moving into the new residence in June 1897.

There followed a period of settled domesticity for Conan Doyle. Touie was holding her own in winter and summer; his two children, Mary and Kingsley, had brought him and his wife considerable happiness; and he had established sufficient reputation to enable him to explore a broad canvas in his literary work. His personality at this time is delineated in a short but telling novella entitled *A Duet* which he produced as a light alternative to his more serious fiction:

> There was sometimes just a touch of the savage . . . in Frank Crosse. His intense love of the open air and of physical exercise was a sign of it. He left upon women the impression, not altogether unwelcome, that there were unexplored recesses of his nature to which the most intimate of them had never penetrated. In those dark corners of the spirit either a saint or a sinner might be lurking, and there was a pleasurable excitement in peering into them, and wondering which it was. No woman ever found him dull.

Conan Doyle's conception of the psyche as a kind of eternal battleground on which the perpetual struggle for the human soul is forever fought demonstrates the extent to which, even at this more mature stage of his life, the Jesuitical teachings held him in their thrall.

The years at Hindhead were productive ones for Conan Doyle the short-story writer. The 'darkling figures' that still haunted his rich imagination found their expression in a series of atmospheric pieces, published principally in the *Strand*.

The first of these, 'The Fiend of the Cooperage', appeared in the *Manchester Weekly Times* in October 1897. The story, which has echoes of Conan Doyle's voyage to West Africa, relates the experiences of one Captain Meldrum, the owner of a private yacht, who pulls in to the estuary of the Ogowai river, near Sierra Leone. There he meets two expatriates, Doctor Severall and Walker, who represent a provisions company serving ships that pass up and down the coast. According to these hard-headed men, the local inhabitants believe the riverside cooperage to be haunted by an evil spirit, and there have been dark rumours circulating about the power of voodoo ever since the disappearance of two native watchmen from the place some days before. Severall and Meldrum agree to stay on guard in the cooperage. A storm blows up during the night, forcing them to leave their watch near dawn, and when the two men call upon Walker they enter his bedroom and find his crushed and twisted body huddled on the bed. Horrified by the death of his companion, Severall accompanies Meldrum in a canoe on the swollen river until they reach the yacht. Here at last they are able to glimpse the mysterious assassin as it arches upwards like the figure-head of a ship, 'flattened, malignant, as large as a small beer-barrel, of a faded fungoid colour, . . . the neck which supported it . . . mottled with a dull and yellow black'. The night visitor is none other than the great python of the Gaboon.

'The Sealed Room', which appeared in the *Strand Magazine* the following September, relates the curious case of a young man whose millionaire father has disappeared several years previously, leaving him without a profession and with the house as a legacy which he is not entitled to sell. Before disappearing the father leaves instructions with his wife that a certain sealed room in the house is not to be opened until the son, Felix, is 21 years of age. In the interim Felix's mother dies, having suffered from a heart condition for many years. The narrator, Stanniford, who comes across the case by a chance encounter, soon forgets about the plight of the young man. Then one day he is visited by Felix's solicitor, told that the sealed room is to be opened, and asked to act as a witness to the proceedings. When the room is finally entered, the shrivelled cadaver of the father is found slumped over his desk. Unable to meet his debts, he took poison and kept his death a secret to avoid placing undue stress upon his wife. 'The Sealed Room' is an unlikely story, yet with its emphasis upon the macabre and the guilty closeting of the father one is reminded of Charles Doyle's own incarceration and subsequent demise.

'The Japanned Box' (January 1899) also reflects Conan Doyle's preoccupation with death and family misfortune. The story concerns a private tutor who secures a job at an ancient ancestral home in the Midlands. The owner of this Gothic pile, Sir John Bollamore, is a widower who has been left to care for his two sons and their younger sister. It transpires that Sir John, now a singularly silent and retiring individual, led a reckless life in his youth. Described as once being 'bruiser, driver, gambler, drunkard, the greatest rip and debauché in England', he closets himself several times a day in a turret chamber whence is heard the voice of a woman.

Following the collapse of the turret's ceiling, Sir John moves to the library, which the tutor has been asked to index. Falling asleep after self-administering a pain-killer, the tutor wakens to become the unwilling witness of a most bizarre scene: Sir John, seated before a phonograph, playing back his wife's entreaties not to indulge in the drinking bouts which had ruined him as a young man.

Like 'The Sealed Room', this story's theme of the power of the dead over the living provides its ultimate twist. We have the central 'sin' or misdemeanour (alcohol abuse) uppermost in the author's imagination and the image of the locked room which contains the guilty secret. This image of the room was for Doyle a symbol both of the subconscious and of the creative process. In a poem he wrote entitled 'The Inner Room' he depicts a variety of fictional entities fighting for the control of his identity:

There are others who are sitting
Grim as doom
In the dim ill-boding shadow
Of my room.
Darkling figures, stern or quaint,

Now a savage, now a saint,
Showing fitfully and faint
Through the gloom.
And those shadows are so dense,
There may be
Many – very man – more
Than I see.
They are sitting day and night
Soldier, rogue and anchorite;
And they wrangle and they fight
Over me.[6]

In May 1899 Conan Doyle published 'The Brown Hand'.
One of the more horrific of his short stories, this recounts
the experiences of a doctor who finds himself summoned to
his uncle's house on Salisbury Plain. The narrator, who has
been asked to assist his ancient relative over a particularly
distressing and macabre matter, is a member of the Psychical
Research Society and 'had formed one of a committee of
three who spent the night in a haunted house'. (This is an
autobiographical reference to the Dorset poltergeist phenomenon some five years earlier.) The owner of the house,
Sir Dominick Holden, is the victim of a restless spirit, but he
appears loath to explain his plight. The narrator spends a
night in the laboratory and sees the ghost of an Indian who
had his hand amputated by Holden many years before. The
visitations are explained by the ancient superstition that if a
limb is amputated, the life-after-death existence can never be
satisfactory until the limb is restored. Having obtained
advice from an occult text ('in the case of earth-bound spirits
. . . some one dominant idea obsessing them at the hour of
death is sufficient to hold them in this material world . . . As
a rule it springs from some unfulfilled wish, and when the
wish has been fulfilled the material bond relaxes') the
nephew obtains a suitable replacement for the amputated
original and leaves it in the laboratory. The phantom Indian
claims his grisly trophy and the ghostly visitations cease.

The macabre details of 'The Brown Hand' were sufficient to
make the story a popular one, and it is fairly typical of the
horror genre in which writers like H.G. Wells and E.F. Benson
were working at the time. What makes it particularly impressive even today is the combination of medical detail and Gothic
atmosphere Conan Doyle injects into the narrative.

Although Conan Doyle was not yet prepared to commit

himself regarding the existence of a life after death (although he certainly believed in the power of hypnotism and telepathic communication), he was at this stage becoming increasingly occupied with the possibility of psychic survival, and he paid considerable attention to the experiments that were being carried out in Britain and on the continent. Now and again, through his contacts in the SPR and elsewhere, he became aware of a number of occult groups and societies, including the Rosicrucianism which had attracted a number of writers and intellectuals to its ranks. Conan Doyle's attitude to them was strangely dismissive.

In his memoirs he recalled an encounter with a general practitioner named Pullen-Bury, 'probably in 1898'. The doctor, a student of the occult, had one room in his house which he had reserved for 'mystic and philosophic purposes'. Having ascertained that Conan Doyle himself was interested in psychic research, Pullen-Bury invited him to join a secret society of students of the esoteric, apparently something like the Rosicrucians:

> 'What shall I get from it?'
> 'In time, you will get powers.'
> 'What sort of powers?'
> 'They are powers which people would call supernatural. They are perfectly natural, but they are got by knowledge of deeper forces of nature.'
> 'If they are good, why should not every one know them?'
> 'They would be capable of great abuse in the wrong hands.'
> 'How can you prevent their getting into the wrong hands?'
> 'By carefully examining our initiates.'
> 'Should I be examined?'
> 'Certainly.'
> 'By whom?'
> 'The people would be in London.'

Like many of these esoteric sects, this branch of the Rosicrucians depended on certain teachings which were available only to those initiates who had passed the required examination. Some while later Conan Doyle awoke in the early morning having experienced an extraordinary sensation. 'It was not', he recalled, 'a nightmare or any prank of a dream . . . I can only describe it by saying that I was tingling all over. It was not painful, but it was queer and disagreeable, as a mild electric shock would be.' A few days later he was visited by Pullen-Bury, who informed him that he had passed the test. Having had time to consider the affair in detail, Conan Doyle declined to join the order and made his apologies to the doctor.

A month or so later he was again visited by Pullen-Bury, who this time was accompanied by a Dr Felkin, who was known to Conan Doyle in connection with the tropical service. The two men sat and talked in Conan Doyle's presence about their out-of-body experiences. 'It was not spiritualism and it was not theosophy,' Conan Doyle recalled, 'but rather the acquisition of powers latent in the human organization, after the alleged fashion of the old gnostics . . . One thing I am very sure of, and that is that morals and ethics have to keep pace with knowledge, or all is lost.'[7]

Conan Doyle's preoccupation with the occult was somewhat overshadowed by world events during 1899 and 1900. In January 1899 he had chaired a meeting at Hindhead to discuss the Tsar's peace conference initiative, but by the end of the year his pacifist inclinations had been forgotten as he succumbed to the wave of jingoism which was sweeping Britain. In October of that year South Africa declared war on Britain. By December British troops had suffered a series of setbacks and Conan Doyle was eager to join the fray. He attempted to join the Middlesex Yeomanry, but before his application was processed a friend of his, John Langman, asked if he would act as a doctor and medical supervisor at the Langham Hospital. When Conan Doyle finally reached the capital of the Free State conditions at the hospital were appalling. Though there were only beds for 50, 120 patients were crammed into the hospital, and the place was littered with dying men. It was an experience he was never to forget.

After several agonising weeks spent among excreta, flies, and rotting cadavers the army continued the march to Pretoria, and Conan Doyle was able to see some action from the sidelines. 'I felt happy,' he recalled in his memoirs, 'because I had always wanted a baptism of fire and now I had a fairly good one.'

When Conan Doyle returned to England he settled down with Touie (she had returned, much refreshed, from a visit to Naples) and began work on his *History of the Boer War*, a book which has been rarely equalled as a first-hand account of the British campaign. He also issued a pamphlet entitled

The War in South Africa, Its Cause and Conduct, which set out the British viewpoint and countered many of the unfounded anti-British rumours circulating at the time.

Meanwhile, in the *Strand Magazine* of March 1900 his short story 'Playing With Fire' had appeared. Of all his fictional forays into the occult, this short piece deals most extensively with the trappings of the seance room. Described by the narrator as an account of 'what occured on the 14th of April last at No. 17 Badderley Gardens', the tale begins with a critique of its main character, John Moir, a student of the occult. Moir's researches, 'which had begun with an open mind, ended unhappily in dogma, and he became as positive and fanatical as any other bigot'. Conan Doyle is talking about spiritualism, which he evidently regarded with considerable scepticism.

Moir's sister is found to be mediumistic, having 'a battery of that animal magnetic force which is the only form of energy . . . subtle enough to be acted upon from the spiritual plane as well as from our own material one'.

In the artist Deacon's studio at Badderley Gardens hangs an unfinished picture depicting animals, fairies and 'allegorical figures of all sorts'. In the foreground stands a magnificent unicorn which Deacon has had difficulty in depicting. Enter Monsieur Paul Le Duc, a famous student of occultism, seer, medium, mystic, and agent of the Rosicrucians. Le Duc, who holds that 'thoughts are things', admires the unicorn and claims to be able to materialize it.

The seance commences, Moir's sister falls rapidly into a trance, and after a short while a greenish-yellow phosphorescent light rolls and wreathes its way around the seance table. A spirit is contacted and a dialogue begins in which the subject of evil forces figures largely. (This dialogue is fairly typical of the results recorded by Conan Doyle and his contemporaries at numerous seances during the period 1916–18.) Determined to invoke a significant manifestation, Le Duc concentrates his mental energies. In the corner of the room a shifting patch of radiance builds from the darkness. And then

> Some huge thing hurtled against us in the darkness, rearing, stamping, smashing, springing, snorting. The table was splintered. We were scattered in every direction. it clattered and scrambled amongst us, rushing with horrible energy from one corner of the room to another. We were all

screaming with fear, grovelling upon our hands and knees to get away from it. Something trod upon my left hand, and I felt the bones splinter under the weight . . .'

This phantasmagorical tale of a unicorn is surely the most powerful of all Conan Doyle's accounts of the supernatural. Unlike some of his earlier pieces, the writing is economical, sharp, and possessed of a powerful intensity. The descriptions of the seance, obviously based on close observation, read very convincingly. The characters of the piece carry weight, whilst the description of the phantom unicorn is without question one of Conan Doyle's finest forays into pure fantasy.

In March 1901 Conan Doyle's health showed signs of deterioration. He had already suffered from illness during the Boer War, and now his 'iron constitution' gave way to a recurrent fever, diarrhoea, and insomnia. On his doctors' advice, he went to Cromer in Norfolk for a holiday. There he met up with an old friend, the journalist Fletcher Robinson. The latter, who was a student of folklore and the supernatural, told Conan Doyle a legend concerning a phantom hound which haunted the Dartmoor family of Cabell. Cabell, a seventeenth-century squire and heir to the manor of Brook, maltreated his wife and she escaped on to the moor. Cabell pursued her, stabbing her and her hound to death in the process, but afterwards he was haunted by the phantom of the hound. The legend is an interesting variation on the 'wisht' hounds of the West Country and probably has its origins in Norse mythology.[8]

The story intrigued Conan Doyle. His avid interest in the supernatural led him to devise a method of bringing back Sherlock Holmes, who would play the central part in a murder mystery with supernatural elements. He was inspired partly by the enormous success which William Gillette's play *Sherlock Holmes* had been enjoying in the winter of 1899, first at selected cities in the USA and later at the Garrick Theatre, London. Since the play would reopen in London in the autumn of 1901, what better than to produce a new full-length Holmes tale for the readers of the *Strand* early in 1902?

The play and the new novel were an immediate success. Conan Doyle was truly in the public eye at this period. Gillette's play was running at the Lyceum to packed houses, *The Hound* had given the *Strand* a new lease of life, whilst revised and expanded versions of his *History of the Boer War* appeared in 1901 and 1902, under the title *The Great Boer War*.

Conan Doyle's services to the nation at the Langham Hospital and his authorship of *The War in South Africa, Its Cause and Conduct* led to a knighthood shortly after King Edward VII's accession to the throne. Although he showed some reluctance to accept the honour, believing it might detract from the force of his political arguments, Conan Doyle relented to pressure exerted upon him by the Ma'am and sister Connie. He was subsequently knighted at Buckingham Palace on 9 August 1902, and whilst he was there an additional honour was bestowed upon him: he was appointed Deputy Lieutenant of Surrey. At Buckingham Palace he was especially pleased to meet for the first time Oliver Lodge (also being knighted), whose views on psychical research and spiritualism concurred somewhat with his own. In the years to follow his friendship with the brilliant physicist was to result in a fascinating correspondence regarding the whole range of psychic phenomena and their credibility.

Conan Doyle's attitude to death was constantly changing, as can be seen from an examination of his fiction during these busy years. Sometimes he appeared to believe that consciousness could survive dissolution, if the will prevailed, at other times he seemed sceptical.

In a story he published in 1903, his concern with psychometry (the power of certain sensitive individuals to visualize the history of objects by touching and experiencing them) is powerfully demonstrated.

The main character in 'The Leather Funnel' is Lionel Dacre, a 'wealthy man of refined and eccentric tastes'. Dacre is an occultist whose experiments into the unknown 'have passed all the bounds of civilization and of decorum'. We are informed that in his large house in the Avenue de Wagram, Paris, 'the worst excesses of the black man have been perpetrated' and that his eyes were those of 'a sensualist and an egotist'. The profile of Dacre bears a marked similarity to the infamous magician Aleister Crowley, who at this time was making something of a name for himself in occult circles.

Dacre presents the narrator (his guest) with a large black funnel and invites him to sleep next to it in the hope that his dreams may reveal something of its history. He is clearly much preoccupied with dreams and their significance, a fact which surely reflects Conan Doyle's own interest in this area. (He had read with fascination Sigmund Freud's *Interpretation of Dreams*, 1899.) At one point Dacre presents his evolutionary view of scientific belief, a view closely akin to Doyle's own:

> The charlatan is always the pioneer. From the astrologer came the astronomer, from the alchemist the chemist, from the mesmerist the experimental psychologist. The quack of yesterday is the professor of tomorrow. Even such subtle and elusive things as dreams will in time be reduced to system and order . . .

Dacre goes on to explain that any object which has been intimately associated with a human trauma will retain a certain atmosphere or association which then transmits itself to the sensitive mind. Uneasily the narrator submits to the experiment, sensing some hidden horror connected with the funnel.

Once asleep he experiences a nightmare of such clarity and grotesque dimensions that he awakes screaming. He sees a small blonde woman, her face 'comely, yet feline', surrounded by sinister black-clad inquisitors. The woman is strapped spread-eagled to a wooden 'horse' and buckets of water are brought into the chamber. When the leather funnel is presented the dreamer realizes the function it is about to fulfil. He has recalled the torture of the notorious Marquise de Brunvilliers, a murderess from the reign of Louis XIV who dispatched members of her own family. Known as the 'Question', the torture consists of forcing vast quantities of water into the mouth of the victim.

Interestingly, Conan Doyle does not specify the orifice in question, although we are told that the funnel carries the Marquise's teethmarks about its base. This ambiguity only serves to heighten the sense of sexual perversity which runs through the narrative. It is certainly one of Conan Doyle's most disturbing stories and reflects the darker side of his nature.

In the summer of 1903 an extraordinary book appeared. Entitled *Human Personality and Its Survival of Bodily Death*, it was a labyrinthine attempt to define the human personality in terms of its physical and mental components. The work, which was published posthumously, had been written over a period of many years by Conan Doyle's friend F.W.H. Myers. Conan Doyle was excited by the book. He wrote to the Ma'am in October 1903 that he believed it to be 'a great root book from which a tree of knowledge will grow'.

Although the book appears dated today, at the time it represented something of a revolution in the area of psychical research. The two-volume edition, prepared largely by Myers's friends and colleagues in the SPR, falls neatly into two sections: the philosophical dissertations, and the vast number of transcripts, letters, and submissions which provide the evidential backbone of the book.

Briefly stated, Myers's contention was that human personality, represented by the conscious self, is merely the outward manifestation of a larger, unseen personality which itself connects with the super-consciousness of the universe. Upon this central theory hangs Myers's explanation of mediumship, telepathy, and other hitherto inexplicable phenomena.

Conan Doyle was impressed, for Myers's book at last offered a scientific interpretation of the known facts. It meant that if the human personality was (as Myers suggested) indestructible and truly supernatural, the problem of death could be looked at afresh. Naturally he still demanded *proof* of the existence of the personality after death, but Myers's book provided the hypothetical basis. Writing in *The New Revelation* some 15 years later, Conan Doyle remarked:

> [Myers's] was an enormous advance. If mind could act on mind at a distance, then there were some human powers which were quite different to matter as we had always understood it. The ground was cut from under the feet of the materialists, and my old position had been destroyed . . . if the mind, the spirit, the intelligence of man could operate at a distance from the body, then it was a thing to that extent separate from the body. Why should it not exist on its own when the body was destroyed?

Although Conan Doyle at this time was busy with a new series of Sherlock Holmes stories (he had accepted a cheque from *McClure's Magazine* for $5,000 for six stories), he continued to study with great interest the researches of psychic investigators in Britain and abroad. One case which greatly intrigued him in 1907 was that of the medium known as 'Eva C'.

In April 1906 Dr Charles Richet, Professor of Physiology in the Faculty of Medicine of the University of Paris, had published in the *Annales des sciences psychiques* details of a bizarre series of events which had taken place at the Villa Carmen in Algiers. Richet's experiments, conducted in the presence of the villa's owner (a General Noël of the French Army), had begun in the 1890s, using an Arab medium, Ahmed, who appeared to be able to contact an ancient Hindu entity, Bien Boa. Bien Boa created a variety of phenomena, including writing on slates, table levitation, and coloured lights.

In 1899 'Eva Carrière' (her real name was Marthe Béraud) was recommended to General Noël as a sensitive with extraordinary powers. (She later became engaged to Noël's son, Maurice, who himself died from a tropical disease in 1904.) Eva had a cabinet created to which she retired. A few minutes later a white-robed figure would emerge (whose name was Bergolia), often accompanied by the 300-year-old Bien Boa and Maurice Noël.

Richet investigated the case with some scepticism but was favourably impressed by Eva. The experiments were held in a small, isolated building over a stable, and those present were the General, Mme Noël, and others, including Eva's two younger sisters Marie and Paule. A black maid, Aischa, sat next to Eva in the cabinet. Eva was not tied, nor were her hands held, so that there was considerable potential for deception. Nevertheless, this did not seem to worry Dr Richet. 'After a variable period . . . sometimes after an hour, or even two hours,' he recalled, 'the curtains drew apart, and we could see Marthe and Aischa each sitting on her chair seemingly asleep.'

During these experiments Marthe was not undressed but wore only a thin dress. Richet, who observed in his account that she was 'intelligent . . . lively and a bright-eyed brunette', periodically passed his hands over her body to check that 'she had nothing on but this thin garment'. Convinced that there were no theatrical accessories or in-strumentation, Richet observed that the materializations were very complete:

> The phantom of Bien Boa appeared five or six times under satisfactory conditions in the sense that he could not be Marthe masquerading in a helmet and sheet. Marthe would have had not only to bring, but also to conceal afterwards,

the helmet, the sheet, and the burnous. Also Marthe and the phantom were both seen at the same time. To pretend that Bien Boa was a doll is more absurd still; he walked and moved, his eyes could be seen looking round, and when he tried to speak his lips moved.[9]

Excited by these phenomena Richet returned to Paris to write his report. Simultaneously a lawyer named Marsault issued a report in the magazine *Les Nouveaux Horizons* attacking Richet. He claimed that Eva had told him Bien Boa and Bergolia were fakes. Eva C. and her servant dressed up in masks and beards to dupe the General and his wife, and when Richet arrived the seance room was modified to heighten the illusion.

Conan Doyle was fascinated by the whole affair. He had followed Richet's research work with interest and known him to be a reliable and sometimes sceptical scientist. He was prepared to ignore Marsault's (as he saw it) scurrilous attack and wrote to Richet asking to be kept informed of this wonderful young medium.

As the new century advanced Conan Doyle found more and more of his spare time being taken up with the investigation of psychic phenomena. He remained cautious and non-committal about many of the mediums he encountered during this period and was well aware of the possibility of fraud and deception on the part of some professional practitioners. Conan Doyle is popularly criticized for his gullibility – a suggestion which is demonstrably at variance with the facts. One particular incident involved the medium Frederick Foster Craddock. Conan Doyle had been invited to attend a seance of this medium by his spiritualist acquaintance Admiral Moore. He was, to say the least, somewhat uneasy about the whole affair since only the previous night Craddock's spirit control, Rosetta, had been seized, revealing Craddock himself in a disguise. During the subsequent seance, the Admiral took matters into his own hands and grabbed at the phantom which purported to be his own father. When the lights were turned on Craddock was revealed standing in a sheet, his face covered by a rubber mask and a turban wrapped around his head.[10]

Whilst Conan Doyle was the first to admit that there were many fraudulent mediums, he still retained a belief that many of the reported phenomena (especially those investigated by the SPR and other bodies) were substantially real.

A case in point was that of Mrs Leonara Piper, who came to England in 1906 for an investigation by the SPR. Mrs Piper did not produce 'physical phenomena' but concentrated her efforts on telepathic cross-corespondences in which certain mediums could link up messages from the deceased. The SPR produced an impressive amount of evidence to back up her reputation as a genuine psychic, although certain authorities such as Richet considered that her communication with the late Myers and Gurney were mere figments of her imagination.

In the summer of 1906 the tuberculosis which Touie had so heroically held at bay, finally engulfed her. She passed away on the morning of 4 July aged only 49. Conan Doyle was distraught and for some while was unable to do any work. Towards the end of the year, however, the case of the wrongly accused Parsee George Edalji came to his attention, and he was able to throw himself into the matter in an attempt to prove the man's undoubted innocence. In September of the following year he had remarried (much to the pleasure of the Ma'am). The lady in question was Miss Jean Leckie, whose family he had been acquainted with for many years. To be nearer to Jean's parents, Conan Doyle sold his house and bought a new residence at Crowborough which he named 'Windlesham'. He also took on a London flat, 15 Buckingham Palace Mansions. His family was soon to expand. In addition to Mary and Kingsley, he and Jean had three children: Denis, Adrian, and Lena Jean (known in the family as 'Billy').

His marriage to Jean Leckie, for whom he had harboured a platonic affection throughout his first wife's declining years, marked a new departure for Conan Doyle. He became more relaxed, more genial, and less bound by convention. Moreover, his well-established reputation as a writer and man of public affairs gave him a new confidence. In the years that followed, his slow but inevitable conversion to spiritualism would be well served by a capable and supportive soul mate.

CHAPTER 5

The Vital Message

After his second marriage, Conan Doyle devoted much of his enormous energy to literary matters. 'Windlesham' offered him the perfect setting. The house was situated in a quiet tree-lined road and was possessed of a magnificent garden whose cottage Conan Doyle frequently made use of as his 'snug'. He produced a good crop of ghost stories during this period of settled domesticity. Among the best of them is 'The Silver Mirror' (*Strand Magazine*, August 1908), which uses a diary form to convey the nightmare experiences of a junior partner in a law firm whose task is to examine the suspect accounts of a firm in a deserted office. The young man in question is typically neurasthenic, possessed of a sensitive (and therefore highly psychic) nature.

Alone in the room, the narrator dwells upon a silver mirror given to him by a friend and clearly of great antiquity. The mirror has a strange feeling of perspective to it and at night develops an opacity from which shadows of the past emerge. As he sits by the mirror, night after night, the young man becomes aware of two eyes, 'full of intense, vivid life'. They are the eyes of a woman in great distress. As he peers intently into the mirror, he notices what at first appears to be a bunch of white ribbons on the left side of the woman's dress. Later this is proved to be a man's hand. Similarly what at first glance seems to be the shape of an animal in the background turns out to be a terrified courtier.

Dimly now I begin to see the figures in the background.

Fierce faces, bearded and dark, shape themselves out of the mist. There is one terrible creature, a skeleton of a man, with hollow cheeks and eyes sunk in his head. He also has a knife in his hand. On the right of the woman stands a tall man, very young, with flaxen hair, his face sullen and dour. The beautiful woman looks up at him in appeal. So does the man on the ground. This youth seems to be the arbiter of their fate. The crouching man draws closer and hides himself in the woman's skirts. The tall youth bends and tries to drag her away from him . . .

Finally the full nightmare reveals itself. The narrator has witnessed the murder by Darnley of Rizzio, the lover of Mary Queen of Scots, and the mirror itself has come from Holyrood Palace, the scene of the grisly murder (and a place with which Conan Doyle was acquainted through his father's work). The mirror stood in the very room where the deed was done.

Another story, 'The Terror of Blue John Gap', written by Conan Doyle in 1909 (and published the following year), also features a neurasthenic young bachelor, Seaton, who is staying with two elderly women at a farm in a remote region of Derbyshire. Seaton, who is a keen walker, chances upon a large horizontal shaft dug by the Romans which is reputed to be haunted according to a local man, Armitage, who strikes up a friendship with the visitor. Dauntless, Seaton explores the cleft and discovers, some distance down, a huge footprint as of some gigantic primaeval beast. Ill-health renders further exploration useless, but meanwhile Armitage disappears without explanation. Seaton summons up his courage and makes a last foray into the cave. There he encounters a threatening, amorphous beast, resembling something more from the subconscious mind than anything identifiable from prehistoric times:

> I was conscious of the loom of some enormous shape, some monstrous inchoate creature . . . As I ran, I saw the great beast lurching before me . . . Its hair looked like coarse faded oakum, and hung down in long, dense masses which swayed as it moved. It was like an enormous unclipped sheep in its fleece, but in size it was far larger than the largest elephant . . .

The years 1908 and 1909 were difficult for Conan Doyle, and the obsessive themes of these two tales may well be a reflection of his mental state at the time. In January 1909 he developed a blockage in the intestine. He was operated upon on the 11th and was for some while afterwards in a critical condition. Nevertheless, in addition to short stories, he devoted considerable energy to a theatre production, an adaptation of his novel *The Tragedy of the Korosko*. Entitled *The Fires of Fate*, the play opened at the Lyric Theatre on 16 June 1909 and was initially very successful. However, heavy production costs forced him to launch a second play, entitled *The House of Temperley*. This production, staged at the Adelphi Theatre, was a precursor of his boxing epic, *Rodney Stone*. Again, production costs were heavy, Conan Doyle opting for elaborate costumes and real boxing sequences. Sadly, the success of this new venture was marred by the death of Edward VII. Not to be defeated, Conan Doyle embarked on a third project. This was an elaboration on a Sherlock Holmes story he had written years before, 'The Speckled Band'. (It was his favourite Holmes story.) The play was a sure-fire success and ran for 169 performances at the Adelphi, subsequently going on tour. An American production of the same play met with more limited success.

Throughout the pre-war years Conan Doyle's obsession with the possibility of life beyond death continued unabated. Now and again he was told first-hand experiences of persons who had been bereaved and who had received remarkable revelations through mediums. One such person was Edward Marshall Hall, a young lawyer whose wife had died tragically at the hands of an abortionist. Hall told him of a strange episode which had taken place in 1894.[1] A friend of Hall's (a Miss Wingfield) had developed the power of automatic writing. To test her abilities, Hall handed her a letter, sealed in a blank envelope, which he had received recently from his brother, a remittance man who lived in South Africa. The medium declared that the writer of the letter was dead, a fact which was subsequently proved.

Stories of this kind intrigued Conan Doyle and made him even more convinced that the human consciousness could leap the gap between life and death. A wonderful fictional interpretation of this concept is developed in the short story 'Through the Veil', published in the historical collection *The Last Galley* (1911). In this brief narrative, a Scots couple, the Browns, drive out to see the excavations of a Roman fort at Newstead. There they meet the farmer on whose land the site stands. He tells them of the skeleton of a man, spear in hand, which has been discovered down a 14-foot hole. Returning home, Brown experiences a vivid dream in which he finds himself part of a Celtic tribe attacking the Roman fort. In the midst of the fray Brown encounters his own wife, whom he grabs and pulls out of the burning remains of the fort. He is intercepted by a Roman soldier whom he stabs to death. The Roman soldier is none other than his wife's other-life husband. 'For an instant,' Conan Doyle concludes, 'the curtain of the past had swung aside, and some strange glimpse of a forgotten life had come to them'.

When he was not spinning stories of the afterlife and reincarnation from his fertile imagination, Conan Doyle was writing science-fiction. In 1912 his magnificent novel *The Lost World* appeared. Probably inspired by the many discoveries which had been made of the fossilized footprints of prehistoric reptiles, Conan Doyle's novel features a larger-than-life character, Professor Challenger. Conan Doyle, who based this bull of a man on Professor Rutherford of Edinburgh University, placed him into the centre of a narrative which is rich both in fantasy and humour. The story, which is narrated by an Irish reporter, Ed Malone, concerns an expedition to South America. Following a request by his editor to investigate a possible fraud, Malone visits the violent and quixotic Challenger, who has recently returned from South America with stories of seeing and photographing prehistoric beasts. After Challenger has given vent to his hatred of reporters (Malone is hurled downstairs after a brief struggle), he invites Malone to a lecture at which he receives sufficient support for his theory to be able to form an expeditionary team. The team travels to a remote area of the South American jungle where they discover a plateau which has been geologically preserved and which hosts an environment both fascinating and dangerous to the scientists. The subsequent adventures of Challenger and his companions owe something to the work of Jules Verne, but the writing is in many ways superior, and at points seems more reminiscent of Conrad's *The Heart of Darkness* (particularly the description of the change from the forest to the alien plateau).

The dream-like quality of *The Lost World* and the powerful, dominating character of Challenger made the novel a tremendous and well-deserved success. Much encouraged by the enthusiastic reception given to his new fictional creation, Conan Doyle composed a shorter follow-up, entitled *The Poison Belt*, in which the world is stricken by a poisonous substance from outer space. Challenger and his companions go out equipped with oxygen cylinders, and are able to witness a vast tableau of humanity, stricken and motionless in the very midst of activity. Fortunately for humankind the condition is a temporary one and the world soon returns to normality.

Two other stories are of interest from this productive period. 'The Horror of the Heights' (*Strand Magazine*, November 1913) concerns the discovery of a diary in a field not far form 'Windlesham'. The diary turns out to be a record of the extraordinary flight of aviator Joyce-Armstrong 5,000 feet above Salisbury Plain. As the pilot ascends into the rarefied atmosphere above the earth's surface he encounters a vast jellyfish, a sort of guardian of the upper-limits. Conan Doyle's ability to summon these disturbing entities from the dark recesses of his subconscious was never more clearly delineated than in his description of the monster:

> The whole aspect of this monster was formidable and threatening, and it kept changing its colour from a light mauve to a dark, angry purple . . . On the upper curve of its huge body there were three great projections which I can only describe as enormous bubbles . . . The creature moved swiftly along . . . and for twenty miles or more it formed my horrible escort, hovering over me like a bird of prey which was waiting to pounce . . . So elastic and gelatinous was it that never for two successive minutes was it the same shape, and yet each change made it more threatening and loathsome than the last . . .

The second story, 'How It Happened', purports to be a piece of automatic writing and relates the experience of a motorist who loses control of his car and crashes into a bank. When he regains consciousness the first person he catches sight of is a former college friend who, he recalls, had been killed in the Boer War. 'How It Happened' is a slight piece, yet it reminds us of Conan Doyle's continued fascination with the trauma of death and the possible survival of the soul.

In July 1913, Conan Doyle began a correspondence with Captain Hubert Stansbury, the author of a short book entitled *In Quest of Truth*. He had thought so much of this philosophical tract that he had covered his copy with annotations in neat copperplate handwriting. Yet there was one vital aspect with which he took issue, and that was the author's assumption of a materialistic and mechanistic universe. As he wrote to Stansbury:

> I find myself . . . in opposition . . . concerning the nature of the soul and the possibility of continued life. I admit that your considerations against it have great force, and that some of them are new to me. But I don't see how anyone can read such a book as Myers's *Human Personality* – a reasoned book from a man whom I know to have been a most careful and critical observer – without being convinced that there are powers and peculiarities in the soul or spirit which prevent it from being in the ordinary sense an emanation from matter – a secretion of brain as bile is a secretion of liver, to use the simile which some materialist employs.

If telepathy had been proved as a verifiable fact of human consciousness, why not also accept the possibility that an independent soul or spirit could exist? In spite of the presence of frauds, Conan Doyle concluded, there was a residual proof in the claims of spiritualism which could not be ignored.

Stansbury quickly replied to the letter. Unlike Conan Doyle, who was a theist, he could not accept that there was a central organizing intelligence. If this were so, how could Conan Doyle explain the existence of evil in the universe? And how could catastrophes like that of the *Titanic* be explained? Conan Doyle would not back down. On the contrary, he was eager to defend his belief in an omnipotent and benign consciousness:

> I see all around me things which show me the presence not merely of power, but of a very singular loving kindness, often in small matters. To take an example: there is the beauty of flowers and their scent. Every utilitarian object of life could be served without that. It fulfils no function. It seems an extra thrown in out of kindness – a luxury among the necessities of life. So, too, the infinite variety of flavours . . .

Stansbury throught Conan Doyle naïve. If the beauty and scent of flowers showed a beneficent influence at work, then the argument must cut both ways. Equally the vice of the slums and even the blight on flowers must show the *lack* of that loving-kindness.

Conan Doyle was willing to accept that the overall design and function of the universe was beyond his immediate comprehension. Stansbury saw no reason to limit the power of the intellect. The universe was not infinite, and if the human mind could study an infinitesimal selection, then there was no reason why it should not understand the universe.

Conan Doyle persisted. Although he admitted that evil was a problem in a universe inspired by a benevolent deity, 'yet now and again one catches a glimpse of its ultimate effects, and sees purpose once more'. Typically, he used the example of the drunkard and the promiscuous person to illustrate his point:

> It is a horrible evil on the face of it. What is its ultimate effect? The drunkard dies, his offspring are enfeebled, and a branch which had moral weakness in it is pruned from the human tree. The same applies to veneral disease. It extirpates the moral weakling, and causes his offspring to miscarry. As in a glass darkly, no one sees good emerging out of evil.

Conan Doyle's preoccupation with moral laxity and the sins of his own father are here only too apparent, and he found himself hard pushed to provide a convincing answer to Stansbury's next letter. As Stansbury was only too ready to point out:

> To insist dogmatically that anything is beyond our intelligence is surely no argument and no proof. If there be a First Cause, I see no reason why it should be beyond our understanding. But if the universe be eternal, like a closed curve it can have no beginning, and then the idea of a First Cause, or power which began it, is really unthinkable.
>
> You say concerning an eternal nature that 'it could not come of itself'. But if nature be eternal, the very word means that it never came at all – that it has always existed . . . Your questions, 'Who ordained – ?', 'Who made those laws?', and 'Who made harmony a quality of nature?' will all answer themselves if you will try to regard the universe as eternal.

Reluctantly, Conan Doyle had to admit a partial defeat. Yet it bothered him to think of an order and structure within the universe endlessly unfolding without purpose. To him, evidence of design pointed to an organizing intellect: 'I can afford to let a hundred points go, and profess ignorance of them, if on the hundred-and-first I can give reasonable proof of purpose in creation.' As regards the question of evil, whilst he admitted that he did not understand its function in the scheme of things, at the same time 'the good enormously preponderates'. As to the question of eternity, he regarded Stansbury's use of the circle as dangerous, for 'it takes us back to symbolism. It is like the triangle with an eye inside it, which represented the medieval Deity. It gives a false sense of knowing something when we don't really.' In his opinion, it was absurd to think of an eternal universe and one still had to face the question 'Who ordained it so?'

Conan Doyle's correspondence with Stansbury provides a clear picture of his position prior to the Great War. The Darwinian interpretation and its structure of the universe had not changed fundamentally since his Portsmouth days. He had become more convinced of the possibility of the survival of human consciousness, although he was still sceptical about the claims of certain mediums. What he lacked was a personal revelation.

In the spring of 1914 Conan Doyle and his wife accepted an invitation from the Canadian government to see the National Reserve Park in the Rockies. The couple sailed in May and arrived in New York after a severe thunderstorm. While in the city he had visited some years before under the guidance of his impresario, Major Pond, Conan Doyle spoke to the press, saying that he supported Home Rule for Ireland and was opposed to the methods being employed by the women's suffrage movement. However, he studiously avoided all mention of psychic matters since at this time he was still undecided about his beliefs. William J. Burns, head of the New York Police Department took the couple around the Tombs and Sing Sing prison, where Conan Doyle's sensitive nature was much affected by the plight of the prisoners.

When he reached Canada he and Jean immediately fell in love with the place. In his memoirs he recalled: 'It was wonderfully impressive to travel swiftly all day from the early summer dawn to the latest evening light, and to see always the same little clusters of houses, always the same distant farms, always the same huge expanse stretching to the distant skyline . . .'

No sooner had he returned from Canada than war broke

out. Conan Doyle described the realization of the European catastrophe as a waking nightmare which haunted him for four years. As always, feelings of impotence made him act. A local plumber left him a note which said: 'There is a feeling in Crowborough that something should be done.' With Conan Doyle it was no sooner said than done. He posted a thousand notices, had them put up around the village, and within a few days had organized the Crowborough Civilian Reserve, a sort of Home Guard which spent its days drilling and camping in readiness for the war effort. After some initial problems with certification at the War Office, the reserve was issued with rifles and large numbers of local men were soon attracted to the unit.

Meanwhile Conan Doyle divided his spare time between trying to persuade the War Office to equip the British soldier with shields and body armour and, with the approval of Prime Minister Asquith, working on a history of the war, entitled *The British Campaign in France and Flanders*.

The initial jingoism expressed by Conan Doyle soon gave way to a mood of despairing resignation as it became clear that the war would not be over in a matter of months. He turned to fiction, producing the powerful novel about the much-maligned Irish-American secret society known as the Molly Maguires. Conan Doyle set his new murder story in the heart of the Sussex Weald but, like his earlier Sherlock Holmes novels, *The Valley of Fear* is a story within a story, much of it taking place in the coalfields of Pennsylvania.

Although Conan Doyle himself was too old to take part in the war, many of his friends and relatives were engaged at the Front, among them his eldest son, Kingsley, his brother, Innes, and his wife's brother, Malcolm Leckie. Eager to visit France (his accounts of the conflict had hitherto been based on newspaper reports and dispatches), he gratefully accepted an invitation from Lord Newton of the Foreign Office to go to the Italian front and was then able to spend some time in Flanders visiting Ypres. The pock-marked landscape and the debilitated state of the British troops had a profound effect upon him. It was some small consolation to him to be able to meet Innes, now an adjutant general of the 24th Division, and Kingsley, a medical officer in the First Hampshires.

He visited Paris, a dead-and-alive place with darkened

streets and shops nearly all closed, before travelling to Padua and thence to Udine, the Italian headquarters. Here he came under heavy shelling, a small shell coming close to his motor convoy. He retreated to Paris and there learned of the death of Lord Kitchener when the *Lusitania* was sunk. He went abroad again in 1916 and whilst there examined the Autralian troops whose immense spirit and bawdy humour impressed him. 'They were great soldiers, these Australians,' he wrote. 'There was a reckless dare-devilry, combined with a spice of cunning, which gave them a place of their own in the imperial ranks . . . Conan Doyle's excursion into the margins of battle provided him with an excellent insight into the conditions of men engaged in the long struggle. Moreover, his respect for the British and German soldier intensified.

When peace was finally declared, many of the families who had suffered bereavement turned to the solace of spiritualism, and it has often been said that Conan Doyle's own whole-hearted acceptance of the spiritualist creed was due to the great losses suffered by him and his wife. This is, of course, a vast over-simplification of the facts. Unlike many people who embraced the new religion, Conan Doyle had been a student of psychic phenomena since his early years, although, as we have seen, he had not been prepared to commit himself to a final rejection or acceptance of the evidence.

Nevertheless Conan Doyle watched the spread of spiritualism's popularity with growing interest. For many converts to the new religion (for it certainly was a religion) the promise of a hereafter in which their beloved sons would enter paradise physically entire was the fulfilment of their deepest wish. Many newspaper reports circulating at the time reported ghostly faces of the departed hovering over graves and 'physical' phenomena at seances. Some soldiers reported seeing the Angel of Mons, whilst others glimpsed the ghost of Lord Kitchener, leading the troops into battle.

During the war years a series of 'proofs' were given to the Conan Doyle family which provided Conan Doyle with undeniable testimony about the reality of the hereafter. A young woman had come to stay at 'Windlesham' in the early part of 1914. Lily Loder-Symonds had been a bridesmaid at Conan Doyle's second wedding and was a long-time friend of Jean. Employed initially as a nanny to the Conan Doyle children, she suffered from ill-health and her worsening bronchial condition meant that she found herself in the position of an invalid.

Lily was a keen spiritualist and devoted much of her time to the art of automatic writing. A number of messages started to come through from 'the other side' whilst Lily lay in her small bedroom at 'Windlesham', many of them from deceased friends and acquaintances of Jean and Arthur. Sometimes the messages made little sense; at other times they were remarkably prophetic in content. On the day that the *Lusitania* went down, for instance, Lily received a message foretelling that the event would have a profound impact on the course of the war.

As the conflict progressed, Lily and the Conan Doyles experienced many bereavements. Jean's brother Malcolm Leckie fell at Mons in August 1914; Lottie's husband, Captain Oldham, died, as also did Connie's son, Oscar. Then in the spring of 1915 three of Lily's brothers were killed in action.

In the autumn of 1916 Lily's condition worsened. At the same time she produced a series of long messages from her dead brothers. Deeply fascinated (although not totally convinced of this testimony), Conan Doyle quizzed her about a conversation he had had with Malcolm Leckie years back. He was amazed to find that Lily was able to recall the precise content of that talk. There and then Conan Doyle became convinced of the truth of spiritualism.[3] It was the personal revelation for which he had been waiting.

Conan Doyle always emphasized the importance of actual experience and fact, particularly when dealing with automatic writing. In *The New Revelation*, he commented:

> Of all forms of mediumship, this seems to me to be the one which should be tested most rigidly, as it lends itself very easily not so much to deception as to self-deception, which is a much more subtle and dangerous thing. Is the lady herself writing, or is there, as she avers, a power that controls her, even as the chronicler of the Jews in the Bible averred that he was controlled?

And referring to Lily Loder-Symonds, he confirmed his belief in her reliability as a medium:

> . . . she foretold the arrival of an important telegram upon a certain day, and even gave the name of the deliverer of it – a

most unlikely person. Altogether, no one could doubt the reality of her inspiration, though lapses were notable. It was like getting a good message through a very imperfect telephone.

By the summer of 1916 he had come to accept out-of-body experiences as a demonstrable fact, having received 'many private instances' of this phenomenon. In a letter to the spiritualist magazine *Light* on 30 April 1916 he described the soul during unconsciousness as 'like a captive balloon on a psychic rope by which it can be drawn instantanously back'. 'The instances are so numerous,' he commented, 'so well attested, and so utterly beyond the reach of coincidence that one marvels that any man calling himself a scientist could dismiss them as unworthy of scientific consideration.' He went on to argue that the scientists should look at the evidence rather than interpret psychic phenomena from an *a priori* conception of the universe.

On 4 November 1916 another, much longer letter appeared in the pages of *Light*. Although the tone was cautious, the contents revealed a wide acceptance of the principles of the spiritualist movement. Conan Doyle began by defending his right to uphold such principles:

> If anyone were to look up the list of subscribers to *Light* for the year 1887 I think that he would find my name. I am also one of the oldest members of the Psychical Research Society . . .

He went on to argue that, despite the occasional frauds and 'wild imaginings', there remained a substantial core in the spiritualist movement which was closer to the truth than any other religious movement. There was an infinite quantity of phenomena; what was needed was careful interpretation. Gone were the days when spiritualism offered a scientific novelty to its participants. Now it was (or should be) 'taking shape as the foundations of a definite system of religious thought, in some ways confirmatory of ancient systems, in some ways new'.

At last Conan Doyle was able to fit spiritualism into the broad humanism which he had perceived played a role in all major religions. Spiritualism confirmed a life after death; it showed the unhappy results of sin; it demonstrated the existence of higher spiritual beings and of a 'summerland' or heaven wherein the individual found his or her resting-place.

The question of the nature of death was central to Conan Doyle's belief:

> . . . death makes no abrupt change in the process of development, nor does it make an impassable chasm between those who are on either side of it. No trait of the form and no peculiarity of the mind are changed by death but all are continued in that spiritual body which is the counterpart of the earthly one at its best, and still contains within it that core of spirit which is the very essence of the man. Nature develops slowly, and not by enormous leaps, so that it would seem natural that the soul should not suddenly become devil or angel but should continue upon its slow growth.

The place he termed 'summerland' was a kind of simulation of our present reality, possessing a similar atmosphere, but etherealized in accordance with the demands of the reborn body. Since the conditions on either side of death were so similar, the idea of communication between the living and the dead became feasible. The proof of such communication lay in the testimony of the countless clairvoyants, psychics, and mediums who were able to demonstrate the existence of this other dimension by means of the direct voice, automatic writing, spirit control, etc. Conan Doyle concluded his letter:

> Such, in brief, is the spiritual philosophy where faith . . . is replaced by actual demonstration. The evidence upon which this system rests is so enormous that it would take a very considerable library to contain it, and the witnesses are not shadowy people living in the dim past and inaccessible to our cross-examination but are our own contemporaries, men of character and intellect whom all must respect.[4] The situation may . . . be summed up in a simple alternative. The one supposition is that there has been an outbreak of lunacy extending over two generations of mankind and two great continents–a lunacy which assails men or women who are otherwise eminently sane. The alternative supposition is that in recent years there has come to us from divine sources a new revelation which constitutes by far the greatest religious event since the death of Christ . . . a revelation which alters the whole aspect of death and the fate of man. Between these two suppositions I can see no solid position. Theories of fraud or of delusion will not meet the evidence. It is absolute lunacy or it is a revolution in religious thought, a revolution

which gives us as by-products an utter fearlessness of death, and an immense consolation when those who are dear to us pass behind the veil.

Although Conan Doyle had reached the point where conviction was almost absolute, he still insisted on a certain degree of verification where mediums were concerned. During the winter of 1916 he visited several well-known mediums and reported his findings to his friend Sir Oliver Lodge. In December he sat with Vout Peters and wrote to Lodge about the experience. The seance which involved a French control, yielded much which was fascinating but not conclusive.[5]

Like Conan Doyle, Lodge felt uneasy about the number of fraudulent mediums who were capable of bringing discredit to the movement. Both believed that the police machinery for dealing with such malefactors was totally inadequate and that it was often difficult to distinguish between the genuine and the fake. Conan Doyle complained to his friend Lodge that the law was indiscriminate in the way it dealt with mediums so that the innocent suffered along with the guilty. The phoney medium caused irreperable damage to the movement.[8] Conan Doyle's interest in mediums also extended to spirit photographs, and in the early part of 1917 he undertook a sitting in the company of the psychic photographer William Hope. Conan Doyle was suitably impressed by the results he obtained. He wrote to Lodge about the episode, explaining that Estelle Stead and his sister-in-law were the sitters. A fine profile photograph of his nephew was obtained. Conan Doyle who was convinced that such a profile shot had never been taken during the subject's lifetime, explained to Lodge that Mrs Forbes had brought the plate and developed it herself and that it was only after development that the head was observed. He concluded his letter by suggesting to Lodge that Hope, who suffered an impoverished life style, should be set up in London where he could continue to provide positive testimony.

In the same letter Conan Doyle announced his intention to write a psychic work which would be a 'whole-hearted acceptance' of the movement and which would influence even 'the humblest' of people. Clearly then by April 1917 he had finally suspended any disbelief he might have hitherto harboured regarding the spiritualist cause and was already thinking about the evangelistic aspects of his own role.

On the morning of 4 April 1917 Conan Doyle had a most unusual psychic experience. He awoke early with the strong feeling that some information of importance had been conveyed to him in his sleep. The one word 'Piave' rang in his head and was clearly of significance, although it meant nothing to him. He at once went to his study and looked the name up in an atlas. He discovered that Piave was the name of a river about 50 miles in the rear of the Italian front, which was at that time advancing with some rapidity. Puzzled, but convinced that the name would eventually be of crucial importance, he drew up a witnessed statement to the effect that he believed some great event of the war would centre on the Piave.

Some six months later his suspicions were confirmed when the Italian army was driven from its positions and came to an eventual halt on the line of the Piave where it remained until February 1918. In June of that same year the first battle of Piave was fought and it was a victory for the Allies. From that date the Allied forces never looked back, and on every front enjoyed a consistent record of victory, culminating in the second Piave battle.

The sealed letter written by Sir Arthur was received by the secretary of the SPR on 7 November 1917 and read on 20 November 1918.[9] Conan Doyle remarked in a subsequent communication to the SPR that he fully believed in the psychic implications of this event:

> . . . how could this be accounted for by coincidence? That is unthinkable. Even if my subconscious self had known there was a river called Piave, that would not have shifted the Italian army back to it. Was it then telepathy? But no one in the world could have conjectured such a series of events. What then was it? I claim that the only possible explanation is that my friends on the other side, knowing how much I worried over the situation, were giving me comfort and knowledge. The ordinary spirit has, so far as my reading and experience teach, only a very limited and uncertain gift of prophecy. Therefore I have some reason to hope that my information came from a high source. Why I should have been so privileged above others is the one point which is beyond my conjecture.

In October 1917 he gave a lecture in the company of Sir Oliver Lodge before the London Spiritualists Alliance entitled 'The New Revelation'. This was to be his first public declaration about the degree to which he was now prepared to champion the cause. He said that if it had taken him a long time to arrive at the conclusion he now held, this was because psychical research involved questions which were complex, deep, and difficult. When he had finished his medical education, he had been a convinced materialist and was of the opinion that the analogy of nature was against the theory of the survival of bodily death. although he was a theist, he certainly did not believe in an anthropomorphic deity.

As regards spiritualism, which he had once looked upon as the greatest nonsense, his own personal experiences of psychic phenomena and the views of reputable scientists like Sir William Crookes, Alfred Russel Wallace, and Camille Flammarion had convinced him of its truth. The existence of fraudulent mediums did not surprise him, since many of them were paid for their labours, and in any case the physical gift of mediumship bore no relationship to morality.

The war had compelled him to realize for the first time the importance to everyone of a study which aimed at the breakdown of the wall between this world and the next. Through spiritualism a new revelation was in the process of delivery. Although it was still in the 'John the Baptist' stage, nevertheless there was a significant body of fresh doctrine which had been accumulated, mainly through automatic writing, but partly also from direct voice and other sources.

Conan Doyle retained a critical perception of Christianity, which he regarded as too much obsessed with the death of Jesus Christ. In his view it was the life of Christ which should form the basis of Christian belief – a belief which must of necessity adapt or perish.

In January 1918 Conan Doyle gave an interview to a reporter from the spiritualist newspaper *Two Worlds*.[10] When asked whether he did not think it slightly absurd that man's survival of bodily death should be indicated by moving tables, he replied that these humbler phenomena had little connection with the creed of spiritualism. To his mind they were 'a device of the Great Designer, by which public attention is drawn to the matter'. As for the higher phenomena, such as automatic writing and trance speaking, these certainly had much to do with religion since they were the means by which the truth came through. When asked directly about what he saw as the unreasonable side to Christianity he highlighted the doctrine of original sin, the Fall, the 'vicarious' Atonement and the 'placation of the Almighty by blood'. It is clear that he now saw Christ as a psychic with greatly developed gifts rather than a purely supernatural being:

> [He was] A high spirit, in the sense we use the words . . . something more than man. We hold that in both His moral and His psychical attributes He was more than man though, of course, infinitely less than God . . . [one cannot] possibly understand many passages [of the New Testament] unless [He had] a knowledge of psychical matters . . . take His words when the sick woman touched Him. They were 'somebody touched Me, for I perceive that virtue has gone out of me'! This is exactly how a healing medium would feel . . .

Not only was Christ a medium but the early Christians were spiritualists:

> Think of St. Paul, with his 'natural body and spiritual body'; and look at John with his precept, 'Believe not every spirit, but try the spirits whether they be of God'. Is not that exactly what a wise spiritualist would say now who does not accept every message that comes to him, but tests them by his reason and by the general body of information already recorded? The 'lying spirit' is unfortunately a fact now, as then!

When asked whether he viewed spiritualism as a new religion, he replied that he hoped it would not be so, since he did not want to add yet another sect to the list. He perceived it as a rallying, unifying force which would eventually revolutionize all the Christian creeds. Once the Christian lay powerless before the materialist's assertion that death ended all; now the proof of a continued life offered the weapon desperately needed by Christians, if they were ready to use it. Meanwhile the materialists were aided and abetted by the cynicism and disbelief so prevalent among people of all classes. The established Church was powerless, and England 'a mummy wrapped up in ecclesiastical bindings'.

The full declaration of his views on spiritualism was embodied in a short book Conan Doyle issued in March 1918. Entitled *The New Revelation*, it was to provide a cornerstone in spiritualist thinking.

Conan Doyle's intention was to reveal the religious importance of spiritualism and to provide a personal testimony which would be comprehensible to the masses. The book is divided into four chapters: 'The Search', 'The Revelation', 'The Coming Life', and 'Problems and Limitations'.

The 'Search' outlines Conan Doyle's personal quest for truth and tells of how the author had been interested in psychic phenomena since 1886. it details his interest in the literature of the movement and the discovery that many eminent scientists had vouched for its truth.

After mentioning his encounter with General Drayson, Conan Doyle relates how over the years he had held numerous table seances, with sometimes indifferent results. Out of the mass of reported evidence, he chose two which appeared to him to be convincing in their depiction of an afterlife and a previous existence on earth. The first of these concerned Dorothy Poslethwaite, a young Australian woman who had died in Melbourne at the age of 16. Miss Poslethwaite said that the sphere she inhabited circled the earth; that Mars was inhabited by an advanced race; that there was no bodily pain in her sphere (although there was certainly mental anxiety); and that the spirits were given both nourishment and punishment. In short, paradise was a place of light and laughter where Buddhists, Muhammadans, and Christians mingled without restraint or prejudice.

The second spirit turned out to be a famous cricketer with whom Conan Doyle had had some serious conversation in Cairo. Dodd had been a free-thinker who observed that in the spirit world spirits lived in families and communities. Married people did not necessarily meet again, he claimed, but those who loved each other did.

Joining the SPR in 1891 appeared to have some impression on Conan Doyle, although he criticizes the Society for their somewhat over-academic approach to the phenomena. On the other hand he has nothing but praise for Myers's *Human Personality*, which he regards as a major breakthrough in terms of cumulative evidence.

Regarding mediums, he is dubious about the reliability of the phenomena produced by many of those who make a living out of their talent and cites the Italian peasant Eusapia Palladino, who appeared to have practised both trickery and genuine mediumship.

Having traced his own development up until the Great War, Sir Arthur then admits that he 'might have drifted on for [his] whole life as a psychical researcher' if it were not for the tremendous reassessment of beliefs and values which this cataclysm brought about. He goes on to say (with some feeling):

> In the presence of an agonized world, hearing every day of the deaths of the flower of our race in the first promise of their unfulfilled youth, seeing around one the wives and mothers who had no clear conception whither their loved one had gone to, I seemed suddenly to see that this subject with which I had so long dallied was not merely a study of a force outside the rules of science, but that it was really something tremendous, a breaking down of the walls between two worlds, a direct undeniable message from beyond, a call of hope and of guidance to the human race at the time of its deepest affliction. The objective side of it ceased to interest, for having made up one's mind that it was true there was an end of the matter. The religious side of it was clearly of infinitely greater importance . . .

It seems evident, therefore, that Conan Doyle's acceptance of spiritualism relied upon a *religious* interpretation of the known facts. Having rejected Catholicism, he had sought for a theistic system of belief which would accommodate the principle of the survival of bodily death. Spiritualism offered him this with its non-sectarian approach and insistence upon the provable existence of an afterlife. This did not mean (as some of his critics have attempted to show) that he was therefore willing to suspend *all* disbelief. With regard to automatic writing, for example, he admitted that it was not always possible to distinguish between the product of the unconscious mind and a genuine communication from the beyond. However, there was an answer to the problem:

> The answer must be that we require signs which we can test before we accept assertions which we cannot test. In old days they demanded a sign from a prophet, and it was a perfectly reasonable request, and still holds good . . .

All the phenomena received by mediums and clairvoyants were linked; there could be no doubt about it since the evidence was overwhelming and undeniable. From the lowest manifestation of a table-rap to the most inspired

119

utterance of a prophet was one complete whole, a system which enabled humanity to reach the revelation, if only they had the motivation to seek it.

Conan Doyle was careful to distinguish between psychical research and religion. What he claimed was that the results of psychical research confirmed the continued life of the soul and that the nature of the afterlife was affected by the conduct of the individual during his life on earth. Spiritualism was therefore a quasi-religious system which brought its influence to bear on organized religions and demanded their adaptation and reform. It not only confirmed the existence of an afterlife but also demonstrated the results of sin, the existence of higher spiritual beings, and the concept of purgatory. Thus the new revelation, far from destroying old beliefs, should be hailed by mankind as a powerful ally and positive reforming force.

To Conan Doyle, Jesus Christ provided an example which was much misinterpreted by the early Church and later, with the emergence of the established Church, twisted out of all proportion. In his view the divinity of Christ as traditionally interpreted was open to dispute. As a messenger from the 'other world' his life on earth had an importance and he left behind him an example which might be matched by others should they wish to emulate him. However, such notions as atonement and redemption were, in Conan Doyle's view, entirely irrelevant. His reading of the New Testament convinced him that the teaching of Christ was in many ways lost by the early Church and did not survive. Moreover, the psychic abilities of Christ mentioned in passing in the New Testament had been overlooked by the established Church. In reality they were central to his teaching. (For example, the list of gifts which St Paul gives as being fundamental to the Christian disciple is essentially the list of gifts one would expect a powerful medium to possess.)

Conan Doyle's picture of the afterlife at this period seems to have been pieced together from a variety of sources. In 'The Coming Life' he describes in considerable detail the gradual awakening of the spirit after the barrier of death has been passed. The spirit self, a simulacrum of the self-in-life, soon finds itself surrounded by those entities it knew in life. The spirit, far from being 'a glorified angel' or 'goblin damned', is simply the person himself, containing all his strengths and weaknesses.

The reborn spirit then finds himself plunged into a long period of sleep. Having wakened from this condition his strength (previously diminished) soon returns and the new life commences. This appears to be a largely utopian version of life on earth, full of interest and occupation from which the spirit would not wish to be separated. However, this life beyond lasts only for a limited period. After that the self passes on to other phases. This bears something of a resemblance to the Buddhist spheres of Tibetan philosophy. The spirits of the lower sphere are not permitted to ascend whereas the higher can descend at will:

> These, roughly speaking, are the lines of the life beyond in its simplest expression, for it is not all simple and we catch dim glimpses of endless circles below, descending into gloom and endless circles above, ascending into glory, all improving, all purposeful, all intensely alive.

Conan Doyle had his own theories about the nature of spirit communications. He believed that there were two forms of dreams experienced, the first being those of the released spirit and the second the 'confused action of the lower faculties which remain in the body when the spirit is absent'. The spirits themselves had limitations and did not always know what impression they were making upon the minds of the living. Their ability to connect with our own world was therefore intermittent. This, he believed, explained many of the mistakes that were made in seances. The spirits also appeared to have an estimate of time which was at variance with our own.

Above all, Conan Doyle insisted, the 'new revelation' was a confirmation of what had been revealed to mankind time and again in past centuries. Materialism had helped to destroy the intuitive and psychic abilities of man which in former times had been of great importance to him. Now its influence had to be battled against and the convictions of spiritualists translated into actions:

> It must be repeated that while the new revelation may seem destructive to those who hold Christian dogmas with extreme rigidity, it has quite the opposite effect upon the mind which, like so many modern minds, has come to look upon the whole Christian scheme as a huge delusion. It is shown clearly that the old revelation has so many resemblances,

defaced by time and mangled by man's mishandling and materialism, but still denoting the same general scheme, that undoubtedly both have come from the same source. The accepted ideas of life after death, of higher and lower spirits, of high teachers, of an infinite central power, of circles above circles approaching nearer to His presence – all of those conceptions appear once more and are confirmed by many witnesses.

Although it is true that Conan Doyle's philosophy of spiritualism was formulated over a long period of time and based on a wide and informed variety of experiences, there is evidence that the cultural and psychological effects which the war had on him were considerable. Far more than ever before he felt the need to bring home to people the message of hope which he thought spiritualism offered. The mass slaughter of a generation had wrought immeasurable harm and it was a burden which many believed they could not bear. The (as he saw it) overwhelming evidence of a life after death mitigated this universal anguish and provided a renaissance in religious terms.

Before 1918 drew to a close Sir Arthur gave two important talks, one in Leeds, the other in his much-loved Southsea. He had, it seems, decided to follow up his public declaration of faith with a concerted effort to preach to converted and unconverted alike anywhere and everywhere in the British Isles. At Southsea he spoke about the war bringing about a great need for a first-hand knowledge of what happened after death and recalled the 13 mothers who had written to him about their sons who, having been killed in the conflict, had contacted them. Two cases were known to him of girls of 13 who by automatic writing were giving to the world valued testimony of a force 'extraneous to themselves'. One had even written 'in the purest Greek' the Gospel according to St John. Conan Doyle defended mediums as a profession, comparing them with ministers of other religious denominations, and he advised his audience to pursue their investigations 'rationally, critically, sympathetically and earnestly'.[11]

By the beginning of 1919 the die had been cast. Arthur Conan Doyle had finally reached a stage in his existence where the roles of public defender of causes, writer, and psychic investigator could unite under a new banner. It was a banner offering hope, consolation, and fresh inspiration to the many who were prepared (as he saw it) to be reasonable and willing to sustain a hope in the spiritual future of mankind. His 'enemies' were the materialists, for spiritualism was the antithesis of materialism, that much was certainly clear. 'The fact is manifest', he wrote, 'that if the spirit can live without matter, then the foundation of materialism is gone, and the whole scheme of thought crashes to the ground.' In the decade that followed he was to realize how hard the 'good fight' would be against the cynics and the disbelievers who were only too willing to impede his quest.

CHAPTER 6

A Spiritual Breakthrough

In February 1919, Sir Arthur Conan Doyle and his wife attended a seance held by the Thomas brothers at Penylan, a mining village in South Wales. Since the 1914-18 War there had been a tremendous revival in Wales and spiritualism was undergoing a renaissance even rivalling the popularity of Welsh Methodism. The Thomas brothers were typical of the groups who spearheaded the movement. The family was well known in the area of Cardiff, where they impressed believers with their phenomena. Mr Thomas senior, an avowed spiritualist for nearly 40 years, was a self-educated democrat, well loved among the local community as a councillor and alderman. Having been employed as a miner's agent in Merthyr Tydfil for many years, he retired and founded the Merthyr Spiritualist Society, of which he was president. Like his son Tom, he was at the outset non-sensitive to outside influences, but his wife and his three daughters were all mediumistic. For nearly 40 years the family had established and maintained a home circle and were proud of their spiritualistic achievements.

The eldest son, Tom (born in 1881), had an ambition to become a public speaker, but in the restricted culture of the Welsh mining community experienced some frustration. He had therefore turned to psychic matters at an early stage and worked assiduously for the spiritualist movement, being a founder member of the Merthyr branch. Will, the youngest child, shared his older brother's desire to make a name for himself. Having been told that he was clairvoyant in 1911 by a medium operating at Swansea Sands, he participated in

Tom's abortive expedition to South America before establishing himself at Gorseinon as part of the home circle. As trance mediums, Tom and Will were capable of producing a variety of phenomena, including the playing of musical instruments, spirit voices, and the removal of small objects from the clothes of participants. Like many mediums of the period, they preferred their own domestic setting and performed in the presence of the whole family. Their spirit guide was a North American Indian called White Eagle.

The seance in which Conan Doyle participated was held at the house of Mr Wall (a local medium) in the presence of Mr Leo Joseph, a local MP, the Chief Constable of Cardiff, and about 20 other spiritualists. Before commencing, the Thomas brothers invited the assembled company to conduct a detailed search of the room and its contents. The Chief Constable and his assistant then roped Tom around his middle and strapped him to the back of the chair which stood near to the cabinet. After communal hymn-singing, the lights were switched off and a number of objects were then thrown around the room, including a doll and a tambourine which had been placed inside the cabinet. After several minutes had elapsed Tom, who had now fallen into a trance, enquired whether Lady Conan Doyle felt cold. Having replied in the affirmative, a jacket belonging to one of the brothers was then dropped into her lap. More objects were then to be seen floating around the participants' heads, including a guitar and a child's trumpet. Throughout these chaotic proceedings, hymns and sentimental songs were continually sung, thus sustaining the quasi-religious ambience. At the close of the seance, when the lights were switched on, it was observed that the floor was littered with about a dozen articles and the cabinet was empty. The police then examined Thomas, who was found to have the rope intact and the knots untampered with.

Conan Doyle was convinced of the genuineness of these phenomena:

> I believe that we are dealing with a thoroughly material generation, with limited and self-satisfied religious and scientific lines of thought, which can only be broken up and finally rearranged by the shock of encountering physical phenomena which are outside their philosophies. The whole campaign is, I believe, engineered from the other side, and one can continually catch glimpses of wisdom and purpose

beyond that of the world. The levitation of a tambourine or the moving of furniture may seem humble and even ludicrous phenomena, but the more thoughtful mind understands that the nature of the object is immaterial, and that the real question has to do with the force that moves it.[1]

Predictably, the press were sceptical about the proceedings attended by Sir Arthur. Foremost among the London papers in this respect was the *Sunday Express*, whose editor, James Douglas, had made exposés of fraudulent mediums a regular feature in his columns. A few weeks after the South Wales seance he offered a reward of £500 to any medium who could produce a bona fide materialization of the spirit of any person who had died within living memory. The appearance, he insisted, must take place before a small jury of experts who would include men of science, qualified engineers, and professional conjurers. Interviewed in Cardiff, the Thomas brothers were understandably cautious about 'public' performances. Tom in particular wanted nothing to do with publicity. 'We have been misrepresented by people who were camouflaged into our meeting,' he told an *Express* reporter. 'These conjurers may be able to do "tricks" but can they accomplish them through the agency of spirit?'

Nevertheless the test took place, being conducted at the offices of the *Sunday Express* in Shoe Lane. Although Tom Thomas declared from the outset that he was reluctant to participate in what he regarded as a 'dangerous attempt to undermine the health of the medium', the two brothers agreed provided that Maskelyne, the famous magician and anti-spiritualist, was excluded from the proceedings. The results were somewhat non-conclusive, a fact which the brothers ascribed to an atmosphere of hostility and scepticism engendered by the audience. Some of the persons present witnessed a 'white form or efflorescent cloud' gathering in a corner, whilst a shirt suspender and a pair of braces were deposited in the hands of some of the committee members. (This was regarded as significant evidence to the spiritualists present, since both brothers had been roped securely to their chairs.) Even the genuineness of these phenomena was disputed by one of the sitters present, who argued that since most of the company were convinced spiritualists, the results obtained were extremely suspect.

Conan Doyle remained dubious about the value of such

public demonstrations and refused point blank to take part in the testing of the Thomas brothers. In his view it led to nothing but confusion:

> A conjurer put up a similar challenge of £1,000 once before, which was won by the spiritualists but the result was litigation and trouble for all concerned. On the one hand, spiritualists claim, as the result of their experience, that harmonious conditions of mind are essential for good results. On the other, the sceptics must approach the sitting in an acrid, argumentative spirit. These conditions are incompatible and no good can result.[2]

It was not long before another condender entered the fray in order to claim the £500 offered by Douglas. A professional conjurer by occupation, he had spent years performing with faked mediums but now claimed that he could produce a 'genuine materialised phenomenon'. The medium in question was to remain anonymous since her spiritualist friend, in whose flat the seance was to be held, might object to publicity. The seance duly took place at the flat in the West End of London, and the reporter Sydney A. Moseley gave an account of the proceedings.[3] There were seven people present including the owner of the flat, his wife, and her girl-friend.

The medium, referred to as 'Miss Smith', first described to Moseley details of his past, present, and future. She then described, with considerable accuracy, his greatcoat which he had hung in the adjoining room. Although Moseley was impressed with this initial display of her powers, he conceded that the coat might have been examined by the medium on a previous occasion. However, it was the events that followed which convinced him that he was dealing with a genuine medium.

First, the door of the seance room was sealed. Then the medium was tied, hands and feet, with stamp paper, the seal being signed by Moseley. This was to ensure that the slightest movement would tear the paper, thus indicating that cheating had taken palce. The lights were then extinguished and in the darkness 'the white form of the medium stood out with weird prominence against the background of pitch blackness. If you strained to see,' remarked Moseley in his account of the case, 'a kind of white vapour soon emanated from the outlines of the white figure of the medium.'

After some initial wrestling with an unwanted spirit, the sitters were then rewarded with a great beam of light which lit up the end of the curtained wall. Moseley recalled:

> It was of a beautiful brilliance, but faded away as suddenly as it had appeared. Then another light, wan and cloudy, seemed to emanate from the back of the medium. It hung, first of all, just above her head, a thin curl of cloud, and then grew in size and contour till it resembled an aged woman in a shawl. It remained for a few seconds stationary, and then glided to the side of the medium. I leaned forward and tried to make out any details of this apparition, but beyond the outlines nothing was discernible. Now and then the figure seemed to grow in brilliance, and at one time looked as if it were coming towards us, but it turned, and remained all the time in the vicinity of the medium and the black curtains.

> The more closely one looked, the stranger became the form of this ghostly looking light. Now it seemed as if it were a woman carrying a child, then as a woman bent with age, and finally just as a beacon of light. Whatever it was, it moved freely about from one side of the room to the other.

Moseley seemed impressed by the phenomena he had witnessed, although he was careful to point out that the issue was not entirely proven. For instance, the friends of the medium might easily have seen his coat and dipped into the pockets before the commencement of the seance. Equally the 'manifestation' might have been the result of a well-constructed and manipulated lighting effect.

The week following this seance Sir Arthur joined a committee of investigators who sat with the medium. They included Lady Glenconner, Sir Henry Lunn, Dr Wyn Westcott, a coroner, Superintendent Thomas from Scotland Yard, and the editors of *Light* and the *Occult Review*. About 12 other people also attended the proceedings.

After a few preliminary comments by Selbit, the medium's agent, Miss Smith was brought into the room wearing a veil. She then said that she would attempt to identify some particulars about several articles which had been placed in a box. After some initial difficulties, she was able to read two words in a sealed packet which had been left in the box and the owner of the letter was pleased to confirm their accuracy.

The medium next pictured a black swan, which puzzled her since she pictured it being carried about in a pocket. This turned out to be a Swan fountain pen belonging to Sir Henry Lunn.

The third article to be envisaged was a ring which had belonged to Sir Arthur's eldest son. Kingsley, who was Sir Arthur's favourite child, had been wounded at the Somme and had died of pneumonia in London in 1918. Sir Arthur was anxious to establish contact with him. The medium gave the initials on it correctly, and Sir Arthur reported that the engraving of these initials was so faded and worn that they could not possibly be seen except in a strong light. Other articles were described in minute detail by the medium, and the owners were greatly impressed by her accuracy. Sir Arthur said that the demonstration was an extremely clever one, and Lady Glenconner agreed that it was convincing. Following this psychometrical display the medium was searched in an adjoining room and then tied securely to a chair by three of the men present. The door having been sealed, the lights were dimmed and the medium fell into a trance. After a short while the ghostly, efflorescent form curled up from behind the medium and gradualy assumed the outline of an old woman. After the phantom had vanished there were sounds of heavy breathing from the medium which then ceased. After an interval the lights were switched on, and it was observed that the anonymous stranger had turned her chair round to face the door at her left. However, the seals and bandages which had secured her were still intact.

Conan doyle told the *Sunday Express* reporter:

She was able to tell me the initials on the ring of my boy – who died some months ago – although the average person examining it would perhaps make nothing of it. It was so worn that it would be excusable if you could not make anything of it even if you had the ring before you. So far as the second part of the programme is concerned, that is a different matter. Before a decision can be made, one must attend several seances with the same medium. One certainly saw a floating light. But although I was sitting in the front row, and was quite close to it, I could not make anything of it. I should have to see it again before passing a definite opinion on it. In any case, I think the proceedings were instructive and clear. But I have my doubts about the whole thing.

It is worth reporting this comment in full to illustrate how cautious Conan Doyle was in assessing the powers of the mediums whom he encountered. Although posterity would prefer a picture of a gullible and easily satisfied dupe, nothing could be further from the truth. By 1919 Sir Arthur had seen many demonstrations of this kind and knew exactly how liable mediums were to practise trickery and deception. And whilst the psychometry had impressed him in this case, he was by no means satisfied with the physical phenomenon.

In showing caution Sir Arthur had acted wisely. A few days later Sydney Moseley called on Selbit and in the course of conversation extracted a full confession from him. Selbit explained that the box containing the articles gathered from the audience was removed from the room during the seance and the medium held a substitute box while the original box was being examined in an adjoining room. The contents were then described to the medium detail by detail. As for the 'ghost', it was an accomplice. However, Selbit was reluctant to supply further details about this trick.

At about the same time as Sir Arthur Conan Doyle was investigating the 'masked medium', he had received a series of letters from a number of people. These concerned a medium in London to whom he had sent mothers who had asked him for some proof of the existence of their departed sons. Sir Arthur's idea was to place the details of these correspondents in the hands of a committee of six newspaper investigators (these included representatives of the *Daily Chronicle*, the *Evening Standard*, the *Daily Sketch*, the *Daily Mail*, and the *Sunday Express*). Many of the correspondents had received detailed messages from their departed relatives through 'Mrs B', but Sir Arthur himself was uncertain about her powers since on occasion she could be quite unsuccessful in obtaining positive results. On the other hand she had been able to describe most vividly to him Lily Loder-Symonds and the 'spirit' had used a phrase which was known only to her intimate friends. More impressively, she had described an officer who had a gold coin. This at once called to mind Malcolm Leckie, who had been presented with a spade guinea by Sir Arthur on receiving his first medical case.

It was, however, the third of these sittings which had convinced Sir Arthur of the latent powers of 'Mrs B'. This had taken place shortly after the death of his son Kingsley.

The significance of 'Mrs B's' testimony lay in the fact that throughout the seance she referred to 'Kingsley' and this name was not used outside the family circle, his full name being Alleyne Kingsley L.N. Conan Doyle. Sir Arthur recorded:

> My boy tried to console me at his death and said that in any case he would not have stayed in England, as he had intended to go abroad in the medical service. He told me that he had suffered pains in the lungs – which was quite true, because he died from pneumonia after serving in the army three years. He referred to other friends who had passed over and said: 'When I was alive I did not believe in spiritualism. Now I believe in it. I was a chuckle-headed ass not to believe it'.[4]

At the fourth sitting even more satisfactory results were obtained. Conan Doyle was able to contact his brother Innes, who had also died in the war and who told him that he would have liked to live for another three months so that he could have seen the conclusion of the war.

Sir Arthur remained confident of 'Mrs B's' powers, yet others were not so easily satisfied. *Truth* magazine regarded her purely and simply as a telepath and was of the opinion that 'Mrs B' 'had consciously humbugged Sir Arthur Conan Doyle and twenty-four of the twenty-six people he has sent to her'. Sydney Moseley, who underwent two successive sittings (and who was not unsympathetic to spiritualism), experienced no success whatever. He reported:

> I could not recognise the name of one spirit-friend who hovered near me. 'Mrs. B' once gave the name of Nellie. When I said I did not know Nellie she said: 'Perhaps it is Annie'. Then she gave the name of Clara, and when that failed she said it might have been Sarah. She also gave the name of Gertie, and when that elicited no recognition on my part said it might have been Bertie. 'Mrs. B' also described in detail a man who purported to be my father and a woman who was supposed to be my mother, but I failed to recognise either of them from my own knowledge or from the knowledge of my family.

By the summer of 1919 Conan Doyle estimated that he had already addressed over 50,000 people on the subject of spiritualism at various locations. Despite the occasional disappointment he experienced at the hands of certain professional mediums, he continued to protest at the cynicism of the unconverted. The constant assumption, he pointed out in numerous letters to the press, was that all mediums were rogues. However, this was an exaggeration of the facts. Genuine phenomena could be observed, but this depended on a certain amount of sympathy on the part of the investigator. The spiritualists themselves were derided in the press, but unfairly so. They were, in reality, far from being the credulous dupes who were to be found 'gaping and marvelling' at the displays produced by mediums.

Conan Doyle was eager to extend his campaign to every section of the community. He was therefore delighted when in October 1919 the Bishop of Worcester invited him to give an address on spiritualism in Worcester Cathedral. The address, which caused considerable controversy in the local and national press, was followed by a counter-address given by Canon James Wilson, a traditional Christian and an opponent of spiritualism. Wilson thought that spiritualism had made a fundamental error in assuming that the human personality would continue to exist after death in human form. To him human personality had no form and therefore the life hereafter must be conceived of in terms of formlessness and a non-material structure.

Conan Doyle was quick to reply to this attack and wrote a letter to the *Worcestershire Advertiser*, the newspaper which had published an account of Canon Wilson's lecture. Because we could not imagine the Divinity in a human shape in the next world, he argued, there was no reason at all why our own spiritual or etheric bodies should not retain their present appearance. In fact there was every reason to believe in the transference of the bodily form, for this would explain the appearance of the departed as visions at the time of death and in seances.

Wilson replied to Conan Doyle's letter in a second lecture in the cathedral. Visions at the time of death were, he maintained, more subjective impressions and were not verifiable. In a second letter to the *Worcestershire Advertiser* Conan Doyle assured Wilson that 'they have been certified by every scientific man, so far as I know, who has ever earnestly investigated them. These verifications are accompanied by copious photographs of the spirit body, so far as it can be made visible to our physical eyes.'

In his second lecture, Wilson gave a brief potted history of the spiritualist movement from the orthodox Christian point of view. The phenomena and beliefs of spiritualism, he admitted, were of great antiquity and deserved scientific study. Indeed, certain aspects of the movement were worthy of acceptance. Psychotherapy, hypnosis, and telepathy were accredited forms of psychic power emanating from the subconscious mind. When it came to mediums, however, the evidence was uncertain in the extreme, fraud and self-deception being all too common. Nevertheless, there *were* rare instances when a force was employed (this he referred to as 'teledynamism') which led to the displacement of objects.

Wilson then addressed himself to the central issue: could spirits of the departed communicate through mediums with the living? (This he regarded as a question of scientific fact.) He based his conclusion on two main sources: the conclusions of the SPR (who had found to date no evidence to justify a belief that hallucinations might be due to telepathic influence exerted by the dead), and of Sir Oliver Lodge, who in his spiritualist classic *Raymond* emphasized the role of the 'secondary personality' of the medium.

Conan Doyle's third letter to the *Worcestershire Advertiser* provided a much more detailed and informative counter-offensive. He began his letter by explaining that he had talked 'face to face again and again' with his dead relatives and that he wanted no scientific expert to tell him the truth of it. Neither was he overly impressed with the testimony of scientists. He believed that the ordinary man was quite capable of deciding whether he was or was not in touch with the dead and the letters he received from countless correspondents who had themselves communicated with the departed were, as a rule, well balanced and reasonable.

Wilson had been only too ready to attack Sir Arthur's concept of the 'etheric body', which he had defined as a mould of 'bound ether' (a term invented by Fresnel, the French scientist). Conan Doyle believed at this time that each human body carried with it a mould of indestructible ether which would be capable of surviving bodily dissolution and that the existence of this mould explained the post-mortem visions so frequently reported. Sir Arthur concluded his letter:

We are bringing to the world the greatest tidings which have ever reached it for two thousand years, and in spite of the determined opposition of the clergy on one side and of the materialists upon the other, it is spreading more quickly than any other religious movement that has ever come to enlarge the bounds of human thought and to bring hope into weary hearts.[5]

Sir Oliver Lodge found himself in a somewhat difficult position when asked to comment on Canon Wilson's utterances. On the one hand he was not such a vociferous spiritualist as Conan Doyle was. On the other he did not agree with everything Wilson had to say on the subject. He regarded his treatment of mesmerism as cavalier, and he disputed Wilson's assumption that mediums carried out their actions whilst under self-hypnosis. When it came to the central issue regarding the survival of bodily death, he had to admit that 'communication across the veil' was both 'possible and genuine'.

The Wilson–Conan Doyle affair represents an interesting excursion into the question of how far the Anglican Church was prepared to attack spiritualism. Clearly it saw the spiritualist movement as a major rival offering a misinterpretation of the facts of the Christian faith, although judging by Canon Wilson's performance it had not as yet organized itself in terms of a consistent theological approach.

Throughout the autumn of 1919 Sir Arthur had continued to communicate with his friend Sir Oliver Lodge on various aspects of spiritualism. Lodge had lost a much-loved son in the Great War and through various mediums had become utterly convinced that the young officer had survived the grave. His detailed account of the various seances he attended and the evidence he accumulated are to be found in the book *Raymond*, published soon after the end of the war and a bestseller in those days of sorrow and bereavement.

On 7 September Conan Doyle himself broke through the barrier of death and was able to contact his son Kingsley. The medium in question was Evan Powell a Welsh spiritualist from Merthyr Tydfil who had travelled, like Conan Doyle, to Portsmouth to address a meeting. What impressed Sir Arthur about Powell was that he did not operate as a commercial medium and therefore his psychic powers were 'free from that deterioration which comes from over-strain'.

After the conclusion of the lecture Powell agreed to return to Sir Arthur's hotel room and there gave him a sitting. The other persons present at this gathering were Lady Conan Doyle, Frank Blake, president of the Southern Countries Spiritualist Union, Mr and Mrs MacFarlane, leaders of the Portsmouth branch, and Harry Engholm a cinema producer. All present were therefore sympathetic to the cause.

Powell first insisted on being searched and was then bound thoroughly by Sir Arthur to a wooden armchair. A small megaphone was placed beside him and this was circled with luminous paint so as to be visible in the dark. The lights were then turned out and the room plunged into total darkness. The assembled company sat around the medium, though none touched him.

Within a few minutes the breathing of the medium became loud and stertorous. A voice then addressed the company, deep, strong, and quite unlike that of Powell. This announced itself as the Red Indian spirit Black Hawk, Powell's control. Conan Doyle having been christened 'Great Chief' and Engholm 'Little Chief', there was then an interval of silence during which the luminous band of the megaphone was seen to rise into the air and circle around the company's heads. Having momentarily vanished, the megaphone subsequently returned with flowers taken from the mantelpiece.

The Indian control now announced that 'Leely is here' and 'Leely wishes to speak with the Lady of the Wigwam'; a moment later a quick, excited voice said, 'Jean, Jean, I am here.' Lady Conan Doyle, convinced that she was speaking to her departed friend Lily Loder-Symonds, exchanged words of affection. Then came silence again. The lights were turned on and the spiritualists discovered that a huge wooden pedestal weighing approximately 50 pounds had been brought from the corner and placed in the centre of the semi-circle.

The following evening Sir Arthur and the assembled company again sat with Powell. Numerous physical phenomena were again noted and the pedestal again lifted into the circle. As Conan Doyle recorded:

> Then came what to me was the supreme moment of my spiritual experience. It is almost too sacred for full description, and yet I feel that God sends such gifts that we may share them with others. There came a voice in the darkness,

a whispered voice, saying 'Jean, it is I'. My wife felt a hand upon her head, and cried, 'It is Kingsley'. I heard the word 'Father'. I said 'Dear boy is that you?' I had then a sense of a face very near my own, and of breathing. Then the clear voice came again with an intensity and note very distinctive of my son, 'Forgive me!' . . . I told him eagerly that I had no grievance of any kind. A large, strong hand then rested upon my head, it was gently bent forward, and I felt and heard a kiss just above my brow. 'Tell me, dear, are you happy?' I cried. There was silence, and I feared he was gone. Then on a sighing note came the words, 'yes I am so happy' . . . a moment afterwards another gentle voice, claiming to be that of my wife's mother, recently deceased, was heard in front of us. We could not have recognised the voice as we could the other. A few loving words were said, and then a small warm hand patted both our cheeks with a little gesture which was full of affection. Such were my experiences.[6]

In Conan Doyle's view the evidence v.as overwhelming. He wrote to Lodge,[7] explaining that he and his wife were completely convinced by the authenticity of the phenomena, and noting that Powell had promised him a complete materialization at the next seance on December 3.

In Wales Powell produced four spirits in quick succession, each of them known to Sir Arthur. The fourth was his brother, who announced himself as 'Innes', a name known only by his family and intimate friends. Sir Arthur discussed Innes's widow, who was ill in Copenhagen. Innes suggested the name 'Sigurd Frier' or 'Trier' (Conan Doyle could not quite make the name out) as a source of psychical treatment for her condition. The next day Conan Doyle wrote to a young Danish friend in London, asking him if the name meant anything to him. The young man replied that it was the name of a well-known psychic who operated in Copenhagen. Conan Doyle was amazed since the other members of the circle could not possibly have known that the conversation would have led to this single, demonstrable fact regarding Copenhagen.[8]

During the early months of 1919 Conan Doyle was hard at work on a sequel to his spiritualist tract *The New Revelation* – a work which had enjoyed considerable success among the converted. Part of his new book (which he entitled *The Vital Message*) was an attempt to relate the war to the spiritualist creed. In Sir Arthur's opinion 'The shock of the war was meant to rouse us to mental and moral earnestness, to give us the courage to tear away venerable shams, and to force the human race to realise and use the vast new revelation which has been so clearly stated and so abundantly proved . . .'

He was particularly antagonistic to the Fundamentalists. In his view the Bible was a compound of the living and the dead and there could be no clear thinking until Christians realized that the Old Testament was interesitng only as a collection of poetry, historical accounts, and folklore. The concept of an anthropomorphic, tribal God filled with rage, jealousy, and revenge no longer had any role to play in modern religious belief and should be discarded. The Old Testament, he reminded his readers, was a document which 'advocates massacre, condones polygamy, accepts slavery, and orders the burning of so-called witches'.

The other basic adjustment he thought necessary to Christian belief lay in the Christian conception of Christ. The whole belief system had come to centre around Christ's death, whereas the emphasis should be on the example shown by his life:

> All the religious wars, the private feuds, and the countless miseries of sectarian contention, would have been at least minimized, if not avoided, had the bare example of Christ's life been adopted as the standard of conduct and of religion.[9]

A large part of *The Vital Message* attempts to set out the case for the spiritualist movement from an historical and evidential point of view. Having sketched the development of the spiritualist revival from its origins in Hydesville, New York State,[10] Conan Doyle went on to describe the achievements of the famous nineteenth-century medium D.D. Home and the accomplishments of a number of modern investigators, including Professor Crawford of Belfast, Hope the psychic photographer, and 'Mrs B'. The results of these practitioners' researches were, he claimed, quite undeniable:

> The physical basis of all psychic belief is that the soul is a complete duplicate of the body, resembling it in the smallest particular, although constructed in some far more tenuous material. In ordinary conditions these two bodies are intermingled so that the identity of the finer one is entirely obscured. At death, however, and under certain conditions in the course of life, the two divide and can be seen separately.

Conan Doyle had much to say about the messages received form the spirit world. The dead pursued happy and active lives in much the same way as the living. There was 'action for the man of action, intellectual work for the thinker, artistic, literary, dramatic and religious for those whose God-given powers lie that way'. There was no physical aspect to love, although there was close union between married couples and friendships between the sexes. Age disappeared and the individual reverted to his or her full normal growth and appearance.

It was also a world of sympathy. 'The sullen husband, the flighty wife' were no longer there to plague their spouses. They coexisted in domestic bliss, against a background of 'pleasant homesteads', beautiful gardens, green woods, and lakes.

It was an equitable world in which social divisions and class enmity no longer applied. 'Brain, energy, character, driving power, if exerted for good, make a man a leader there as here, while unselfishness, patience and spirituality there, as here, qualify the soul for the higher places . . ,'

Finally, the primitive notion of heaven and hell had no place in this scheme of things. Instead Conan Doyle envisaged a gradual rise in the scale of existence rather than judgement based on the individual's earthly life. The commonest of all sins in this afterlife was the sin of conventionality and sluggish spirituality. The undeveloped soul would be placed in a position where it would be able to develop and flourish in order to improve its condition. Such was the world revealed to the spiritualists by the messages from beyond.

Conan Doyle ended his work with an examination of the psychic abilities of Christ and his disciples, which, he maintained, the established Church had chosen to ignore. He was pessimistic about the future of the Church. 'It is still beyond all doubt', he commented, 'that Christianity has broken down, and that this breakdown has been brought home to everyone by the terrible catastrophe which has befallen the world.' Christianity had plunged into a decline and men no longer took it seriously. This in turn had given rise to the growth of materialism and in its wake the ugly nationalism which had been witnessed in Germany. It was up to the world religious leaders to adapt their dogmas to the increasing demands of the human intelligence and perceive the importance of the psychic dimensions. Only then would they be able properly to interpret the teaching of the Master whom they had for long misrepresented.

The year 1919 had been a gruelling one for Conan Doyle. In addition to his family and professional commitments, he had endured a back-breaking series of lecture tours of the British Isles. On 16 January he spoke to 2,000 in Birmingham; on 17 March he was in South Wales touring the villages and towns; and in April he went to Glasgow to speak on behalf of the Glasgow association of Spiritualists. In May he was at Doncaster, where he stamped his foot and uttered repeatedly, 'I tell you what I know to be true'; thence to Huddersfield to address an audience of 2,000 in the Town Hall, and so to Manchester, Leicester, Northampton, Portsmouth, Wolverhampton, Worcester, Glasgow, and a wide sweep of the north. Throughout these intensive tours the message was the same: established religion had failed to grasp the significance of the 'new revelation' but the movement was gaining momentum and would soon vanquish materialism utterly if only because its message of hope and deliverance from despair was undeniable. By now Sir Arthur and his wife had gone beyond the tentative position they had occupied at the time of the publication of 'the new revelation'. Spiritualism was no longer just an inspiration to religion; it *was* a religion. In September 1919 Conan Doyle told a reporter:

> Men have largely ceased to go to church. It is not that they are irreligious. It is that they have outgrown this presentiment of religion. Is it not remarkable that in the lectures that I have delivered up and down the country quite half my audience are men? [Spiritualism] is a religion that approaches that of the Early Christian Church. Christ was the great Psychic, and his disciples, I believe, were chosen because they were his psychics . . . It is essential, therefore, to hold the sittings in a reverent and religious atmosphere. Thus may they be 'the communion of saints'. We begin with prayers and hymns. It is either the most solemn thing in the world or it is absolute nonsense. There is no middle ground between these extremes.[11]

Before the year was out, Sir Arthur was able to spare the time to visit Dr W.J. Crawford, Extra-mural Lecturer in Mechanical Engineering at Queen's University, Belfast. From 1914 onwards Crawford had been conducting a series of detailed experiments with a family of mediums known as the Golighers. The most important member of this remarkable family was Kathleen, the youngest of four daughters, who had inherited strong mediumistic tendencies.

Crawford's seances were held in an attic in the house occupied by the medium's family, and it has to be pointed out that although Dr Crawford always ensured that they were attended by no fewer than eight people, all of these individuals were entirely sympathetic to the cause. The room was sparsely furnished, the furniture consisting of a series of wooden chairs, a seance table, and a small cabinet in the corner, placed there for 'materializations'. The only lighting available was a gas jet enclosed in a lantern with a red glass sliding front. The members of the seance began with the singing of a hymn and a prayer. This would then be followed by a series of what Crawford described as 'purely physical phenomena'. Crawford claimed that psychic energy was at the root of the whole thing and that the movements of matter produced by this energy were telekinetic.

In his first detailed account of the sittings,[12] Crawford defined two classes of phenomena: (1) impacts, and (2) movements of material bodies against the action of forces such as friction and gravity. The impact phenomena consisted of raps and their variations and were caused by psychic force being applied to a material body. The second class included the levitation of the seance table and the displacement of small objects in the room.

Crawford's last book, *The Psychic Structures at the Goligher Circle* (1920), was published shortly after his death (he committed suicide for reasons unconnected with his work) and contains a fascinating record of the phenomena which Conan Doyle must have witnessed. By now Crawford had developed a theory to explain the phenomena. The movements of objects in the seance room were due to the action of 'psychic rods' which protruded from the body of the medium. When the table was levitated, for example, the rod acted as a cantilever, fixed to the body of the medium at one end and gripping the under edge of the table or its legs with the other end. The psychic rods which issued from the medium's body varied in diameter at their extremities from about half an inch to three or four inches, and the free end of the rod assumed various shapes and sizes. In one experiment Crawford describes the handling of a rod:

Towards the end of the seance I asked the 'operators' . . . if they could place the end of the structure in one of my hands. On the reply 'yes' I went inside the circle, lay down on my right side on the floor alongside the table, and placed my gloved right hand between the two nearest legs of the table. Almost immediately I felt the impact of a nearby circular rod-like body about 2 inches in diameter on the palm of my hand, which was held palm upwards . . . The circular rod-like body was flat at the end, *i.e.* as if the rod were sawn across. It maintained a steady pressure evenly distributed over the area of impact, and was soft but firm to the sense of touch . . . This was accompanied by a sensation of rough-ness, as though the edge were serrated, such a feeling . . . as would be given by a substance similar to *very* fine emery paper . . .

In order to trace the origin and effect of these rod-like structures, Crawford devised a number of methods. First he encased Kathleen's feet in a box, then he asked the spirit operators to bring the structure out of the box, which itself had been held over a piece of phosphorescent paper. In a short while a curved body something like the 'toe of a boot' advanced over the inner edge of the cardboard then retired.

Crawford was fascinated by another aspect of the phe-nomena, which he called 'plasma'. It appeared that whenev-er phenomena of the physical order occurred a sticky, glutinous substance issued from the body of the medium. At first he believed that the substance was being generated by the feet of the medium. Then he devised a method of placing quantities of carmine between Kathleen's toes and in her stockings, which enabled him to trace the source of the plasma.

Before each seance commenced Kathleen was asked by Crawford to change into clean knickers, clean black stock-ings, and clean shoes. The 20-year-old girl duly obliged, and her feet were then locked into the box. At the conclusion of each seance he would unlock the box and examine her feet. On the ball of the foot of each stocking slight traces of carmine would be present. Crawford then asked the young medium to open her legs. He was then able to trace the splashes of carmine running in an irregular fashion between the thighs and around the bottom of the knickers.

Night after night Crawford subjected the young girl to these intense examinations – something of an ordeal, since

Kathleen had to stand in her underwear whilst Crawford made detailed notes of the stains and their distribution. At last he became convinced that the plasma must originate from one place only: the vagina. (Of course he could not be that explicit, but his detailed notes make it abundantly clear that this was so.) Determined to prove his point, he resorted to physical manipulation and was rewarded:

> The medium was sitting on a chair placed on the platform weighing machine. I asked the operators to take psychic matter from her in the ordinary way. I put my hand on the lower part of her back just above the buttocks. The rise and fall of her flesh was very apparent, as psychic matter was supposed to be taken from her and put back. I put my hand on her haunches just above the seat of her chair. The flesh did not seem to move bodily, but her flesh seemed to fall in. It could be distinctly felt filling out as the psychic stuff apparently returned to her.

How far Crawford remained objective in his 'manipulation' of Kathleen's thighs remains open to question. However, he was utterly convinced of the existence of the plasma and was careful to point out that, besides the photographs he had included in his book, he had 'many others which are scarcely suitable for publication in a popular book'. They all indicate the fact that once the plasma is extruded from the body of the medium, the spirit operators can mould it into the various shapes and forms required to produce the phenomena.

Conan Doyle, who had witnessed these bizarre phenomena, was most intrigued by Crawford's explanation of the plasma emanating from Kathleen's body. He believed that spirit operators acted upon the brain of the sitters and thence on their nervous systems. Small particles were drawn out through the nervous system and thus out through the bodies of the sitters. The streams of energized particles then coalesced to form a pattern, and when the medium was at her highest pitch of tension the band of particles was re-energized. The operators, now having generated a strong supply of the nervous energy they required, then acted upon the body of the medium, 'who is so constituted that gross matter from her body can . . be actually temporarily detached from its usual position, and projected into the seance room'.

Conan Doyle wanted answers. What was the plasma?

Who determined it? Was it the mind of the medium or the mind of the observer? Or was it some independent mind? In his *History of Spiritualism* he commented:

> Among the experimenters we have a material school who urge that we are finding some extraordinary latent property of the normal body, and we have another school, to which the author belongs, who believe that we have come upon a link which may be part of a chain leading to some new order of life. It should be added that there is nothing concerning it which has not been known to the old alchemists of the Middle Ages . . . Personally the author is of opinion that several different forms of plasma with different activities will be discovered, the whole forming a separate science of the future which may well be called Plasmology.[13]

Conan Doyle based his remarks largely upon the results of a series of spectacular seances conducted in France at the Institut Métaphysique by a close friend and scientist, Dr Gustave Geley.

Geley had heard of the extraordinary ectoplasmic powers of the mediums Mme Bisson and Eva C. and invited them to undergo at least two seances a week under laboratory conditions between December 1917 and March 1918. Geley was cautious in his approach, the seance room being always locked in the intervals of the work and bolted during experimentation. The medium Eva C. was completely stripped in an adjoining room before each experiment and then reclothed in tight black knitted combinations, sewn down the back and at the wrists. Her hair, mouth, and throat were examined with care, and Geley was careful to record that a vaginal examination was conducted 'on two or three occasions'. The seances were then conducted in good light, and when photography was intended red electric lights 'of 30 to 60 candle-power' were used.[14]

The phenomena would appear after a variable interval, sometimes short, at other times long (an hour or more). They always began by painful sensations felt by the medium, who would sigh and groan intermittently. These groanings were greatest when the manifestations began to appear, and they disappeared when they ceased.

The ectoplasm first appeared as a series of bright luminous liquid patches on the left side of the garment worn by the medium. After approximately three-quarters of an hour larger quantities of the material emanated from the whole body, but chiefly from the extremities of the body, especially the mouth, the nipples, the ends of the fingers, the top of the head, and the vagina. Geley was able to observe the ectoplasm (for he was working in good light) actually exuding from the inner surface of the cheeks, from the arch of the palate and the gums. When examined, it was seen to adopt diferent forms. Sometimes it appeared to be like a form of protoplasmic paste; at other times it resembled a number of fine threads. On occasion it formed a widely spread membrane with fringes and swellings, reminiscent of a caul. To the touch it seemed soft and inelastic when spread wide but hard and knotty when it formed cords.

Geley found that ectoplasm was mobile. Sometimes it developed slowly, descending over the medium's shoulders and breasts with a creeping movement; at other times it moved quickly, then disappeared in an instant. The substance was highly sensitive both to light and to touch. In fact when Geley attempted to squeeze the ectoplasm, Mme Bisson experienced considerable pain akin to that of a touch on raw flesh.

Once the ectoplasm had established itself it began to assume a variety of structures. Sometimes these were indeterminate and inorganic, but mostly they were organic. Geley witnessed representations of faces, fingers with nails, and on occasion complete hands with their bones and joints. The following account is typical of the materializations he recorded both in narrative form and by photography:

> As soon as she 'slept' she was affected, and moaned like a woman in labour. Little by little she became calm without anything coming to pass . . . Suddenly Mme Bisson exclaimed 'There it is . . . at the curtain'. It was so; above the medium's head, in the opening between the curtains and coming from the right, the head of a woman was visible at about the normal height of a person standing. Only the head emerged from the curtain. The materialisation was perfect; it was a living face of normal size, of fresh tint, and with expressive eyes. The face was beautiful, and the experimenters gazed at it with expressions of admiration spoken in low tones. I was so moved and surprised that I omitted to press the button for the flashlight . . . At last the head, reduced by two-thirds in size, placed itself on Eva's breast, in profile, and I pressed the button . . . After the flash I saw the head

for a moment on Eva's knees; I saw no shoulders. Then everything disappeared instantaneously . . .[15]

Conan Doyle read Geley's reports with considerable interest. It seemed logical to him that when spirit descended into matter it required a material basis. Once manifest it could then be moulded by the medium's mind and respond to her subconscious, which in turn was fed by the spirit world. Conan Doyle speculated that several different forms of plasm with different activities would be discovered, 'the whole forming a separate science of the future which may well be called Plasmology'. He also believed that all psychic phenomena external to the medium, including clairvoyance, could be traced to this source.

Anxious to see the extraordinary phenomena for himself, Conan Doyle corresponded with Geley and was duly invited to the Institute Métaphysique. A number of pressing commitments prevented him from attending until the autumn of the following year. However, he had reason to be satisfied. The year 1919 had furnished him with first-hand evidence of the survival beyond death of members of his own family; moreover he had lectured in the far corners of the British Isles and spread the word to the populace in his own inimitable way. It only remained for him to take the good news abroad to the far-flung corners of the Colonies where spiritualism was still in its infancy.

The year that followed gave him just such an opportunity.

CHAPTER 7

A Missionary Zeal

By 1920 spiritualism had attained the status of a successful popular religious movement. Although it lacked the funding enjoyed by its mainstream rivals, it did not lack publicity. The press, although not prepared to take spiritualism seriously, nevertheless kept the public alert to the great controversy which continued between its supporters and detractors. Sometimes the criticisms which were levelled against spiritualism were wholly justified, for many of its adherents were undoubtedly conned by extremely proficient hoaxer mediums. On other occasions such criticisms were either totally without foundation or grossly exaggerated. Sir Arthur Conan Doyle was in the vanguard of the movement and did his best to ensure that justice was done. He was willing to admit that there were fraudulent mediums at large and was only too happy to warn fellow spiritualists and the popular press about their existence. On the other hand he was not prepared to accept the often vitriolic and ill-informed attacks mounted by journalists and psychic investigators.

One such 'exposer-general' was the writer and rationalist Joseph McCabe. In January 1920 he addressed an assembly in the Patrick Burgh Halls, Glasgow, on the theme of 'Sir A. Conan Doyle's Ghosts'. He informed his audience that Conan Doyle had complained to him about his attacks on the spiritualist movement, which had caused considerable harm. Warming to this theme, McCabe described how he intended to take Sir Arthur to task at a debate in London. It was both misleading and unkind to tell mothers that they would meet their children after death. As to table-rapping, tilting, and moving, this was completely explainable by conjuring. Spirit messages which purported to come from the spirit world through the medium to the recipient were none other than a wireless system between the two.

McCabe got his chance at the Queen's Hall, London, on 11 March. Conan Doyle believed that by agreeing to participate in the debate he would be able to promote the truth of spiritualism, and he felt confident as its spokesman. The debate drew a great deal of public interest, for by now Sir Arthur was well known as a defender of 'the new revelation' whilst McCabe was considered an able opponent by the Rationalist Press Association whom he represented.

McCabe opened the debate by roundly declaring that spiritualism was 'born in fraud, nurtured in fraud, and . . . based today to an alarming extent all over the world on fraudulent performances'.

McCabe had hard words to say about the nineteenth-century psychic and medium D.D. Home, one of the pioneers of psychic phenomena. He was particularly sca-thing about the medium's supposed levitation in front of witnesses. Doing his best to discredit Home, McCabe pointed out that Home lived on his spiritualistic gifts from the age of 16 until he died; that he married twice in order to augment his wealth; and that he unjustifiably inherited a sum of £36,000 from a follower, Mrs Lyon, by suggesting that her dead husband had commanded her to hand this sum over to him.

McCabe was equally scornful of Conan Doyle's own psychic experiences. In his view the 'Piave' revelation was worthless since the very day before Sir Arthur had his vision *The Times* had published a long article from its military correspondent on the expected advance of the Austrians upon the Venetian plain. In other words 'Piave' was nothing but a piece of auto-suggestion. McCabe concluded his address with these words:

> I submit to this jury that, like every man who has gone into that dim supernatural world, he [Conan Doyle] has lived in clouds, in a mist. Whatever other witnesses there may be, you will find . . . that distortion of judgement, that blearing of vision, which occurs whenever a man enters that wonder-ful world, that world of almost unparalleled trickery in the history of man.

Conan Doyle responded to the attack magnificently. The

evidence, he claimed, was undeniable. If McCabe would care to examine it, he carried with him a small book containing the names of 160 people of high distinction, many of them eminent, including over 40 professors. These were all willing adherents of the cause of spiritualism:

> They have not been to one seance, like Mr. Clodd, or to two or three, like Mr. McCabe. Many have studied for twenty or thirty years, and been to hundreds of seances. When it comes to people who have never had any practical experience, simply because they think and reason so, arguing against men who have taken the trouble and done the work, then I say they are out of court.

As for D.D. Home, Sir Arthur regarded him as beyond reproach. He never took any money for anything he did and showed his powers in all kinds of light. Regarding the levitation affair, the facts when condensed were that two noblemen and a Guards officer saw him go out of one window and come in at another. All that Mr McCabe could say was that they were mistaken. Niether was he a confidence trickster. Certainly Home made the acquaintance of Mrs Lyon. Certainly she gave him £24,000 (not £36,000 as McCabe alleged), but the sum was given voluntarily, and in recognition of this act Home changed his name to Home-Lyon. Soon afterwards Mrs Lyon changed her mind and brought an action for the restitution of the money. However, Home was acquitted by the court.

Conan Doyle went on to defend his 'Piave' revelation. Since he had not read the article in *The Times*, the fact of its existence did not detract from the genuineness of the experience. Moreover, he had experienced a number of equally convincing revelations in the company of certain mediums, chief of whom was the Welshman Evan Powell.

One of Sir Arthur's main areas of interest, he told his audience, was ectoplasm. In the early days spiritualists used to state that a materializing medium exuded a kind of viscous gelatinous material, which they claimed to have felt and handled and which was used by spirits to build up temporary forms and show material evidence of their presence. Recent investigations had shown this to be correct. He then went on to describe in some detail the series of remarkable experiments conducted by Mme Bisson and her medium Eva C.:

The book [by Mme Bisson] contains 201 photographs, showing this viscous ectoplasm pouring out of the medium
forming an amorphous cloud, and finally moulding itself into
human faces and human figures . . . You can see the ectoplasm here pouring from the medium's nose, her eyes, her
ears, and her skin. They are repellent photographs; but many
of nature's processes are repellent . . . Now, these sittings
were not held with Madame Bisson alone . . . When she
began her experiments this young German, Dr. Schrenck-
Notzing from Munich, was with her. He went back to
Munich, and found he could get another medium with the
same power. She was a Polish lady in reduced circumstances. She produced precisely the same effect, and he
brought out a book with 168 photographs, many of them
Madame Bisson's, but the others his own, and . . . there is
the same result with this identical ectoplasm pouring out . . .
Then Dr. Geley took it up. He worked for months, and had
100 scientific men in to check his results. He published
photographs which show exactly the same results again.
Don't you think it is simply the insanity of incredulity to
wave that aside?

McCabe was quick to reply to this mainspring of Sir
Arthur's argument. Mme Bisson's book was written by
Schrenck-Notzing and not by Mme Bisson, who merely
translated the work into French. McCabe believed Eva C. to
be one of those abnormal human beings called 'ruminants'
who can swallow items of a large size and then bring them
up from their stomachs. Conan Doyle refused to accept this.
Anyone who had read the book, he retorted, would have
seen the photographs showing that the medium had a
fine-meshed net placed round her head. This net was
fastened or pinned on to the dress which she was obliged to
wear when in the seance room, but this did nothing to stop
the outpouring of ectoplasm. The theory of regurgitation
just would not do.

What was the evidence put forward by Schrenck-Notzing?
In 1920 the English translation appeared of his *Phenomena of
Materialization*, subtitled 'A Contribution to the Investigation
of Mediumistic Teleplastics'.[1] The work contained no fewer
than 225 illustrations, most of them photographs taken by
Mme Bisson under the direction of Schrenck-Notzing. In the
first year of the experiments with Eva C. (1909) the photographs often turned out to be failures, but by 1913 the author
met Stanislava P. (the 'Polish lady' mentioned by

Conan Doyle), who offered remarkably similar results to those of Eva C. The whole period of experimentation thus covered (with intervals) 10 years. Two mediums were involved, plus a number of official observers.

Eva C., the first of these mediums, was a young and attractive blonde in her mid-twenties. According to Schrenck-Notzing she was received into the Bisson family in the autumn of 1910 but lived at first in the studio flat of Mme Bisson, a sculptress. (Mme Bisson's husband was a well-known French dramatist who spent a considerable amount of his spare time 'collecting' mediumistic phenomena.) From the outset, it would appear that the conditions under which these seances were held at the Bisson house were tightly controlled. Here, for example, is an extract from Schrenck-Notzing's account of a sitting held on 25 May 1909:

> Before commencing the experiments the medium was undressed and Mme. Bisson performed a gynaecological examination.
>
> Eva was today only hypnotised by her relative after the net had been lowered and fastened. Mr. R.M. (physician) touched her fingers through the meshes and hypnotised the medium by Braid's method. I sat immediately in front of the curtains and saw, as a first phenomenon, a white and apparently soft mass, ascending on the side of the left ankle of the medium in the shape of a white column about 2 inches wide. It attained a length of about 20 inches and then disappeared. During this occurrence the left hand lay quietly visible on the left knee.
>
> Shortly afterwards we saw during the next very short exposure a white-clad figure in front view, with its head surrounded by a turban-like bandage. The face was beardless . . . the body was bent over in front, but no arms or legs were visible . . . Mme Bisson undressed the medium, and assisted her to dress in my presence. Neither by me nor by any other observer was any white material or anything else found which gave rise to suspicion.

As the experiments progressed Schrenck-Notzing insisted upon even tighter controls and was most rigorous in his examination of the young woman. In order to ensure total visibility of Eva C.'s body, Mme Bisson devised a loose dress made of a fish-net material which was translucent enough to ensure that no trickery was taking place. As always, Eva undressed completely before Mme Bisson and Schrenck-Notzing. Mme Bisson would then ask Eva to sit on a chair, where a detailed vaginal exploration, using a speculum, would take place. Tight black knitted combinations would then be put on and, after careful examination a thin black dress which had one opening at the neck. Before the dress was sewn up the witnesses would be asked to examine the medium at close quarters. Schrenck-Notzing recalls how he

> made her breathe before every sitting through the nose (each side separately), asked her to open her mouth widely, examined her cheeks, external ears and passages, her armpits and the felt slippers on her feet, as well as her hair and scalp . . . Immediately after every sitting the author examined all the seams of the dress, the hair, the dress, and body surface again, without ever discovering any suspicious change either in the medium or in her dress.

As with Professor Crawford's experiments with Kathleen Goligher, much of the ectoplasmic material appeared to have generated itself in the medium's vagina. Although Conan Doyle could not present these details of Schrenck-Notzing's experiments to his audience, an examination of Schrenck-Notzing's text reveals how carefully Eva C. was examined for traces of concealment. Mme Bisson reported to him in December 1911:

> Yesterday I hypnotised Eva as usual and she unexpectedly began to produce phenomena. As soon as they began, Eva alowed me to undress her completely. I then saw a thick thread emerge from the vagina. It changed its place, left the genitals, and disappeared into the navel depression. More material emerged from the vagina, and with a sinuous serpentine motion of its own it crept up the girl's body, giving the impression as if it were about to rise into the air. Finally, it ascended to her head, entered Eva's mouth, and disappeared.

Schrenck-Notzing, fascinated by the phenomenon, insisted on conducting his own gynaecological examination. This, he notes, was done with the index finger in a good light, but no trace was found of any alien substance. Often such interference would produce a hysterical response (understandably, one would have thought) in the medium. Schrenck-Notzing observes:

> The character of the somnambulic Eva is not fundamentally different from that of the medium in the waking condition. But her whole nature appears spiritualised . . . Displays of

anger, as a rule, occur only in consequence of interference, possibly necessary by the sitters, which hurts her feminine sense of honour or modesty. Any abrupt and unexpected procedure e.g. awakening her (pin-pricks), touching the materialisations (attempted exposure), making a thorough gynaecological examination, . . . may produce anger, violent disturbances of pulse and respiration, hysterical cases and fainting fits . . . As already mentioned, she feels the phenomena to be something foreign to her, and a sort of compulsion, in spite of the efforts she herself has to make in producing them.

At last he became convinced that it was not humanly possible for Eva to have concealed the ectoplasmic substance within the apertures of her body. Such a possibility defied common sense and made a nonsense of the now regular examinations he had himself conducted.

Assuming that a female medium wished to use the vagina as a hiding-place for closely rolled packets, e.g. chiffon gauze, she would have to attach some kind of cord or ribbon to the packet beforehand in order to be able to withdraw it. This cord would be detected during the exploration at the mouth of the vagina, and any finger introduced into the vagina would feel the foreign body. In the case of persons with a very wide vaginal entrance, it might be possible to withdraw the packets by means of the fingers deeply inserted. But such a manipulation supposes that the genitals are not separated from the hand by any partition, even a knitted one, and that the person is in a standing or reclining position. She might have touched the external genitals through the garment, but could not have penetrated to any depth.

The hiding of objects in the anal aperture, and their withdrawal from it, is even less possible, on account of its closure by a firm ring muscle, which hinders the introduction of a finger. Hidden packets can only be withdrawn by means of a cord of suitable length. The external end of which would have been immediately discovered during the corporeal examination; but never with the sole help of the person's own finger.

As one can observe from this small selection of the evidence available to Conan Doyle, it was extremely difficult for him to quote chapter and verse and thus substantiate his defence of the ectoplasm phenomenon. McCabe claimed that the Schrenck-Notzing experiments were invalid, yet he was not prepared to acknowledge the evidence. Similarly his regurgitation theory does not fit the facts. The fact that hysterics can sometimes bring up in their mouths objects they have swallowed, by an antisperistaltic motion, cannot be doubted. However, such a person cannot make any selection among the contents of his or her stomach. The ruminant must vomit whatever is there at the time, i.e. food diluted with liquids and gastric juices. In the bringing up of a swallowed object, traces of the contents of the medium's stomach would be brought up in addition. In the case of Eva C. any soft or fibrous preparations in the form of small packets would be attacked and decomposed by the gastric juices in the stomach. They could hardly possess the clarity and diversity of form shown in the photographs. 'In any case,' as Schrenck-Notzing observes, 'Eva, as a rule, took her dinner two hours before the sitting, and was sometimes observed during the five, or even seven, preceding hours, so that the swallowing of artificial products would have been noticed.'

The Conan Doyle–McCabe debate ended on friendly terms. Both men had argued dispassionately and presented their cases with a certain degree of conviction. Nevertheless Conan Doyle had the edge, being the master of his subject. In his closing remarks Conan Doyle admitted that McCabe was 'a man of moral courage and that he says what he means'. However, his knowledge of psychic matters was superficial. 'He has got up a case. He has got it up cleverly and superficially. But he has not read those books . . . Psychic research is not my opponent's business. For some years I have devoted my life to it.'

Sir Arthur's zeal was soon to find a new testing-place. this time it was not the small villages and the cities of Britain which provided his audiences, but the vast pioneer population of Australia.

In 1919 Conan Doyle had been invited by the spiritualist fraternity of Australia to conduct a series of lectures at major cities across the continent. Although it was an attractive prospect in many ways and would certainly provide extra publicity for the movement in international terms, there were also distinct disadvantages. To begin with Conan Doyle was no longer a young man, and the wear and tear of the British spiritualist campaign had begun to tell on him. Secondly he and Jean now had three children of their own, boys of eleven and nine and a girl of seven, and such a long voyage would necessitate a maid. In all seven people would result in a colossal sum of £1,600 to be spent on return tickets.

Conan Doyle got in touch with an Australian agent, Carlyle Smythe, who assured him that there would be no shortage of people to hear him speak, and the tour was subsequently arranged from the British side by Harry Engholm, himself a leading spiritualist.

At a farewell luncheon held at the Holborn Restaurant prior to Conan Doyle's departure for Australia, Sir Arthur reaffirmed both the political and the religious necessity of his 'new revelation':

> German wars and Bolshevism and other things of which we know, have shown us that we have been building on foundations of sand. To me the religious aspect of this question is everything. I am as interested as every intelligent man must be in those psycho-physical powers which have come incidentally to us . . . I am also deeply interested in our converse with the dead, but that, after all, is a little thing, . . . it is not the essence of the matter. The essence of the matter is a religion, a philosophy. What the dead tell us is a description of the universe which is accurate and logical. They give us something to hope for, and make us realise it is indeed not only an all powerful, but an all-loving God. This is the real new revelation which casts a search-light from heaven down upon the darkened earth.[2]

Conan Doyle and his family sailed on 13 August 1920, and after a long and largely uneventful trip they arrived at the port of Fremantle on 17 September. At Adelaide, after some trouble with striking dock workers the party disembarked and were hospitably welcomed by a letter from the Australian premier. On 25 September Conan Doyle plunged into his first lecture, at Adelaide, and was warmly received by an audience comprising not only committed spiritualists but also priests, university professors, and eminent business-men. 'Over all,' the *Register* reported, 'Sir Arthur dominated by his big arresting presence. His face had a rugged, kindly strength, tense and earnest in its grave moments, and full of winning animation when the sun of his rich humour plays on the powerful features.'

By the second lecture at Adelaide Conan Doyle had won over his audience and impressed them by his sincerity and eloquence. He told them that mere phenomena were no hing in themselves; that the real flower of spiritualism was 'what the wisdom of the dead could tell us about their own conditions, their present experiences, their outlook upon the secret of the universe, and the testing of religious truth from the viewpoint of two worlds instead of one'. The audience listened with rapt attention.

The following day Conan Doyle showed his audience a selection of psychic photographs. Some of the audience could hardly believe their eyes. There on the large screen were William Crookes's materializations of Katie King, photographs of Eva C., and the remarkable shots done by Dr Crawford of Kathleen Goligher, the ectoplasmic material pouring from her mouth and from between her legs. The audience were amazed at the clarity of these photographs, whilst the local press reported that no such exhibition had ever before been seen in Australia. Only one newspaper dissented, the *Argus*, which carried a vitriolic leader accusing Conan Doyle and his followers of 'black magic', 'shamanism', 'witchcraft', 'freak religion', and 'black evil'. The article ended by maintaining that Conan Doyle represented 'a force which we believe to be purely evil'.

Conan Doyle's next port of call, Melbourne, was considered particularly attractive by the author, and he recalls in his memoirs of the trip[3] that he found the city oddly akin to his much-loved Edinburgh. Smythe, his agent, had come unstuck with the bookings here, and the lectures took place in the Playhouse, which only housed in excess of a thousand. The Melbourne press were not quite so rapturous in their reports of Sir Arthur's lectures, but the audiences were large and responsive.

Whilst in Melbourne, Conan Doyle was eager to contact the famous medium Charles Bailey, who had been discredited in France in 1910. Bailey specialized in aports – objects brought on the scene at a seance by no visible agency. Among the manifestations he offered were tortoises, live birds, snakes, and jewellery.

Bailey had been discredited at a seance in Grenoble at which he had produced from thin air two small birds complete with nests. Sadly for Bailey, a local petshop owner reported that a man answering Bailey's description had bought the birds two days previously, and when the investigators insisted on an examination of Bailey's rectum, he refused. There had also been other exposés. In 1911 he was accused of hiding birds in his boots (this was never proved), whilst in March 1914 an investigator saw him pull a Babylonian tablet from his mouth. Bailey declared outright that he had been a victim of a plot, and this had been confirmed by Professor Reichel. However, Conan Doyle knew he must tread warily.

A seance took place in Conan Doyle's hotel room, Conan Doyle having taken the precaution of inviting 10 guests along to ensure fair play. The results were very disappointing. Spirit hands were glimpsed in the darkness, but when Conan Doyle tried to grasp them he was sharply reprimanded. A head began to materialize and a written message in bad Italian came through the control. Altogether Conan Doyle remained unimpressed and puzzled. However, he was willing to give Bailey the benefit of the doubt because of the impressive results he had read about:

> The results were far above all possible fraud, both in the conditions and in the articles brought into the room by spirit power. For example, I have a detailed account published by Dr. D.W. McCarthy of Sydney, under the title, 'Rigid Tests of the Occult'. During these tests Bailey was sealed up in a bag, and in one case was inside a cage of mosquito curtain. The door and windows were sealed and the fire-place blocked. The sitters were all personal friends, but they mutually searched each other. The medium was stripped naked before the seance. Under these stringent conditions during a series of six sittings 130 articles were brought into the room, which included eighty-seven ancient coins (mostly of Ptolemy), eight live birds, eighteen precious stones of modest value and varied character, two live turtles, seven incribed Babylonian tablets, one Egyptian Scarabaeus, an Arabic newspaper, a leopard skin, four nests and many other things. I may add that at a previous test meeting they had a young live shark about 1½ feet long, which was tangled with wet seaweed and flopped about on the table.[4]

Conan Doyle's second sitting with Bailey proved to be more productive than the first. Bailey was searched and then placed in the corner of the room. He soon went into a trance and began muttering in an Indian dialect. The voice claimed that he was a Hindu control who was accustomed to bringing apports to the medium. Shortly afterwards the lights were turned on and the medium was found to be holding a tiny bird's nest, 'beautifully constructed of some

very fine fibre mixed with moss . . . In it lay a small egg,
white, with tiny brown speckles. The medium . . . placed
the egg on his palm and broke it, some fine albumen
squirting out, there was no trace of yolk.' When Conan
Doyle questioned Bailey's control about the egg, the control
replied that the spirits were not allowed to interfere with
life, and that if it had been fertilized it would not have been
taken.

The following day Conan Doyle took the nest to a local
museum and had it examined. It was revealed that it was
certainly not of Australian origin, and Conan Doyle opined
that the apport was therefore genuine. However, he was at
some pains to point out that when he took one of Bailey's
Assyrian tablets to the British Museum it was found to be a
forgery. Conan Doyle was extremely disappointed, since
Bailey had informed him that the British Museum had
pronounced the tablets genuine.

On 13 November the Conan Doyle family left Melbourne
and travelled straight to Sydney, where they were given an
enthusiastic reception. ('Men swung their hats high and
cheered,' reported one of the evening papers, 'women
danced in their excitement and many of their number
rushed the party with rare bouquets.') The following Sunday the 'pilgrims' were treated to a 3,500-strong reception
where Conan Doyle warned the assembly about the abuse of
psychic powers. He exhorted the Australians to expose
fraud whenever they found it (he was probably thinking of
Bailey) and to maintain the religious content of spiritualism.
The following night Conan Doyle had an unusual psychic
experience. He had become overtired by his exertions and
was sleeping badly. Suddenly, as he lay in bed, a 'distinct
pungent smell of ether' wafted through the window of the
hotel bedroom and with each fresh wave he felt himself
slowly relax. Within a few minutes he was in a deep sleep.

The visit to Sydney was not without criticism. A man
called Simpson, apparently the president of the Christian Evidence Society, continually asked Conan Doyle to
meet him in a debate, but by now Sir Arthur had become
wise to the methods of his enemies. He refused on the very
reasonable grounds that his whole energy had to be devoted to his spiritualistic mission. So Simpson wrote to the
newspapers, condemning him. Conan Doyle was not slow
to reply:

It is men like you . . . who by your parody of Christianity and your constant exhibition of those very qualities which Christ denounced in the Pharisees, have driven many reasonable people away from religion and left the churches half empty. Your predecessors, who took the same narrow view of the literal interpretation of the Bible, were guilty of the murder of many thousands of defenceless old women who were burned in deference to the text, 'suffer no witch to live'. Undeterred by this terrible result of the literal reading, you still advocate it . . .

Before leaving Sydney for New Zealand, Conan Doyle wrote to his friend and colleague Sir Oliver Lodge, who had been following his mission with considerable interest.

Conan Doyle informed Lodge that he had received a number of photographs of fairies with which he hoped to 'draw the fire' of the materialists. In fact he had first heard about the photographs early in May 1920 as a result of a conversation with Gow, the editor of *Light*. Gow had been in contact with a Miss Scatcherd, who had seen a number of these photographs and believed them to be genuine. Miss Scatcherd had received a letter from the sister of a Theosophist, Edward Gardner, who had made contact with a family living near Bradford. In the summer of 1917 two young girls, 15-year-old Elsie Wright and her cousin 10-year-old Frances Griffiths, had apparently enticed some fairies and a goblin into Cottingley Glen and taken photographs of them. Gardner had taken the two negatives to an expert who had found them to be genuine. Conan Doyle then wrote to Gardner's cousin, Miss E. Blomfield, asking for prints. He was duly rewarded and the two photographs arrived, one depicting a dancing goblin, the other a group of wood elves in a ring. Delighted, Conan Doyle wrote back to Miss Blomfield, suggesting that an enquiry be set up as to the genuineness of the photographs.

In June 1920 Gardner finally contacted Conan Doyle. He explained that the two girls were naturally shy and reserved. Elsie was the daughter of a mechanic and the family did not welcome publicity. Since the photos had been taken, the two girls had started work and were thus some few miles apart from each other. However, he would do his best. Conan Doyle visited Gardner in London and the two worked out a plan:

Neither he nor I had actually seen the girls, and it was

arranged that he should handle the personal side of the matter, while I should examine the results and throw them into literary shape. It was arranged between us that he should visit the village as soon as convenient, and make the acquaintance of everyone concerned. In the meantime, I showed the positives, and sometimes the negatives, to several friends whose opinion upon psychic matters I respected.[5]

Foremost among these friends was Sir Oliver Lodge, who at once refused to accept the photos at their face value. It seemed to him, he advised Conan Doyle, that some Californian classical dancers had been superimposed against a rural British background. Conan Doyle replied that such a trick would be an impossibility for two working-class Yorkshire girls.

Having travelled to Yorkshire, Gardner dispatched the negatives to Conan Doyle, who had them examined at the Kodak Company's offices in Kingsway. There they were examined by two experts who advised him that they could find no evidence of superimposition or other trick. However, they were careful to add that such a trick was not beyond the realms of possibility.

In July 1920 Gardner conveyed some positive news to Sir Arthur. He had visited Mr Wright (Elsie's father), who explained that he simply did not understand the matter. However, he was certain that the plate he took out of the Midg camera was the one he had put in the day that the photos were taken by the two girls. More importantly, Gardner had obtained permission to use and publish the photographs on the understanding that the names and addresses of the girls should remain a secret.

When he left England Conan Doyle had been doubtful whether Gardner would be able to obtain further results. After all, he reasoned, the two girls were now well past puberty and thus their psychic powers were probably considerably diminished. One may imagine his surprise, therefore, when in Melbourne he received Gardner's letter containing three more prints all taken in the fairy glen. 'I have received from Elsie three more negatives taken a few days back . . . The "Flying Fairy" and the "Fairies' Bower" are the most amazing that any modern eye has ever seen surely!' Gardner enthused. Conan Doyle wrote back, convinced of the revelatory significance of the discovery:

It . . . seems to me that those wise entities who are conducting this campaign from the other side, and using some of us
as humble instruments have recoiled before that sullen
stupidity against which Goethe said the Gods themselves
fight in vain, and have opened up an entirely new line of
advance, which will turn that so-called 'religious', and essentially irreligious position, which has helped bar our way.
They can't destroy fairies by antediluvian texts and when
once fairies are admitted other psychic phenomena will find
a more ready acceptance . . . We have had continued messages at seances for some time that a visible sign was coming
through – and perhaps this was what is meant . . .

Gardner's letter had confirmed what Conan Doyle had
hoped would prove true all along. The photos were a
genuine confirmation of the spirit world made manifest, and
it was his duty to inform the world of their significance. He
at once set to work and prepared a detailed account of the
affair which was subsequently published in the Christmas
1920 edition of the *Strand Magazine*, and there, for the
moment, the matter rested.

Conan Doyle's sojourn in New Zealand was not without
interest, although he did not attract the same level of
publicity as he had enjoyed in Melbourne and Sydney. In
Auckland he met a clairvoyant who claimed to be able to
perform psychometry without actually touching the object
in question, whilst in Christchurch he met Mr Michie, a local
spiritualist who some years previously had perfected a
breathing method by which he was able to hypnotize
himself. The results, however, were disastrous, for Mr
Michie soon fell into an insidious illness with certain psychic
symptoms, and within a few months was reduced to skin
and bone. Mr Michie's wife (also a medium) was then visited
by an entity who warned her that his own death had been
caused by using the selfsame method and that her husband
should desist. When Mitchie's wife checked out the address
of the deceased man she found that his widow, a Mrs
Stanley, was able to confirm her husband's death from
consumption.

After a brief stay in Christchurch (where Conan Doyle was
entertained by a number of psychic animals!) the family
travelled to Dunedin, where they found a predominantly
Scottish community. In between motoring explorations of
the countryside, Sir Arthur and Lady Conan Doyle obtained

a sitting with one of the most powerful trance mediums and clairvoyants he had ever met. Mrs Roberts, a 'stout, kindly woman, with a motherly manner, and a sensitive, expressive face', immediately made contact with some of the Conan Doyles' relatives and friends. One thing in particular impressed Sir Arthur. When Mrs Roberts said, 'I see an elderly lady here . . . her name is Selina,' he at once recognized his wife's mother, who had died some while previously. The medium then convulsed, uttering the words: 'Thank God! Thank God to get in touch again! Jean! Jean! Give my dear love to Jean!' Impressed by the fact that both names had been given without prior knowledge on the medium's behalf, Conan Doyle asked for a second interview, at which he was able to contact the scientist and spiritualist convert Dr Alfred Russel Wallace.

Conan Doyle had travelled to New Zealand without his children. When he returned to Melbourne after an uneventful voyage his pleasure at being reunited with them was marred by the news of his mother's death. Although she had been totally blind for some years and had reached the respectable age of 83, Conan Doyle was understandably saddened at the revelation, for he had always drawn considerable inspiration from the Ma'am.

The Conan Doyles subsequently travelled to Brisbane, where in between lectures they were able to explore the surrounding countryside and marvel at the profusion of wildlife. Before leaving Brisbane Conan Doyle's attention was drawn to the fact that when a state photographer, Mobsby, had taken a photograph at a function attended by him, a curious result was obtained. Mobsby developed the film himself and was astounded to find that whilst all other figures in the picture were clear, that of Sir Arthur seemed to be shrouded in a mist. As a Brisbane paper recorded, 'The photograph was taken on an ordinary film with a No. 3A Kodak, and careful examination does not in any way indicate the cause of the sensational result.'

At last the Conan Doyles' missionary tour was nearing completion, and on 26 January the family removed themselves to Sydney, where they prepared themselves for the homeward voyage. For Conan Doyle it had been a most satisfactory visit. He reckoned that in all he had addressed some 25 meetings, averaging 2,000 people in each – a total of 50,000 people in all. Smythe, his agent, described the tour as 'a great dynamic progression of enthusiasm. I have known in my career nothing parallel to it.'

Before leaving Sydney, Conan Doyle attended a third and final seance with Charles Bailey, although this time it was not under test conditions. Conan Doyle had his suspicions that Bailey might have smuggled phosphorescent material inside the spectacle case – the only item he was allowed to take inside his cabinet – but upon examination he found it to be clean. Bailey fell into a trance, and the Hindu control told Conan Doyle that he should place a tin basin in the cabinet and fill it with water. Bailey then emerged, carrying the basin above his head. When it was put down, Conan Doyle and his companions witnessed several minuscule tortoises swimming about. The Hindu control claimed these had been brought from a tank in Benares, and the 12 Australians present swore they had never seen the like. Shortly after this apparition there was a loud crash in the room and a number of Turkish copper pennies appeared.

Conan Doyle remained adamant that Bailey could not have smuggled these items into the seance room, despite the the unwholesome reputation he had gained in France. In a letter to Lodge he opined that the so-called exposure of Bailey in France was a swindle engineered by the Roman Catholics.

After spending a short while in Ceylon (Sri Lanka), the Conan Doyles made their way up the Suez Canal and across to France. They then travelled from Marseilles to Paris, where Conan Doyle was able to visit Dr Gustave Geley at the Institut Métaphysique. There Conan Doyle gave an exhibition of the slides he had used on the Australian tour to a distinguished audience of French scientists, including Charles Richet and Gabrielle Delanne. After the lecture the company were given a performance of mediumistic piano-playing by a medium called Aubert.

The following day Conan Doyle felt privileged to be able to meet Camille Flammarion, the astronomer, who had devoted the latter part of his life to psychic investigation.

Geley had much to show Conan Doyle. He had been conducting a series of experiments with a Polish medium called Frank Kluski, a writer and poet whose paternal uncle, a Catholic priest, often had veridical telepathic visions.

Geley had developed a technique for recording materializations which greatly impressed Conan Doyle. The procedure was to place near the medium a bowl containing paraffin wax kept at melting-point by being floated on warm water. The materialized 'entity' was then asked to plunge a hand, a foot, or even part of a face into the liquid paraffin several times. A closely fitting envelope was thus formed which immediately set in the air or by being dipped into another bowl of cold water. This envelope or 'glove' was then freed by dematerialization of the member. Plaster would then be poured at leisure into the glove, thus giving a cast of the phantom hand.

Conan Doyle inspected the paraffin hands and also the plaster cast which had been taken from the inside of one of them. He saw the impression of a small hand, not much bigger than a boy's but with the skin loose and wrinkled. The materialized figure had also left an impression of its mouth and chin.

Geley's thoroughness impressed Conan Doyle. In order to prevent the possibility of the paraffin hand being concealed in the medium's pocket, he had treated the paraffin in the bucket with cholesterin and this chemical had subsequently appeared in the glove. 'These conclusions of Dr. Geley concerning the paraffin moulds taken from Kluski's materialisations', concluded Conan Doyle, 'are shared by Charles Richet and Count de Gramont of the Institute of France, who take part in the experiments. How absurd are the efforts of those who were not present to contradict the experiences of men like these.'

Conan Doyle had been eager to see for himself some of the ectoplasmic phenomena produced by Eva C. and he was soon rewarded. In the presence of Professor Jules Courtier of the Sorbonne and a number of other scientists, he sat and watched in bright afternoon light as the medium, hidden behind a cloth cabinet, stretched her hands out through an opening and was held by the sitters. After Eva had sat in this position for the best part of an hour, Mme Bisson indicated to Conan Doyle a streak of ectoplasm which had formed on the outside of Eva's bodice. Conan Doyle was invited to handle the substance and he felt it shrink and then contract under his hand. The ectoplasmic 'finger' was approximately six inches long and half an inch wide. In September 1922 he recalled:

The ectoplasm which I saw upon Eva, the much-abused

medium, took the form of a six-inch streak of gelatinous material across the lower portion of the front of the dress. Speaking as a medical man, I should say it was more like a section of the umbilical cord than anything else, but it was wider and softer. I was permitted to touch it, and I felt it thrill and contract beneath my fingers. It seemed to be breaking through the cloth and to be half embedded in it . . . The objection of possible regurgitations of food was made at a very early stage of the investigation . . . it has been met and disproved . . . So far did Dr. Geley carry his precautions that on one occasion a crimson dye was mixed with Eva's food. In spite of this the ectoplasm emitted was of a luminous white. There is no possible test which has not been applied.[7]

Having toured the former battlefields of France and meditated on the enormous loss of life there, Conan Doyle returned to England, delighted by the overwhelming success of his trip and hopeful for the future of the movement. He observed that:

The human race is on the very eve of a tremendous revolution of thought, marking a final revulsion from materialism, and it is part of our glorious and assured philosophy, that, though we may not be here to see the final triumph of our labours, we shall none the less, be as much engaged in the struggle and the victory from the day when we join those who are our comrades in battle upon the further side![8]

The following year was spent in a ceaseless effort to convince the public at large of the significance of the forthcoming revolution. In June 1921 he joined the eminent spiritualist Ellis Powell in Portsmouth and spoke to a large congregation there about the drawbacks of his involvement. Unhappily, he admitted, anyone who became deeply engrossed in these matters found himself on debatable ground and found that his friends, possibly even his relatives, took a different view and sharp antagonisms arose.[9] He detailed a case of spirit photography in which the spirit of a little girl was able to impress itself on a camera plate and talked encouragingly about the survival not only of humans but of animals.

On 5 October he was welcomed by a 2,000-strong company in the Free Trade Hall, Manchester, 'an exponent of the most solemn and beautiful doctrine of life everlasting'. Conan Doyle detailed his lifelong interest in psychic matters and went on to distinguish sharply between phenomena and messages from the dead. Phenomena were finite; messages might tell you the fate which awaited you on the other side. Miracles were done in Judaea to call attention to the preaching, and it was exactly so with modern miracles. Conan Doyle then showed a series of slides illustrating the psychic rods of Dr Crawford and Professor William Crookes arm-in-arm with Katie King, and others illustrating psychic photography taken in the presence of Mrs Hope and Mrs Buxton, Messrs Vearncome, Bowsnell, and Mrs Deane.[10]

In November 1921 the case of William Hope the psychic photographer was to assume considerable importance. The controversy that surounded his work annoyed Conan Doyle, who was satisfied that Hope and his medium friend Mrs Buxton were genuine pioneers in the field of psychic photography. In the summer of 1919 Conan Doyle had travelled to Crewe, the photographer's home, and provided his own photographic plates. At the first sitting a rather unsatisfactory result was obtained, but on the second night Conan Doyle used Hope's own plates and obtained the photograph of the face of a young man next to his own. This appeared to be a likeness of Conan Doyle's son Kingsley as he had appeared some eight years before his death. Conan Doyle examined the print carefully and was able to make out a series of fine dots, indicative of process printing. The third result was the most impressive. Hope asked Conan Doyle to mark a plate and put it in a carrier. The company then joined hands, and after a minute had passed Hope announced that a result had been obtained. When developed the photograph showed not only the face of Conan Doyle's elder sister, Annette, but also the small brooch which she used to wear.

Although Conan Doyle was convinced that Hope had remarkable powers (he believed that a cabinet of ectoplasm for concentration was first constructed and the psychic effect was then developed inside it), others, particularly James Douglas of the *Sunday Express*, thought differently. In April 1921 Douglas investigated some photographs taken of him by Hope and found a face hovering near his arm which had appeared recently in a rival newspaper.[11] He decided to invite Conan Doyle to the newspaper offices where a demonstration would be given of concocted psychic powers. Conan Doyle remained unimpressed by the demonstration, protesting that it proved nothing.

In November 1921 a second experiment was carried out at the British College of Psychic Science in the presence of Conan Doyle and others. 'I invite any expert in photography who claims to be able to produce a photo like Mr. Hope's to do so under the conditions of my experiment,' Douglas said. 'If he can produce such a photograph by a normal process, then it will be necessary to consider whether Mr. Hope should be invited to submit to a stricter test than I was able to impose . . .'[12]

Douglas insisted that he preside over these proceedings and was careful to simulate Hope's own methods exactly. The company sat round a table and Douglas placed on it a packet of 12 plates which he had recently purchased. Hewat McKenzie, honorary principal of the College, then wrote his name on the packet. Douglas objected to this and produced a second packet, which he handed to Mr Marriott, the conjurer specially hired for the occasion. Marriott then placed the packet between his hands, and the other sitters put their hands above his, all the while the chosen packet remaining in full view upon the table. Douglas then took the packet and asked Conan Doyle to take Marriott's pulse, which was found to be about 50 beats above the normal rate. Douglas entered the darkroom, tightly grasping the dark slide in one hand and the packet in the other. Inside the darkroom, with the door bolted, Marriott chose (as Hope had done) the first and third slides for development. Douglas signed the plates and the two men returned to the studio. Marriott took two photos, one of Sir Arthur with Douglas and one of Sir Arthur alone. Douglas then took the dark slide.

Back inside the darkroom the slides were developed, and whilst the plates were in the fixing bath Marriott was searched by McKenzie. The four plates were subsequently examined. On one of them the form of a young woman, her eyes gazing upwards, was found, whilst on the other (the photo of Conan Doyle) was a rather poor parody of one of the famous fairy photographs taken by Elsie Wright and her cousin Frances.

Douglas had proved that even the most experienced investigator could be conned, although, to be fair, he was not willing to condemn Hope as a trickster. Conan Doyle's own response was both cautious and balanced. In *The Case for Spirit Photography* he wrote:

Mr. Marriott, has clearly proved one point, which is that a trained conjurer can, under the close inspection of three pairs of critical eyes, put a false image upon a plate. We must unreservedly admit it. When, however, we are asked to draw the inference that Mumler,[13] Hudson, Bowsnell, Hope . . . are swindlers, we must point out the one huge fatal flaw in the argument. Not one of these men has been shown to have been a skilled conjurer, or, indeed, to have had any knowledge of conjuring at all . . . Mr. Marriott produced a very pretty group of fairies dancing round me . . . But I have a photograph before me as I write which has a deeper meaning. It was given me by Mr. Gibson, a professional photographer, of Nottingham, on my recent visit. He went to Crewe, took the photograph himself and received an extra of his dead son . . . Here we reach a point which can only be psychic, for it is outside the realm of trickery.

Although Douglas himself was extremely professional in his dealings with Conan Doyle this was (sadly) not always the case with other journalists. One particular instance which illustrates this fact occurred in the autumn of 1921 when the journalist Filson Young was offered a chance to attend a seance with Sir Arthur and see the phenomena for himself. Young duly met Sir Arthur, Lady Conan Doyle, and the medium Mrs Johnson, at a house in Highgate. In the presence of a number of spiritualists, Conan Doyle told his guests that they would soon hear a number of voices–those of the medium's guides. These guides were soldiers who had been killed in the war, one a lad from Glasgow and another a Lancashire man. There could be no possibility of fraud or collusion, he added, since the people present were well known to each other.

The room was darkened and the seance continued. Presently, during a tune played on a gramophone, a man's voice could be heard (this was David, the Glaswegian). Trivial conversation then ensued. According to Filson Young:

They spoke to the spirit in a patronizing way . . . The voice came as though sounding through the tube of a trumpet, which seemed to be waving about in the air, and the tapping of finger-nails on its metallic surface could be distinctly heard . . . After some more singing . . . David was asked if his friend Jock was coming. 'Oh aye,' he said, and presently a Lancashire voice was heard uttering fragmentary sentences of greeting and occasionally rather feeble jokes, at which the audience laughed loudly . . . It was during this quarter of an hour that my trained ear made me aware of the following facts:

(1) Certain inflections, characteristic of individual and not of local speech, were common to the voices of both Glasgow David and Lancashire Jock.

(2) The same inflections could occasionally be detected in the natural voice of the medium.

(3) The Lancashire voice spoke in a dialect which would have deceived anyone who had not lived in Lancashire, such as may be heard on a music hall stage . . .[14]

More voices continued to disappoint Young, and the eternal hymn-singing and bawled choruses of well-known ditties made him restless. At one point in the proceedings a low voice was heard which one of the participants assumed might be her mother. 'Encourage her,' whispered the medium, 'perhaps she will touch you.' At this precise moment Young squeezed the knee and arm of the eager enquirer and then, growing bolder, put out a hand in the darkness and felt the broad end of the trumpet (the other end was apparently situated near where the medium sat). The trumpet, which had been held rigid, was now released, and the reporter lifted it over his neighbour's head, placing it on the floor behind Conan Doyle. There were no more voices that afternoon, and before he left the house Young told the eager daughter that he, not her mother, had touched her.

Quite understandably, Conan Doyle was outraged at Young's behaviour. 'I could not have conceived you capable, as my guest,' he wrote, 'of acting in such a manner. I fear that this unpleasant incident must be the end of our acquaintance.' Young wrote back to Conan Doyle that as far as he was concerned no manifestation of supernatural force had occurred at the seance. 'I have an extremely highly-trained musical ear, abnormally sensitive to inflections in dialects and pronunciation,' he added, 'I have also a long experience of organ-pipes, resonators and the acoustic effects of tubes.'

Young remained adamant about the gullibility of the participants–a charge which Conan Doyle refused to believe. 'The only credulity shown by any of our company was believing that you were a gentleman,' he retorted.

The Filson Young episode, like the Bailey affair and the

Hope/Douglas experiment, shows how open to attack Conan Doyle was. He had taken on the mantle of public defender of the spiritualist cause and was now experiencing some of the inevitable adverse consequences. Although Conan Doyle had established a reputation for integrity in his psychic dealings, the same could not be said of many of spiritualism's enemies. The field was open not only to fraudulent mediums but also to a number of highly skilled magicians and hoaxers eager to exploit spiritualism's more sensational aspects. In the year that followed he was to cross swords with one of the most formidable enemies the movement had ever had the misfortune to list among its many critics: the brilliant American showman and escapologist Harry Houdini.

CHAPTER 8

Photographs and Fairies

The bitter and sometimes acrimonious debate which was waged over spiritualism during the early 1920s convinced Conan Doyle that the cause could best be served by a persistent and unremitting propaganda campaign. His mission to Australia had shown him the value of such an approach, and increasingly during the latter part of 1921 his thoughts turned to America where he had been so successful earlier in his career.

Meanwhile there was the home battleground to claim his attention. On 10 January 1922 he spoke to the Jewish Spiritualists' Society at the People's Palace, Mile End Road, where he was given a 'splendid reception',[1] having first displayed his psychic photographs to an appreciative audience, whilst February found him in the far north, touring the urban centres of Scotland. On Sunday 5 February, he addressed a company of 1,400 believers in Edinburgh and spoke about his desire to see a more religious interpretation of psychic matters among the spiritualist community. Four days later he was extolling the virtues of the medium Mrs Dean, in whose powers, like those of William Hope, he implicitly believed. Two new psychic slides were shown to a company assembled in St Andrew's Hall, one being a portrait of Dr Allerton Cushman, an American scientist and spiritualist who had obtained a portrait of his dead daughter through Mrs Deane at the British College of Psychic Science. The other photograph had been obtained by a Glasgow man who knew nothing of spiritualism. He had been visiting West Africa and was obstructed from taking a shot of a kraal by two natives with children in their arms. When the photograph was developed a third native, also with a child in her arms, had appeared on the plate standing beside the other two.

The subject of psychic photography was to occupy Sir Arthur's thoughts considerably during the months that followed. In February 1922 an investigation was carried out into the methods of William Hope and his Crewe circle by Harry Price, a member of the Society for Psychical Research, and a colleague (and fellow magician), Mr Seymour.

Price was, like his American counterpart, Harry Houdini, sceptical of the powers of most mediums and particularly anxious to expose their supposed 'fraudulent' methods. He therefore obtained from the Imperial Dry Plate Company eight plates, all of which had been cut from the same sheet of glass. Six of these were then made up into a single packet and treated with X-rays so that Hope would not know their marked identity. Price and Seymour then kept an appointment they had made with Hope at the British College of Psychic Science.

Having delivered the plates in a wax-sealed packet, Price asked Hope to begin the seance. Before the sitters sang hymns and the proceedings commenced, Price was challenged by Mrs Buxton, Hope's colleague (herself a psychic photographer), but he strenuously denied that the parcel had been tampered with.

After several minutes had elapsed Hope took several photographs by the light of magnesium flares. He then accompanied Price into the darkroom, where the package was opened and the two top plates placed in the plate carrier. Hope picked up the carrier and asked Price to wrap up the rest of the plates. It was at this point that Price maintains he saw Hope 'put the dark slide to his left breast-pocket, and take it out again (another one?) without any talking or knocking'.

The two men now emerged from the darkrom and two photographs were taken using Price's plates. When the plates were developed one was of Price sitting alone, whilst the second had an extra (female) face looking over Price's shoulder. This face had the translucent 'psychic arch' which appeared in many psychic photographs of the period, framing the head of the subject. Price, seemingly impressed by the proceedings, then thanked Hope, and taking the plates with him, returned to the headquarters of the SPR, where he dictated a document condemning Hope as a confidence trickster. These were the specific objections Price made:

(1) On the plate with the extra face on it there were no X-ray marks.

(2) That Price had made thumbprints on the carrier which were not found on the carrier actually used.

(3) That he saw Hope put his hand inside his jacket pocket whilst in the darkroom.

(4) That the glass which the plates were made from and on which they appeared was different in colour and thickness from the glass brought by Price.

Conan Doyle was not wholly satisfied with Price's criticisms. To begin with, he argued, the X-rays would vanish if the plates were over-exposed. As for the marks on the carrier, these marks were so small that they would probably be indistinguishable. Besides, there was no independent evidence as to their existence. Lastly, the suspicious movement made by Hope might or might not have been evidence of deceit, but was not sufficient testimony in itself to condemn him.

On the point of the differing glass, Conan Doyle had to accept Price's criticism and conceded that there had actually been a substitution of plates. However, this did not mean that Hope was guilty of deception. Conan Doyle pointed out that the packet of plates had been in the possession of the officials of the SPR for several weeks before the experiment and was therefore openly available to all and sundry who might wish to tarnish Hope's reputation.

The business did not end there. The SPR later claimed that one or two of the marked plates had been returned to them, but they were not prepared to say exactly how or under what circumstances. After badgering the SPR officials Conan Doyle was permitted to see one of the plates in question. Not only was it one of the original set supplied by the Imperial Dry Plate Company, but it was also an unexposed plate. This meant that no one at Hope's end could have distinguished it from the other plates. Finally – and most importantly – the plate had an image on it which, reported Conan Doyle, 'may or may not have been a psychic extra'.[2]

Understandably, Conan Doyle regarded the appearance of the plate as highly indicative of a smear campaign against Hope. The plate had been sent to the SPR on 3 March, a week after the experiment had taken place. It had been placed in a double wrapper with a note inside asking that the plate be developed. The wrapper itself was formed of Psychic College literature and the package had been posted in Notting Hill.

Conan Doyle used his powers of deduction and began to see an elaborate conspiracy mounted against Hope:

> For twenty-four days after Mr. Price takes his packet of marked plates to the headquarters of the SPR it was locked up not in a safe but in an ordinary drawer, which may or may not have been locked, but could presumably be easily opened. My belief is that during that long period the packet was actually opened and the top plates taken out. Upon one of these top plates a faked photograph was thrown from one of those small projectors which produce just such an effect as is shown on the returned plate. The idea may have been that Hope would claim this effect as his own and that he would then be confounded by the announcement that it was there all the time. This was the first stage. The second stage was that either the original conspirator relented or someone else who was in his confidence thought it was too bad, so the packet was again tampered with, the marked and faked plate taken out and a plain one substituted. The packet was then taken to Hope as described. Mr. Hope then got a perfectly honest psychic effect upon the unmarked plate. Meanwhile the abstracter, whoever he may have been, had the original faked plate in his possession, and out of pure mischief – for I can imagine no other reason – he wrapped it in a sheet of the College syllabus, which can easily be obtained, and returned it to the SPR, to whom it originally belonged. Wherever it came from it is clear that it did not come from the College, for when a man does a thing secretly and anonymously he does not enclose literature which will lead to his detection.[3]

Conan Doyle was justified in his suspicions, for Price and his fellow investigators Dingwall and Seymour were all zealous campaigner against fake mediums and therefore more than likely to twist the facts to suit their opinions. Of the three investigators, Eric Dingwall, the research officer for the SPR, was the most opposed to Hope and also largely responsible for the leaflet which set out to condemn him.

Conan Doyle was not the only one to be suspicious. Among the disinterested parties who examined the evidence was Dr Allerton Cushman, who considered that Price's system of X-ray marking was far from infallible. He was also unconvinced by Price's method of marking the plate carrier.

The matter was finally laid to rest when Hewat McKenzie, honorary principal of the British College of Psychic Sciences, was able to examine the cover in which the original packet of plates was wrapped. He found unmistakable evidence that it had been tampered with and opened. This proved beyond a shadow of a doubt that the marked plates were taken before the packet reached the College and two ordinary plates then substituted.

The Hope case continued to vex Conan Doyle in the months that followed, principally because he saw the attempted discrediting of Hope as typical of the negative approach of the materialistically minded. In his opinion a handful of opportunists had been able to hoodwink the SPR and the general public in a most successful manner. In December 1922 he wrote to his friend Sir Oliver Lodge concerned that Lodge, Barrett and other Council members, all of whom were not opposed to spiritualism, had not been presented with an accurate picture of the whole affair. Conan Doyle clearly believed that Hope had been the victim of a practical joke.[4]

Lodge wrote back saying that the case had to be carefully investigated, but this did not prove that Hope was incapable of fraud when such a result would satisfy his clients. Conan Doyle disagreed. In his view, Hope had been grossly misrepresented by the SPR and the pamphlet 'exposing' him should be expunged from the records. A special impartial committee of investigation should be set up taking the matter out of the control of the people who had made such a hash of the affair and who had placed the Society in such an invidious position.[5]

Although Conan Doyle was not prepared to admit it in public, his private correspondence with Lodge suggests that he believed Seymour rather than Dingwall to be the culprit. In January 1923 he wrote to Lodge insisting that mediums should be protected against injustice. He regarded Dingwall as inexperienced, arrogant and a potential menace to the British spiritualist movement.[6] Dingwall may have had an inflated opinion of himself; he may also have been largely responsible for the attack on Hope, yet this did not mean he was guilty. Seymour, on the other hand, was the silent member of the group. He informed Lodge[7] that he regarded Seymour with intense suspicion and he castigated the SPR for failing to appoint an impartial subcommittee in order to analyse the evidence. Unless the Society did something to rectify matters, he warned, Hope would destroy them. As for medium baiting, it was injurious to the movement and destroyed the psychic process.

In March 1922 Conan Doyle published his detailed study of the Cottingley fairies episode. Entitled *The Coming of the Fairies*, the work presented the evidence unearthed by Gardner in 1919 and contained reprints of the articles Conan Doyle had published in the *Strand Magazine* in December 1920. A good proportion of the work provided instances of personal testimony from a number of sources which Conan Doyle hoped would convince the general public of the reality of the fairy kingdom.

In his preface, Conan Doyle was careful to observe that the existence of fairies did not mean that spiritualism must change its ideology to accommodate the new phenomena. 'This whole subject of the objective existence of a subhuman form of life', he pointed out, 'has nothing to do with the larger and far more vital question of spiritualism. I should be sorry if my arguments in favour of the latter should be in any way weakened by my exposition of this very strange episode, which has really no bearing upon the continued existence of the individual.'

Nevertheless, the existence of fairies had to be explained in rational terms. As a man of scientific training, Conan Doyle was only too willing to admit this. He likened these creatures to amphibians who 'may dwell unseen and unknown in the depths of the waters, and then some day be spied sunning themselves upon a sandbank, whence they slip into the unseen once more'. One could well imagine that in the psyche there was a dividing line, much like the water's edge. The line would be affected by what he called 'a higher rate of vibrations':

> Taking the vibration theory as a working hypothesis, one could conceive that by reusing or lowering the rate the creatures could move from one side to the other of this line of material visibility, as the tortoise moves from the water to the land . . . This, of course, is supposition, but intelligent supposition based on the available evidence is the pioneer of science, and it may be that the actual solution will be found in this direction.[8]

Although Conan Doyle had hoped for a positive response

from the public the book did not do particularly well, partly because the issue had been well aired in the press already, and partly because he was not taken seriously by the reviewers. The *Spectator* reviewer, for example, observed that Conan Doyle had not proved the fairies to be animate. 'One must freely admit that the children who could produce such fakes would be very remarkable children,' he wrote, 'but then the world, in point of fact, is full not only of very, but of very, very remarkable children.'[9]

Throughout 1921, a remarkable thing had happened to the Conan Doyle family which would profoundly affect the course of their lives. Conan Doyle's wife, Jean, had accepted the broad faith of spiritualism only after considerable persuasion and first-hand evidence of survival. Chief among the many instances which had convinced her of its certainty had been the evidence provided by her friend Lily Loder-Symonds, who had received messages from 'the other side' through automatic writing. When Sir Arthur discussed with her the possibility of trying automatic writing she had at first been reluctant, holding back her natural impulse to contact her deceased relatives because of the fear that the messages might emanate from her own subconscious self. Gradually, however, the many allusions and pieces of information which started to come through began to convince her that she was possessed of psychic powers. Contact was made with Willie Hornung (Conan Doyle's brother-in-law), Conan Doyle's eldest son, Kingsley, who had died in 1918, and Lady Conan Doyle's brother Malcolm Leckie. Most encouraging of all had been the communications with Lily Loder-Symonds, who advised Lady Conan Doyle that the messages were not from her subconscious self and that they were genuine reports from the beyond.

In March 1922 Conan Doyle heard from a number of new entities who informed him that he would leave his mark 'for ever upon America'. He determined there and then that there was work to be done. 'My own personal powers were little enough,' he wrote, 'but when immortal forces are behind you, your real personality counts for nothing. Therefore I was bound to try . . . The churches had to be spiritualised. Mankind had to face its problems . . . Materialism and comfort and legend had to yield to truth and duty and the beauty of the new revelation.'[10]

On 9 April Conan Doyle and his family arrived in New

York. Tired by the rough crossing he had endured, he found the American press men difficult to handle and his temper almost got the better of him. Nevertheless, he gave them an *aide-mémoire* which he had prepared for just such an onslaught. Spiritualism was the one great final antidote to materialism, he claimed. Although it had been degraded, the psychic movement existed to revivify religion, which had been long decaying. The new knowledge united real science and real religion, each supporting the other.

The press were not especially tolerant of Conan Doyle, despite his popularity as the creator of Sherlock Holmes. The *New York Times* observed: 'With each of the interviews he gives it becomes harder to be patient with him,' and remarked that he had become a laughable figure. Was he senile? one reporter asked him. Was the visit an exercise in profit-making? another enquired. Did spirits drink and smoke in Paradise? a third wanted to know. What about sex and marriage in the hereafter? Conan Doyle gritted his teeth and tried to provide accurate low-key answers which would satisfy the appetites of the press.

Two days later, after experiencing the exhilarating hustle and bustle of New York city life, he lectured at Carnegie Hall. 'I'd give family, title, whatever fortune I possess, my literary reputation . . .' he told the crowd, 'they are all as mud in the gutter to what this thing is to me. I know that it explains all of life to me, and know how inexplicable life was before.'

He described the actual process of death, and said he would show them a photograph of the 'etheric body', which had resided in the human body and was an exact duplicate of it down to the pores of the skin. He insisted that the evidence he presented warranted no sneers and no levity. Honest-minded people must accept it as proof.

He continued his lecture with an account of his reading of spiritualistic literature and his own investigations. He told them of how he had seen and heard his own son, who had died in the war, and of the communications he had received through automatic writing, so accurate in the smallest detail and so faithful in handwriting that he could not doubt that 'the dear boys were really there'. 'I realised', he said, 'that it was the dead who were visiting us. I saw that all these physical phenomena are puerile things, signals to direct our attention to higher things which the human race has been very backward in seeing.' Having realized the tremendous importance of spreading this knowledge, he and Lady Conan Doyle had vowed to pass the rest of their lives carrying the message to everyone.[11]

The following day the *New York World* seemed impressed by Conan Doyle's earnestness and honesty. 'Sir Arthur Conan Doyle made an extraordinary impression . . .' it remarked. 'The effectiveness of his talk depended on the fact that in spite of the imagination of his writings, he seems to be a downright person. He does not look a man who could be easily stampeded. His audience was profoundly attentive.'[12]

Conan Doyle delivered seven lectures in New York, all of which were well received. A photographic lecture followed the religious one, and soon the crowds began to flock in and watch with open mouths the large screen which displayed the grotesque Crawford–Bisson–Notzing photographs. By now the press had grown sympathetic, won over by the sensational nature of the evidence. The *New York Times* noted: 'To an audience which filled every seat in Carnegie Hall, Sir Arthur Conan Doyle showed spirit photographs of every kind – men, women, and children, landscapes and birds – taken with the greatest precautions against fraud. Many were strangely pathetic. One ghost, plainly transparent, was seated beside a printed page containing five verses of St. Mark's Gospel in Cingalese, a language unknown to the medium.'

Whilst in New York, Conan Doyle busied himself when not lecturing by investigating a number of mediums. On 14 April he attended a seance with the young Italian medium Nino Pecoraro, in the presence of Dr Cushman, Hereward Carrington the magician and psychic investigator, and three friends of the medium. Pecoraro sat in a cabinet, and after a short interval the spirit control announced that Eusapia Paladino, the controversial medium, was present. Despite several entreaties from Conan Doyle, however, Eusapia refused to reveal herself.

Two days later, Conan Doyle had a sitting with a Mr Ticknor, a well-known amateur medium whom Conan Doyle described as 'a stoutish, rather Pickwickian figure'. Sitting in an armchair, Ticknor closed his eyes and within a minute was in a deep state of self-hypnosis. Ticknor's control then spoke to the sitters, a North American Indian called Black Hawk (Black Hawk was also Evan Powell's control or spirit guide – a curious coincidence). Conan Doyle was then given messages from a host of his relations: John Doyle, his grandfather; Richard, his artist uncle; his father, Charles; Mary, his mother; and Kingsley, his eldest son. Malcolm Leckie, his wife's brother, gave his name, and so did an old patient of Conan Doyle's at Southsea. Conan Doyle was suitably impressed.

One evening in New York he came fact to face with a pair of fake mediums and, contrary to public opinion, immediately recognized that he was the victim of a rather clumsy hoax. Eva and William R. Thompson, along with Anna Hartmann and Alice Moriarty, sang hymns before the lights were dimmed and the seance commenced in front of several members of the New York press. A figure (Thompson), dressed in a shawl and long lace dress, then emerged from the cabinet in the corner of the room. The face, partly concealed by spectacles, bore something of a resemblance to Conan Doyle's mother. One can imagine Conan Doyle's disgust, therefore, when he gripped the figure only to find a muscular pair of shoulders concealed under the thin dress. Ever the gentleman, Conan Doyle refused to expose Thompson and was then vilified in the popular papers. Some days later the Thompson twins were arrested by the New York police and charged with fraud. 'I trust that the American Spiritualists will not condone or try to cover up such scandals,' Conan Doyle observed. 'The rotten twigs must come off. When the man was doing the direct voice I put my hand on his larynx, and could say with confidence that it was working, and that beyond all doubt the voice was coming from himself.'

Having left New York behind, the Conan Doyles travelled to Boston, their next port of call. Here at Symphony Hall, before a large audience, Conan Doyle launched into his address with customary gusto. He spoke of the devastating sense of loss caused by the First World War: 'Out of my own family ten went and there did not one survive.' He added that with the evidences they received of communications from the departed, he and his wife, seeing all the misery around them, felt they must go out and alleviate that misery. The evidences were received both in automatic writing and through mediums, although he stressed that he accepted automatic writing only with great caution. As for fraudulent mediums, he was at pains to point out that many of these cases were grossly exaggerated and that the vast majority of mediums were entirely reliable. Recounting some of his own experiences at seances, he told of the occasion when, during a sitting with an American medium in the children's nursery at 'Windlesham', as they were singing 'Onward, Christian Soldiers' he heard a beautiful baritone voice above the heads of the small group joining in. Still another case was that in which, during a sitting with an American medium in London, he saw in a halo of light the face of his mother, and found a note, signed with a pet name by which she had been known.

These and many other examples were recounted by Conan Doyle before he reached his description of the afterlife, a place where there was work but also abundant leisure; a place in which a person might retain his earthly creed, but where there was a growing appreciation of the points of unity rather than of difference in religious belief.

To the objection that here was a material heaven, Conan Doyle answered that this was only the first rung of the ladder. From here the spirit could ascend to higher spheres. 'Whatever opinion may be entertained by his hearers concerning the doctrine that he preaches,' the *Boston Transcript* concluded, 'the fair-minded among them will not deny to Sir Arthur Conan Doyle credit for absolute sincerity and the ability to set forth with vigour and compelling interest the belief that with him is a certainty.'[13]

Before leaving Boston for Washington, Conan Doyle consulted the clairvoyant medium Mrs Soulis, who had previously given excellent results to the American Psychical Research Society. Whilst in trance the medium reported that Conan Doyle's son was present, a fact which did not surprise him. However, when she said that he wrote down the word FLOREAT, Conan Doyle had to take the matter seriously since 'Floreat Etona' was the motto of Eton, where Kingsley had been educated. He also received at the same sitting a long message from F.W.H. Myers. 'I believe that the attitude you have assumed is the only true and helpful one for the advance of the Kingdom of God,' wrote Myers. 'I wish I could stand by your side in the body just to give you that satisfaction that comes from feeling that the old workers do not desert the new ones.'

Having visited the grave of one of his spiritual and literary fathers, Oliver Wendell Holmes (the American physician and essayist), and spent some time in the library at Harvard, Conan Doyle left for Washington, stopping at New York *en route* to pick up his family. After a somewhat hostile reception by the press, Conan Doyle set up in an hotel where he soon made the acquaintance of Dr Allerton Cushman, who had obtained evidence of his daughter Agnes's survival through a sitting with Mrs Deane, the psychic photographer. After lunch, Cushman read to the Conan Doyles two letters received from his wife and daughter on the other side through the automatic writing of one of his family. They spoke of themselves as being on the fourth plane. The daughter had seen Christ once and 'wrote words which were as vibrant with emotion and awe and wonder as are those of Raymond or Agnes Cushman when they also tell of that great episode – that glimpse of something never to be forgotten'.[14]

Among other visitors to Conan Doyle's hotel room were Julius Zancig and his wife, the mind-readers who had enjoyed such a resounding success in London in 1906. Although Conan Doyle admitted that the Zancigs might have used codes to perform their remarkable act, he maintained that much of it was based on genuine thought transference. 'No word passed at all,' he recalled, 'but Mrs. Zancig, standing with her face turned sideways at the far end of the room, was able to repeat names and to duplicate drawings which we made and showed to her husband . . . Possibly it is a real ectoplasmic formation, like the figures of Eva. Telepathy has been imagined by some spiritualists to be a real carrying of messages by some Familiar. This is certainly so.'

After lecturing in Philadelphia and Buffalo, Conan Doyle moved to Detroit, where he met another remarkable amateur medium, an Austrian lady married to a Greek. Mrs Economus, a tall, beautiful woman with 'commanding features', made a lasting impression on Conan Doyle. 'One seemed to see a Pythian priestess at the shrine of Apollo,' he recalled. 'She spoke with tremendous force and emphasis, but nothing which could really be called evidential came through.'

At Toledo, Conan Doyle addressed an audience of 3,000 people who had fought through torrential rain to see him. A local reporter remained unimpressed by what she saw. 'The visitor was dressed in an ill-fitting grey suit which was in bad need of pressing, and he wore a frayed white collar. His hair was grey and his head partially bald.' Another, more complimentary, reported: 'There is no doubt of the good your coming has done. Many were thoroughly convinced. Thousands of others who heard you at the Colosseum or through the Press are ready to give sane and intelligent consideration to the subject.'[15]

Conan Doyle could not leave Toledo without a sitting with the famous medium Miss Ada Bessinett. He had already sat with her four times when she had visited England and on one occasion had been considerably impressed by a materialization of the Ma'am which had occurred during the seance held at the British College of Psychic Science.

The seance in Toledo was, according to Conan Doyle, 'one of the most remarkable experiences [he] had ever had', and confirmed his belief in her powers as a medium. The Conan Doyle party, consisting of Sir Arthur, Lady Conan Doyle, Captain Wilson, Sir Arthur's secretary, and Lee Keedick, the manager of Conan Doyle's tour, sat round a large oak table which had been extended to accommodate some of Miss Bessinett's acquaintances. The lights were extinguished and the room was then in complete darkness. Almost immediately lights began to appear, some coming from the direction of the medium, others going towards her. As the Victrola gave out a tune, one of the tambourines in the room was snatched up and proceeded to play in time with the music. It then tapped each sitter on the hands and on the head. Meanwhile Miss Bessinett had apparently fallen into a deep trance.

As the Victrola moved on to play 'Where the Four Leafed Clover Grows', a low contralto took up the melody. Simultaneously soft hands stroked the hands of several of the sitters.

More songs followed, accompanied by a strong baritone and a high soprano. There was a sudden illumination, and a figure that was seen in the centre of the table vanished. A face then flashed out of the darkness three times before Sir Arthur and Lady Conan Doyle, obscured by what appeared to be wraps of ectoplasm. As this was going on, Conan Doyle cried out that a hand had seized his and placed it on that of the medium. The red light was then ordered on by the control (an Indian called Black Cloud) and the sitters, having left their chairs to examine the medium, found her right hand tied to that of Sir Arthur. In both cases the cords cut deeply into the flesh. The light was then turned off and a minute later the cords thrown on to the hands of the sitters.

Then materialized faces began to confront the sitters in rapid succession, many of these being visible to below the waist. A face came to Lady Conan Doyle which she said was that of her mother, and she said, 'Oh Mumsie, you are patting me on the cheek and on the head.' Then came the figure of a woman under a brilliant light. The sitters gasped at this apparition, the body draped in white and the face wrapped in draping. It was an exact reproduction of the photo of Katie King taken by Sir William Crookes years before and used by Conan Doyle on his American tour. There were several other vivid materializations, visible for between two to five seconds: one of a boy, one of a man, one of an elderly woman, and several of younger women. At intervals the voice of a child spirit known as Pansy was heard, who sometimes talked with the sitters and at other times directed the music.

The voice of the Indian control now instructed the sitters that if the trumpet touched their hands they should stand and place the large end of it next to their ear. Each of the sitters did this. Conan Doyle heard the voice of his eldest son, Kingsley, and heard how he was aiding the work of his father. Lady Conan Doyle also talked with several deceased relatives and was given information about how the relatives had entered the next life. This was followed by a number of handwritten messages given to members of the seance circle.

The Conan Doyles were enchanted by the results they obtained. 'We are having most marvellous results,' he exclaimed at one point, and then, with considerable concern, asked 'Are we not in danger of overworking the medium? We cannot be too careful of her. Her gift is too valuable to be endangered by overwork.' Lady Conan Doyle said afterwards of Miss Bessinett: 'She is simply wonderful. She is such a splendid character that she lends great value to what is obtained through her mediumship.'[16]

A week before the Bessinett seance, Conan Doyle and his wife had undergone a very different sort of seance. This time it was with the great escapologist and impresario Harry Houdini.

Conan Doyle had first met Harry Houdini in 1920 after

watching his show at Portsmouth, part of his English tour, and a firm friendship had quickly been cemented between the two men. Houdini, who was an avowed enemy of the spiritualists, had since communicated with Conan Doyle at regular intervals and enjoyed a good-natured series of disagreements with him about spiritualism. In a letter written in 1920, Conan Doyle advised Houdini:

> I see that you know a great deal about the negative side of spiritualism – I hope more on the positive side will come your way. But it wants to be approached not in the spirit of a detective approaching a suspect, but in that of a humble, religious soul, yearning for help and comfort . . . These clairvoyants, whose names I have given you, are passive agents in themselves and powerless. If left to themselves they guess and muddle – as they sometimes do. When the true connection is formed, all is clear . . . Most investigators have ruined their investigation before it began. It really does depend upon psychic or mental vibrations and harmonies. To disregard this is folly . . . Most of our great mediums at present are unpaid amateurs, inaccessible to any but spiritualists. I have sampled nearly all of them, and they are beyond suspicion.[17]

When the SPR investigated Eva C. and Mme Bisson in 1920, Houdini was permitted to sit in on the experiments. He wrote to Conan Doyle about his findings:

> We had success at the seance last night, as far as productions were concerned, but I am not prepared to say that they were supernormal.
> I assure you that I did not control the medium, so the suggestions were not mine. They made Mlle. Eva drink a cup of coffee and eat some cake (I presume to fill her up with some food stuff), and after she had been sewn into the tights, and a net over her face, she 'manifested'.
> 1st. Some frothlike substance, inside of net . . .
> 2nd. A white plaster-looking affair over her right eye.
> 3rd. Something that looked like a small face, say 4 inches in circumference . . .
> 4th. Some substance, frothlike, 'exuding from her nose' . . .
> 5th. Medium asked permission to remove something in her mouth; showed her hands empty, and took out what appeared to be a rubberish substance, which she disengaged and showed us plainly; we held the electric torch; all saw it

plainly; when presto!, it vanished . . . I found it highly interesting.[18]

Although Houdini was not prepared to commit himself about the origin of the Eva C. phenomena, he was nevertheless quite impressed. He was less impressed by Dr Crawford of Belfast, whom he visited and communicated with on several occasions. After a considerable correspondence had ensued between the two men, Conan Doyle invited Houdini to Crowborough before the latter's return to America. Afterwards, Houdini confided in his diary:

> Visited Sir A. Conan Doyle at Crowborough. Met Lady Doyle and the three children. Had lunch with them. They believe implicitly in spiritualism. Sir Arthur told me he had spoken six times to his son. No possible chance for trickery. Lady Doyle also believes and has had tests that are beyond belief. Told them all to me.[19]

Houdini was certainly greatly impressed by the absolute commitment and sincerity expressed by Conan Doyle and at this stage of his career was by no means bigoted. In fact, he told Conan Doyle in 1920, he had gone out of his way for years to unearth mediums who were totally reliable.[20]

In May 1922, whilst the Conan Doyles were staying at the Ambassador Hotel in New York, they visited Houdini's home. Conan Doyle was impressed with what he saw: a vast collection of books, tracts, and photographs, all relating to spiritualism. Conan Doyle was soon to become convinced that Houdini himself must possess occult powers. The following day he wrote to Houdini:

> I think what interested me most was the little 'trick' which you showed us in the cab. You certainly have very wonderful powers, whether inborn or acquired.[21]

It was soon after the Bessinett seance that the Houdinis travelled to Atlantic City, where the Conan Doyles were staying. According to Houdini, Lady Conan Doyle invited him to a private mediumistic sitting in her suite at the Ambassador Hotel. According to Conan Doyle, Houdini requested the seance himself.[22] Whatever the truth may be, the seance took place and messages were obtained purporting to come from Houdini's mother. Conan Doyle recalled:

> It was a singular scene, my wife with her hand flying wildly, beating the table while she scribbled at a furious rate, I sitting

opposite and tearing sheet after sheet from the block as it was filled up, and tossing each across to Houdini, while he sat silent, looking grimmer and paler every moment. We asked him to think a question in silence, and a correct name came instantly through my wife's hand. But then occurred the most marvellous thing of all. Houdini sat playing with the pencil when his hand was suddenly moved and he wrote the name 'Powell'. Now Dr. Ellis Powell, my dear fighting partner in spiritualism, had just died in England . . . I was the man he was most likely to signal to, and here was his name coming through the hand of Houdini . . .[23]

Houdini's view of the proceedings was radically different:

Lady Doyle was very charming. Curtains were drawn, writing-pads placed on the table and also two pencils of the ordinary kind. Sir Arthur, with his head bowed down, just like a simple child, uttered a prayer, calling upon the Almighty to let us have a sign from our friends from beyond.

He placed his hands caressingly upon Lady Doyle's, to give her more power . . .

She took a pencil and, with spasmodic jerks of her right hand . . . started to strike the table . . .

For a few moments she seemed to be struggling with it, but then the pencil began to move. She asked of the spirit, 'Do you believe in God?' Upon having her hand beat the table three times she said: 'then I will make the sign of the Cross' . . . She then wrote:

'Oh, my darling, thank God, thank God, at last I'm through – I've tried, oh so often – now I am happy. Why, of course, I want to talk to my boy – my own beloved boy – Friends, thank you, with all my heart for this!'

[*Marginal Note:* Message written by Lady Doyle claiming the spirit of my dear mother had control of her hand – my sainted mother could not write English and spoke broken English.][24]

Conan Doyle then asked Houdini to pose a question to test whether the spirit really was that of his mother. However, Lady Conan Doyle did not seem to think that the spirit would answer direct questions so Houdini thought that the spirit might attempt to read his mind. No sooner had the thought occurred to him than Lady Conan Doyle had written: 'I *always* read my beloved son's mind . . .' After the seance had finished Houdini wrote the name 'Powell' because, he said, he had been thinking of Powell the magician. A few days later Houdini wrote to Conan Doyle, telling him that the Ellis Powell explanation just simply would not do. When Houdini subsequently published an article in one of the New York papers and wrote of the Conan Doyle sitting in derisory terms, Conan Doyle wrote to him:

> . . . I have no fancy for sparring with a friend in public, so I took no notice. But nonetheless, I felt rather sore about it. You have all the right in the world to hold your own opinion, but when you say you have had no evidence of survival, you say what I cannot reconcile with what I saw with my own eyes. I know by many examples the purity of my wife's mediumship, and I saw what you got and what the effect was upon you at the time. You know also that you yourself at once wrote down . . . the name of Powell, the one man who might be expected to communicate with me. Unless you were joking when you said that you did not know of this Powell's death, then surely that was evidential . . .[25]

Houdini remained adamant. Frederick Eugene Powell was a dear friend of his who had been experiencing financial difficulties. That was the matter which had been on his mind. As for his mother, she could not read, write, or even speak English. How on earth could the automatic writing represent her? Conan Doyle wouldn't accept this. Mrs Wriedt or a trance medium might get Hebrew through, but a normal automatic writer wouldn't. The writing would come in a rush and be translated through the medium's mind. Anyway, there was the direct unspoken question. How did he explain that?

The debate of the Houdini seance created a rift between the two celebrities that was to widen over the years that followed. How does one explain the two mens' dramatically opposed interpretations? Certainly Conan Doyle was convinced of the genuineness of his wife's results. It must be said that he had given frequent warnings about the results obtained from automatic writing, so why was he so adamant about the Houdini sitting? One can imagine that he was extremely eager to impress Houdini, whom he regarded as a possible convert to the cause, and this may well have influenced his judgement. Why did Houdini not express his considerable doubts during the seance itself? Here one must admit that his friendship with the Conan Doyles may not have permitted him that necessary degree of objectivity. When he saw the cross, symbol of Christianity, at the top of each page and read the English manuscript he must have concluded that, sincere as Lady Conan Doyle clearly was, the results could only have emanated from the medium's subconscious mind.

After the Conan Doyles returned to England, further attacks appeared in the American press. A letter in the *New York Times* maintained that Elsie Wright had worked as a darkroom assistant for her father, so that she had had plenty of opportunity to manufacture the fairy photographs. Meanwhile, Clifton D. Wells, the president of Bates College, argued that ectoplasm was nothing more than fabricated animal tissue.[26] Conan Doyle weathered the storm and spent a considerable amount of his time lecturing in Sunderland and East Anglia.[27] Although it had been vastly expensive, the American tour had made a total profit of nearly £1,500. Conan Doyle donated £600 to the London Spiritual Alliance and the Spiritualists' National Union, whilst the remainder was spread between a variety of organizations, including, among others, the London Spiritual Mission, several spiritualist churches, and the Society for the Study of Supernormal Pictures.[28] Clearly the attacks on him in the American press were beginning to wound him, for he told an audience in Sunderland: 'People call me credulous, but they don't know what the evidence is. I say any man who had the evidence I had and didn't believe it would be a lunatic.'[29]

In December 1922 the American magazine *Scientific American* anounced that it would be holding a competition to determine once and for all the genuineness of 'so-called' psychic phenomena. Moreover, the editor, O.D. Munn, declared that the magazine would pay the first individual to produce an authenticated spirit photograph $2,500. A further $2,500 would be paid to anyone producing verifiable psychic phenomena in a seance. A committee was then set up, consisting of the magician Hereward Carrington, Professor William McDougall (a psychologist), Dr Daniel Comstock (a photographic pioneer), the psychologist Dr Walter Prince, and Harry Houdini.

Conan Doyle was asked to help the magazine by examining and then recommending a suitable medium. He was frankly dubious about such a series of proposed experiments, and wrote to the editor raising his doubts. A large money reward, he opined, would 'stir up every rascal in the country', whilst the genuine medium would not bother to apply. It would be far more constructive for a representative to be sent to the various towns in America and Europe so that suitable mediums with a genuine background could be selected.

The editor liked Conan Doyle's suggestions and was eager to comply. As associate editor of *Scientific American*, J. Malcolm Bird, was therefore dispatched to England to make a number of initial enquiries.

Bird found Conan Doyle to be both charming and courteous, and before very long they had struck up a good relationship. A series of mediums were then tested by the two men, the first being John Sloan, the voice medium, and Evan Powell, in whom Conan Doyle placed considerable trust. At the British College of Psychic Science, Powell was attended by Conan Doyle and his wife. Bird insisted that Powell strip to his underwear, but when a rectal examination was proposed Powell refused to co-operate. Bird then strapped Powell to a chair which had been placed inside a cabinet. Bells rang, flowers drifted about the room, and the sitters' hands and faces were caressed. Bird went on to investigate William Hope and Mrs Brixton before moving on to Berlin and Paris.

It was in December 1922 that another important milestone was established in the Conan Doyle quest for psychic confirmation. On 10 December a new entity entered the Conan Doyle home circle. Called Pheneas, the spirit visitor announced himself to be an Arab who had lived in Ur of the Chaldees before Abraham's time. From now on Pheneas took chief control of the seances at 'Windlesham'. He told Conan Doyle and his wife that he must once more visit America and preach the fundamental message of spiritualism. Then Conan Doyle's own mother came through. She corroborated Pheneas's statements. 'Dear ones, your tour in America will be a very great success,' she told the Conan Doyles. 'Strength, enormous strength will be given to you [30] . . .'

Before leaving for America in April 1923, Conan Doyle made copious notes in preparation for his new set of lectures, which he was determined would be even more convincing than the last. One of the issues of the last few months which had preoccupied him greatly was the famous Cenotaph photograph taken by the medium Mrs Deane. This was a photograph which had been taken of the crowd assembled at the Cenotaph in Whitehall on Armistice Day, 11 November 1922. When the plate was developed by Mrs Deane faces were to be seen floating over the crowd. The print was subsequently published in a national newspaper and caused great controversy. Two years later (20 November 1924) the *Daily Sketch* revealed that, following a microscopic examination, the faces on the print were those of 'the famous sporting figures Battling Siki, Jimmy Wilde, and several well-known footballers'. Conan Doyle subsequently denied this accusation, despite the fact that the sportsmen wrote to the newspaper confirming it. Why did Conan Doyle accept the photograph as genuine?

He had his reasons. Mrs Deane, unlike Hope, was a somewhat inoffensive elderly lady of poor origins–in fact the very last person one would have suspected of fraud. Having been forced at the age of nine to work as a cleaner, she was put into service at eleven and subsequently developed a number of psychic powers which she was unable to control. She joined a spiritualist church in Hackney and produced her first psychic photograph in 1920. When her 'gift' first announced itself she was in the habit of taking photos of her friends and neighbours and only charging them what it had cost her to develop the prints. Her reputation then soon spread among local spiritualists and she began producing photographs by the thousand.

When interviewed by Warwick in the 1920s Mrs Deane gave the impression of being a somewhat naïve person, rather limited in intelligence. She would not admit that the *Daily Sketch* faces of footballers, etc., were the same as those in the Armistice Day photograph. As regards the well-known boxer Battling Siki, she commented, all negroes looked much the same to an outsider, and she suggested that the newspaper interviewers seemed to know nothing of the subject which they had been commissioned to write about. She understood roll films but not pack films. However, roll films were a great trouble to develop, being springy and easy to scratch and damage. That is why she still relied on plates. Moreover she did not see the value of using marked or pre-wrapped plates. Warrick found her to be ingenuous and quite unreliable.[31]

Conan Doyle, on the other hand, liked Mrs Deane's apparent honesty. Her lack of professionalism was precisely what appealed to him. In January 1924 he wrote to his friend

Lodge and enclosed a copy of the photograph. He suggested that Lodge examine the photo with a lens and seemed convinced that it showed the presence of both his son and nephew.[32]

Meanwhile, Conan Doyle and his family prepared themselves for the long journey to America. 'All the great cities of the West without one exception had called me, and to all I had to give denial. Can I leave it so?' he wrote in *Our American Adventure*, published in 1923.

Before leaving Britain the Conan Doyles travelled down to the West Country to spread the word. At Torquay he was introduced by the Mayor of the Borough who, although admitting that he was not himself a spiritualist, nevertheless was of the opinion that mankind was on 'the fringe of a new ocean, at present uncharted, and that they must be prepared for any revelation'. Conan Doyle addressed the crowd in his usual buoyant way. Two and a half years had elapsed since he was last in Torquay, he said. During that time he and his wife had travelled all over Australia, New Zealand, and the eastern states of America, as well as a great deal in Britain, lecturing on spiritualism. Why did they do it? He was a home lover, a man who hated travel, and with no more energy than the average man. He did it because he and Lady Conan Doyle believed they could devote the rest of their lives to no greater purpose than making known to others the great revelation which they themselves knew to be true. It was indeed the most important thing that people could consider, for it concerned both their futures and the futures of those who were dear to them.[33]

The past year had not been an easy one for the Conan Doyles. Unlike the Australian tour, the time spent in America and Britain had been one of turmoil and challenge. Although the spiritualist cause was worth fighting for, the going was at times extremely tough. At the same time, Conan Doyle's credibility as a writer and public figure had been challenged on a number of occasions. The case of the Cottingley fairies had certainly not done him much good, whilst the American press and Harry Houdini had presented him as a rather credulous figure, too eager to accept phenomena at their face value and easy to dupe. Whilst this picture was certainly a distortion of the facts, there was, growing steadily in the minds of the public, an image of a writer which they found hard to reconcile with the inventor of Sherlock Holmes, the master analyst and logician. However, as in the past, Sir Arthur Conan Doyle cared little for public opinion. If he considered the cause to be just, then he would fight for it.

CHAPTER 9

Another American Adventure

On 3 April 1923 Conan Doyle arrived in New York, ready for his second spiritualist lecture tour of America. Originally he had not intended to revisit the city but did so on the advice of his tour manager, Lee Keedick, who told him that it was in the best financial interests to do so.

The Conan Doyle family were glad to be ashore, for the unremitting head winds and frequent gales had made for an unpleasant crossing, and Conan Doyle himself had had the misfortune to fall on a wet deck early on the voyage and twist his knee.

Two days later he spoke at Carnegie Hall and gave his usual lecture, this time including the slides. Among the spirit photographs shown was that of the Cenotaph taken by Mrs Deane. As the picture flashed up on the screen the audience tensed and stirred. Then from the darkness of the hall came a high scream. 'Don't you see them? Don't you see their faces?' shouted a voice. For a few minutes there was chaos and a babel of voices. Conan Doyle reassured the audience and had the lights turned up. It was then discovered that a female member of the audience had fallen into a deep trance. When roused, she explained that for some while now she had been possessed by the deceased mother of a dead soldier who now was keen to tell other bereaved mothers what had become of their sons. It was this spirit who had possessed her when the photograph had been shown.

The Carnegie Hall lecture had been so successful and the press coverage of it so sensational that Conan Doyle was asked to repeat it the following Sunday. This proved problematic for him since on the Saturday he had been booked to speak at Rochester (some 200 miles away) and was due in Cleveland the following Tuesday. His trip to Rochester was symbolic, for the city was near the place where the Hydesville rappings first occurred in 1848 and sparked off the spiritualist movement which subsequently swept America. For some while now Conan Doyle had been attempting to raise funds in England and America to build a memorial to the famous Fox sisters, especially since the original house which had been the site of their psychic exploits had been long since demolished.

Before leaving New York Conan Doyle had several sittings with a number of mediums, some of whom, like the Pickwickian Mr Ticknor, he had met before. Through Ticknor he was able to learn more about the control, Black Hawk, and recontacted his mother, who recalled their last talk together in very convincing detail.

The Conan Doyles were depressed at the appearance of New York, which they found to be untidy and slovenly in appearance. Walking through Central Park they noted the trampled grass and the litter, indicative of the neglect which now seemed typical of the city. Whilst there, Lady Conan Doyle was asked to broadcast a radio message on spirit teaching. She spoke of her husband's gradual conversion, of her brother's death, and the evidence which had come to her of his survival. 'I knew the immense consolation that this new knowledge was to me,' she told her audience, 'and when he proposed that we should devote our lives to this end, I eagerly agreed.'

While Lady Conan Doyle stayed in New York with the children, Sir Arthur travelled to Cleveland, Pittsburgh, and then Cincinnati. In the latter town he visited, among other mediums, Mrs Pruden, renowned for her slate-writing. Conan Doyle wrote a number of questions down which were then answered between closed slates. 'This is not your last visit to America,' she told him. 'You will come here again two years hence.' Next on his itinerary were Indianapolis and Columbus, where he enjoyed favourable meetings. From Columbus he wired to his family to join him in Chicago, the next important stage of the trip.

Shortly after the Conan Doyle family had set up in Chicago, Sir Arthur received a visit from a young man of 20 who was eager to be tested for the *Scientific American*

competition. Since J. Malcolm Bird, who had accompanied
Conan Doyle on the trip, was out of Chicago at the time,
Conan Doyle and his family were given a demonstration by
the young Mr Kemp, whose forte was the zinc trumpet. The
group adjourned to the hotel bedroom, where a conversation ensued about American baseball. In the middle of this
dialogue 'a roar like that of a lion . . . burst form the centre
of the circle'. The spirit visitor turned out to be a Red Indian
whom Conan Doyle persuaded to modify his voice. What
sort of an Indian was he? Conan Doyle enquired. For some
time the two chatted about the Five Nations, the Iroquois
describing how he had lost his life in a battle with the pale
faces and had been buried on four sticks raised above the
ground. All this while Conan Doyle grasped Kemp's hand
tightly, but the spirit voice travelled about the room with
remarkable force and rapidity. After the seance had concluded, Kemp and his assistant assured Conan Doyle that
after the sittings long streaks of white matter were often
found in the water tray in which the trumpet was placed.
This, Conan Doyle inferred, must surely be ectoplasm.
Before leaving Chicago for St Louis, Kansas City, and the
Rockies, Conan Doyle was shown around the Chicago gaol,
a dark, forbidding place which left an appalling impression
on him. 'What feeblest reflection of the teaching or spirit of
Christ is there in such an institution, he wrote 'a manure-
heap where human garbage is thrown to reek and fester,
cared for by no one so long as it is decently concealed. You
may conceal your cesspool as you will, but if there is seepage
it will spread death, which will creep back in time to you.
And so it is here.'[1]

After visiting Denver, where he met Harry Houdini and
examined a number of psychic photographs which Houdini
had taken and was impressed with (although Conan Doyle
considered they might well be fakes), the Conan Doyle
entourage moved on to Salt Lake City, the home of the
Mormons. In his first Sherlock Holmes novel, *A Study in
Scarlet*, Conan Doyle had portrayed the Mormons in an
unfavourable light, but when he was received by an attentive audience of some 5,000 who sat spellbound by his
lecture, his opinion altered substantially. Everything about
Salt Lake City seemed to fascinate or intrigue him in some
way. The documents purporting to have been written by
John Smith, the Mormon founder, demanded his attention.

As far as Conan Doyle was concerned, Smith bore all the hallmarks of being a gifted medium. As for Smith's message, it was not very dissimilar to that of the spiritualists, preaching that the Christian religion had wandered far from its original intention. As for its historic side, he considered that Smith had worked into the document many of his own religious memories and conceptions.

When he finally got to Los Angeles, Conan Doyle received an invitation from the president of the Society of Advanced Psychic Research to attend one of their meetings at Altadena, a town some 15 miles away. The mediums in question were Mr and Mrs Jonson, famed for their powers of materialization.

Inside a locked room whose door had been wired up and stapled, Conan Doyle watched as the medium and his wife came out and sat in front of a curtain which shrouded a small recess. Within a few minutes the curtain was drawn aside and a white-robed figure entered the room. Conan Doyle recalled:

> The white-robed figure swayed after its entrance, almost like a dress hung up and blown by the wind. It then seemed to gather strength and form. It advanced about four feet into the room. The medium and his wife, . . . were clearly visible, seated outside the cabinet under twenty pair of eyes. It was explained to me that this white figure was Viola, the guide who controlled the circle. She began to talk in a loud whisper, greeting various sitters by name . . . She then faded away . . .

Several figures now began to appear in rapid succession: an old lady wearing spectacles, another old woman in white, and a small girl clad in white and wearing a coloured sash. The girl sat on the floor with her legs crossed and talked to the company. Was Conan Doyle the man who knew about fairies? she asked. Most certainly, he replied. Could she tell him where they come from? Fairies, the girl explained, were the cherubs in God's kingdom. They had wings because they had never enjoyed an earth-life and didn't understand how to gather the electrons. Therefore God supplied them with wings to propel them. The fairies were all about us in the world and their music could be heard. Frustrated, Conan Doyle asked if the spirit girl could materialize a fairy. This might not be possible, she replied, since the earthly vibrations might be too strong for them.

When one of the company had given the spirit girl a box of candy she faded out before their eyes. Mrs Jonson now said that she had a special visitor for Sir Arthur:

A small female figure . . . advanced from the curtains . . . I came forward and looked eagerly at it. I could not doubt that the general outline of head and shoulders was that of my mother . . . I said, 'Is it you, mother?' She threw up her hands and danced up and down in an ecstasy of delight. Then she vanished and I returned to my seat with no doubt in my mind that the form had reproduced my mother, though I admit that the effect was not an absolutely certain one in the same sense as it was when I saw every smallest detail of her face in the presence of Miss Bessinett.[3]

The seance finished with a young boy called Billy materializing in the room. Billy, it seemed, knew Kingsley well and was also acquainted with Pheneas, Conan Doyle's Arab guide. His name, said Billy (correctly), was Ali Ben Hassen and he was bringing to the Conan Doyles a 'wonderful power'.

Conan Doyle remained deeply impressed by his experience with the Jonsons. How absurd it was, he reflected, that such things should occur in the presence of more than 20 witnesses and that they should be scoffed at by men of science.

After a brief foray along the coast, the Conan Doyles were once more back in Los Angeles on 19 May to receive two most unusual visitors with whom he was to sustain a prolonged friendship. Dr Carl Wickland was a psychiatrist whose work among the deranged had led him to believe that lunacy was the product of spirit possession. In the course of his research Wickland had discovered that static electricity, when applied to the patient in question, had the effect of driving out the incumbent entity.

Wickland's method was to place the patient on a platform and then attach electrodes to his or her body. The spirit was then quietly reasoned with before an electrical charge was applied. At this point the entity left the body of the patient and entered the body of Wickland's wife, who had prepared herself by going into a trance.

In his book *Thirty Years Among the Dead* (1924), a test which has since become a psychic classic, Wickland explains how he first realized his wife's potential when, after a day spent dissecting the body of a 60-year-old-man, he returned home to find Mrs Wickland staggering about and demanding to know why her leg had been cut. Realizing that the spirit owner of the body which he had been dissecting had followed him home, Wickland began to parley with him, first placing his wife in a chair:

> To this the spirit vigorously objected, saying that I had no business to touch him. To my answer that I had a right to touch my own wife the entity retorted: 'Your wife! What are you talking about! I am no woman – I'm a man!'[4]

The spirit then asked for a plug of tobacco to chew, and Wickland was intrigued to note that the teeth of the cadaver indicated the man had been an inveterate tobacco user in life.

Five days later, after an interesting tour of the Goldwyn Studios where the Conan Doyles subsequently met Douglas Fairbanks and Mary Pickford, Sir Arthur visited the Wicklands and saw for himself the electrical apparatus used in the experiments. He sat on the platform, received a sharp shock, and entirely sympathized with the entities in their desire to quit. Later that same day Mrs Wickland demonstrated her skills by enacting a play entirely in Russian in which she played all the characters. Apparently the voices represented a band of strolling players who put on the performance in order to teach the undeveloped dead a moral. Conan Doyle was greatly impressed.

When the Conan Doyles reached San Francisco they found the newspapers full of articles by leading scientists and academics denouncing them. Spiritualism had no scientific basis, the writers argued. There had been a standing offer of $5,000 from Scientific American to anyone proving that spirits could communicate with mortals. It hadn't been won by anyone, and wouldn't be. As for Conan Doyle's theories, they belonged to the realm of religion and had no place in scientific theory or practice. Increasingly tired by the constant journeying and the barrage of negative opinion he had to encounter, Conan Doyle told reporters that the scientists deserved to be shown up as the dolts they were in psychic matters.

Although Conan Doyle seemed at odds with San Francisco, which he regarded as particularly lacking in psychic potential, the work of one individual, Dr Abrams, did attract his attention. Abrams showed Conan Doyle an electronic machine which acted like a wireless receiver and which was sensitive to minute vibrations from organic matter. Conan Doyle watched in fascination as Abrams demonstrated its use to him thus:

> You take a little bit of cancer in a bottle. You approach it to the loose antenna hanging from the radio receiver. When it gets a few inches off, you hear a loud buzz, like an angry hornet. Keep it there. The buzz will be repeated every four seconds. That is cancer.

Abrams was not only able to determine the vibration of plants and animals with his receiver, but he also claimed to pick up the vibrations of the dead. 'The psychic atmosphere of a haunted house', Conan Doyle remarked excitedly, 'might perhaps be amenable to this magnetic vacuum cleaner.'

At Portland, his next stop, Conan Doyle came across one of the two Rosicrucians who had approached him many years before when he was living in South Norwood and enjoying the fruits of his success as a writer. The 'little bearded messenger' of the White Lodge had much to tell Conan Doyle about the Order of the Rosicrucians–of how it had fallen into decline since the disclosure of its occult knowledge and of his own group's attempts to strive against the evil forces which threatened to engulf the world:

> The psychic epochs, I learned, were always known by Zodiacal names, and this Aquarian one was that which was to see the substitution of knowledge instead of faith, and also, as I gathered, the end of the competitive commercial era, and the beginning of an age of equal opportunity for all men . . . Presently, amid many mean streets, we entered a humble dwelling and found two female members of the secret cult . . . The little bearded man sat down, and so did I. After a long desultory talk, the seeress . . . rose up and began to talk, conveying messages . . . from a great spirit who used her . . . The main thesis was that I was a teacher sent down specially for the work that I was doing. That work was superficial, but all the more valuable as people must first learn the psychic alphabet.[5]

Conan Doyle learnt much else: that the world was in imminent danger of terrible cataclysm and that materialism would lead to the downfall of the economic and social systems. There was also a prophecy for his son Denis and a confirmation that on the astral spheres there existed an Order of the White Star of Love which would provide help to earthly mediumship.

In Seattle, one of his last ports of call before leaving the USA for Canada, Conan Doyle encountered another scientist who believed that through experimental methods he had been able to demonstrate psychic powers. Dr Littlefield had discovered, through the use of photomicroscopy, that the saline constituents of blood, when mixed with certain other salts, produced thought images. Even more remarkable was the fact that the scales would apparently answer questions of a philosophical nature. Conan Doyle remained sceptical about this, maintaining that the images on the microscope slide were open to interpretation. Another curiosity which claimed his attention was the psychic photographs of Kanouse, who had photographed a Mrs Lally in her coffin. A different member of the family had stood by the coffin for each of the six shots which were then taken, time-exposures by floodlight. When these plates were subsequently developed not only was a different figure found on each but each also included a spirit figure, so that the plates showed a number of the dead woman's deceased friends. Although the townspeople of Seattle had declared the photographs to be fraudulent, Conan Doyle had been assured by the president of the local psychic research society that Kanouse was genuine and he therefore included the item in his final lecture.

Having reached Vancouver, Conan Doyle at once began to explore the psychic potential of the place. One medium in particular was made available for him to test. Clarence Britton was a tall, neurasthenic individual with penetrating eyes and a languid manner, a disciple of a Michigan farmer who had died when a psychic researcher had pounced on the ectoplasmic figure he had produced from his cabinet. Like his guru, the farmer, Britton also worked from a cabinet. Sitting in the front row of chairs at the house of a bona fide spiritualist, Conan Doyle and his son Denis watched as a succession of different faces, some black-bearded, some white-bearded, emerged from behind the curtains. Conan Doyle felt distinctly uneasy about the whole affair, realizing that 'if they were masks they could have been manipulated' One of the forms bore something of a resemblance to his mother, although by now he was becoming circumspect especially since the report of Ada Bessinett's seance had been so widely publicized.

In Winnipeg he sat with a Scottish medium and a group of scientists who had obtained impressive results. Around a table lit by phosphorus the sitters sat. They watched as the table shot back into a small cabinet only to re-emerge within a few seconds without a soul touching it. Conan Doyle stood by the opening of the curtain and watched the table in the subdued red light:

> One moment it was quiescent. A moment later it was like a restless dog in a kennel, springing, tossing, beating up against the supports, and finally bounding out with a velocity which caused me to get quickly out of the way. It ended by rising up in the air while our finger-tips were on it and remaining up for an appreciable period.[6]

The morning following his lecture at Winnipeg, Conan Doyle completed his last psychic investigation before visiting New York *en route* for Britain. He sat open-mouthed as Mrs Bolton, a woman of Blavatsky-like appearance, but with a broad Lancashire accent, turned water into wine, baptized a nine-week-old child, and then proceeded to inform the sitters in various voices of the conditions of the life heareafter. 'What is one to say of such a performance?' mused Conan Doyle in *Our Second American Adventure*. 'It was against all my prepossessions, for I have a deep distrust of ritual and form and sacraments . . . yet they were solemn and moving, and nothing can exceed the absolute faith of these men and women. Their faith is founded . . . upon long experience in which they have seen miracle after miracle, including materializations of . . . high personages.

Back in England, Conan Doyle seemed pleased with his second tour. He had delivered a total of 40 lectures and visited at least 30 large cities. 'Yet looking back,' he told a *Guardian* reporter, 'I can only find out of those hundreds of papers [who reported his arrival] one that took a definite line against me.'[7] Whether this was through an appreciation of his talents or through sheer indifference it is difficult to decide, yet certainly among the adherents of spiritualism his efforts were appreciated. Of the Carnegie Hall lecture, the *Journal of the American Society for Psychical Research* reported:

. . . he knows how to present his subject and transfer it to his audiences, one hundred per cent effective. There was no sense of over leading, cluttering, confusion or haste. He went into action with clean decks. He had measured the size of the auditorium and the audience, he knew the speed at which the material had to be delivered, the spacing that it required, the simplicity of diction and thought that would bring it within the comprehension of the humblest. He was supported by exceedingly good pictures well chosen, sharp and thrown on a taut screen. The same knowledge of human nature that has won him distinction as a novelist and a historian was revealed in the lectures. The people who think Sir Arthur Conan Doyle a fool are very much mistaken. He is as intelligent and masterful on the lecture platform as he is anywhere else.[8]

If one looks at the contemporary reports of Conan Doyle's lecture tours there is no doubt that he was a gifted speaker and possessed an ability to put across difficult and often highly controversial subjects so that they would appeal to the man in the street. Naturally certain sections of the press were critical of him, but they could not fault him as a propagandist and disseminator of information. By the time he had completed his last major lecture tour in the USA he had demonstrated these capabilities to the full.

At the time of the commencement of his second American tour *Scientific American* had begun to make its first examination of the mediums who had been recommended to them. Over the months that followed Conan Doyle wrote and spoke to Houdini frequently about the work of the committee of which Houdini was a member. Conan Doyle did not place much trust in their abilities, as he revealed in this letter to Houdini, written shortly after his arrival in America:

The Commission is, in my opinion, a farce, and has already killed itself. Can people not understand that 'psychic' means 'of the spirit', and that it concerns not only the invisible spirit or the spirit of the medium, but equally those of every one of the investigators? A delicate balance and harmonious atmosphere are needed. I fear some of your recent comments which I have read would not only keep away every decent medium – for they are human beings, not machines, and resent insult – but it would make spirit approach impossible, for they also do not go into an atmosphere which is antagonistic. Thus a certain class of researcher always ruins his result before he begins.[9]

Conan Doyle had been particularly impressed by the mediumship of the American Mrs Margery Crandon, who with her husband visited Conan Doyle at his flat in Buckingham Palace Mansions. Margery produced a series of impressive phenomena for Conan Doyle and his family. Messages came through from Margery's dead brother, Walter, a bell-box rang loudly without anyone touching it, and a dried flower fell from the ceiling on to Lady Conan Doyle's feet. All the while this was happening Conan Doyle kept a tight hold on Margery's feet.

Conan Doyle wrote several letters to the *Scientific American* committee, recommending Mrs Crandon. They eventually responded, although none too enthusiastically. Their previous mediums had all been found to be either fraudulent or non-productive. Valentine, the Wilkes-Barre medium, was a complete failure. Mrs Elizabeth Tomson of Chicago had been another fiasco, demanding her own conditions and refusing to sit in the place prescribed for her. As for the young Italian Nino Pecoraro, he was able to produce nothing when securely bound and fettered by Houdini.

In 1924, the committee undertook to examine Mrs Crandon and test her phenomena. The members of the committee differed in their opinions. Two of the members regarded the phenomena to be of the first quality and most definitely supernormal. A third member was deaf, whilst a fourth, Houdini, came with his mind already made up before the seances started. The last member of the committee, who examined the evidence on numerous occasions, then decided that it could not be true because he would not believe it.

The phenomena themselves were widely based and included table-tilting, telekinesis by means of teleplasmic rods, the ringing of a bell-box (which contained two dry-cell batteries and electric bell), the movement of a pair of chemical balances, trance-voice, trance-writing, automatic writing, musical sounds, perfumes, supernormal lights, and ectoplasm which emanated from the right ear of the medium. Objects materialized and other objects were made to disappear, and fingerprints appeared which did not match those of the sitters.

In the first sitting it became clear that Houdini was not going to allow Mrs Crandon an opportunity to produce her phenomena under objective conditions. Under cover of darkness he produced a piece of rubber which he then fastened to the bell-box so that the electrical circuit was broken and it would not ring. The control (Walter) at once shouted that it had been interfered with, and the rubber was subsequently found in the box. At the second seance, Margery was shut up inside a box. Houdini, under the pretence of determining if the medium was all right, put his hand inside the box and dropped in a folding carpenter's rule. Walter screamed out, calling Houdini an unutterable cad and putting a curse upon him.[10] The cabinet was then opened and the ruler found. Clearly the folding ruler had been inserted in order to imply that the medium had smuggled in the offending article with the object of unfolding it and poking the sitters in the dark.

Houdini denied all this, of course. In his opinion Margery Crandon was a fake, and in order to prove his point he tied an elastic band round his calf, making his ankle so swollen that he would be able to tell when the medium thrust her foot out to touch the bell-box. Moreover, he was able to convince other members of the committee of her unreliability.

Other leading investigators disagreed with the committee's findings. In June 1926 Eric Dingwall, the research officer for the SPR, made a report on the Margery mediumship, based on experiments conducted by him in January and February 1925. 'I have never on any occasion detected anything that could be called fraud or deceit' he declared, and in a letter to Schrenck-Notzing he explained: 'It is the most beautiful case of teleplasmic telekinesis with which I am acquainted. We can freely touch the teleplasm. The materialized hands are joined by cords to the medium's body; they seize objects and move them . . . I held the medium's hands; I saw [teleplasmic] figures and felt them in good light. The "control" is irreproachable.'[11]

Ever since his return to Britain, Conan Doyle had spent much of his spare time (when not working on his autobiography and an account of his second American tour) conducting home circle seances. Through a number of communications transmitted via Pheneas, his spirit guide, Conan Doyle had become obsessed with the possibility of

Armageddon. On 19 July 1924 he wrote to Lodge telling him that he had collected a drawer full of independent warnings of catastrophe and adding that his wife had also received confirmation of some imminent apocalypse. He would not go public about it but continued to make private inquiries.[12]

Pheneas warned constantly of the impending apocalypse. The spirits had a plan for the world which was like a well-oiled machine. The parts of this machine had been assembled and were even now being put into place. When all was ready the power would be insulated, and the world's journey would commence. There would be no more suffering, no more sorrow, only a profusion of love. However, the whole world must first be cleansed and the centre of the disease eradicated. After the pruning knife had done its work, the fresh life would commence.

On 29 October 1924 Conan Doyle wrote to Lodge informing him that he had had a most useful sitting with Mrs Leonard, the medium. Kingsley, his son, had come through and talked for two hours. He fully confirmed all that Pheneas had said about the coming crisis, but told his father that he must not exaggerate the physical aspect of the cataclysm. Conan Doyle regarded this as final and irrevocable proof of his 'apocalypse' theory. Mrs Leonard had no prior knowledge of the correspondence he had already received and the notion that this evidence was attributable to some psychic conspiracy was quite inconceivable.[13]

As the years passed and the home circle sittings continued at 'Windlesham', Conan Doyle began to collect various pieces of evidence in the form of prophecies and visions which confirmed Pheneas's warning of the apocalypse that was to strike mankind. In a confidential memo sent to Lodge in March 1927, he summarizes no fewer than 87 of these, and in his accompanying letter warns that these forecasts about the future should be treated with considerable discretion and that the press should not be informed for fear of sensationalism. Besides, the apocalypse might never come to fruition, either because of the plans of some higher tribunal or because of a change in the human condition.

The warning, he noted, always seemed to be accompanied by an increase in the seismic activity of the world, which showed itself in those area whence the warnings came. In content, the warnings were most specific – particularly those which had come through Pheneas and which he was loath to include in his final publication of the Home Circle seances, entitled *Pheneas Speaks*. He believed that the crisis would arise instantaneously and that this would lead to the complete destruction and dislocation of civilization. Then, after a short period of total chaos, some return to normality would ensue.[15]

The total period of upheaval would be about three years, and the chief areas of disturbance the eastern Mediterranean, where no fewer than five countries would disappear. In the Atlantic Ocean there would be a rise in the land, causing tidal waves which would affect the American seaboard and much of Europe. There would also be further upheavals in the southern Pacific.

Conan Doyle believed that these physical manifestations of spiritual forces would be accompanied by a 'rending of the veil' so that for a short while spirit and matter would be face to face. After this many spiritualists would pass into their etheric bodies, whilst others of the 'Elect' would stay on earth to establish the new order on a solid basis. The whole chain of events would seem to confirm the notion of a Second Coming.

Whilst he emphasized his utter faith in this apocalyptic vision, Conan Doyle asked Lodge to handle the information with discretion, for he insisted that he had no certainty over these prophecies and if they were to be made public it could cause the spiritualist movement considerable harm. However, he was certain in his own mind that the visions of John and the Book of Revelation were premonitions of this unavoidable cataclysm.

Throughout the latter part of 1924 the great debate over spiritualism continued to intrude and claim Conan Doyle, and when he was not engaged in literary work he was waging war with hostile factions, mainly through the press or by actively campaigning around Britain. On 20 November, the *Daily Sketch* alleged that Conan Doyle's beloved Cenotaph photograph with which he had enthralled the people of America was a 'cruel fraud'. To settle the matter, Sir Arthur sent the photograph to the famous anthropologist Sir Arthur Keith so that he could take anthropometric measurements and compare these with the original photos of the sportsmen which had appeared in the newspapers. 'Not one of the photographs reproduced by The Sketch is identical with any of the representations or photos reproduced in the spirit photos,' Keith wrote back to Conan Doyle.[16]

The spring, summer, and autumn of 1924 were spent travelling, but this time Conan Doyle restricted his wanderings to the homeland. In February he addressed an audience of 2,000 at the Queen's Hall in London. May found him preaching the word in Holloway and Brixton, whilst in November and December he was at Ealing and Surbiton revealing the wonders of ectoplasm.[17] He also found time to reply to a prolonged attack in the *Guardian* newspaper by G.R. Oakley, a Roman Catholic priest, who claimed that 'The great names of Sir Oliver Lodge and Sir Conan Doyle have cast a veil of a philosophical and scientific character over the blatant dangers of popular spiritism . . . they are taken today by the multitude to be the prophets of that which the multitude knows as "spiritualism" and the result is dreadful beyond contemplation.'[18] Oakley argued that the practice of spiritualism led to widespread lunacy, a point with which Conan Doyle violently disagreed. As for spiritualists, he wrote to Lodge, they were noticeable for their sanity and good physical health. The claim regarding insanity had been proved unfounded by statistics many times over.[19]

The winter of 1924–5 saw no let-up in the great public debate which had rumbled on ever since the Great War, and once more Conan Doyle found himself in the limelight. In June 1925 the *Morning Post* ran a long series of articles by Conan Doyle and Sir Arthur Keith on the scientific basis of spiritualism. Sir William Crookes, spirit gloves, and ectoplasm were discussed by the two men in considerable depth, as well as the religious and philosophical implications of the movement. However, the articles were written in a good-natured and objective manner, a fact which relieved Conan Doyle immensely, particularly since the press was usually content to ridicule spiritualist claims or dismiss them outright. The series produced a flood of letters which continued to fuel the debate for some while afterwards.[20]

In February 1925 Dr Crandon, the husband and promoter of Margery, had written to Conan Doyle informing him that the *Scientific American* committee had at last found the evidence against his wife to be non-conclusive.[21] Crandon was impressed by Dingwall who, alone among the investigators, had treated the medium with some humanity:

> He alone of an audience of fifteen hundred dared to get up and tell Houdini he was a liar. January 31, he addressed an audience of one thousand people declaring that the Scientific American Committee had missed an unique mediumship; that they had treated it as a burlesque or vaudeville; that he [Dingwall] had discovered nothing that suggested fraud or deceit at the sittings he had had . . . There was no limit to his enthusiasm here until he had conferences with the ever discreet Scotsman, McDougall, who, alas, is not economically free. McDougall filled him with the hypothesis that Margery and I are putting over a gigantic intellectual hoax with the purpose of finally showing that the best psychic researchers may be fooled with the intent to throw back psychic research forty years. Since then Dingwall has been more gloomy than ever . . .[1]

The Margery mediumship affair did not end there. Two years later, in June 1927, another thumbprint was obtained of the control, Walter. This time the print was so clear that it could be matched with the Navy Department's records. When this was done the print was found to be reversed. Conan Doyle immediately wrote to Crandon and asked for photographs of the prints to be sent to him. He then sent them to an ex-Scotland Yard expert and had them microscopically examined.[22] The results confirmed the American conclusions.

In August 1925 Sir Arthur embarked on a venture which subsequently was to cause him considerable financial heartache. When the lease of the ground floor and basement of Abbey House, 2 Victoria Street, Westminster, became free, he saw it as a wonderful opportunity to establish in the centre of London a psychic bookshop, library, and museum. It had been an idea he had entertained for a long time. Inside the premises he exhibited books, tracts, publications of his own, and those of leading psychic investigators, including Richet, Geley, Schrenck-Notzing, Crawford, and Crookes, and a number of apports and psychic photographs. As he told *Light*:

> It has long seemed to me, that one of the weak points in our psychic movement is the complete disconnection between our splendid literature and the man in the street. He is as a

rule absolutely unaware of its existence . . . I would ask the support of all psychic students for this venture . . .[23]

Although the Psychic Bookshop was an initial success in the propaganda sense, there is evidence that it proved to be a considerable drain on Conan Doyle's resources. Five years later, in a letter to *Light*,[24] he admitted that it had cost him £5,000 (a considerable sum in those days) and he was anxious to turn the business into a limited company.

In September 1925 the highest of all accolades was granted to Sir Arthur when he was invited to Paris as acting president of the International Spiritualist Congress. The Conan Doyle family were both amazed and delighted when they arrived at the first meeting, held at the Salle Wagram. A vast crowd which had assembled to hear the Anglo-Celt pushed and shoved its way through police cordons in order to get into the hall. Outside, as Sir Arthur delivered his address and paid homage to his friend Gustave Geley (who had been tragically killed in a monoplane accident in July 1924), rioting groups continued to battle with the gendarmes. Inside hall the atmosphere was better, if not restrained. The slides got confused, owing to an inept projectionist, an error which gave the sceptics an opportunity to voice their criticisms. Eventually Conan Doyle lost his temper and quit the assembly.[25] The second lecture, on 10 September, started badly but concluded in a more civilized fashion. Despite these ructions, Conan Doyle was pleased with the outcome. After his return, he wrote to Lodge, claiming that the visit had been a great success and expressing his surprise at how eager the French were to obtain the facts.[26]   When he was not addressing the crowds in France, and the inhabitants of Ealing, Surbiton, and the like, Conan Doyle devoted his attention to more permanent matters which would serve as a memorial to the spiritualist movement. Not content with opening a psychic bookshop, he had conceived the idea of writing an authoritative history of spiritualism. He had already written a number of disconnected articles to this end which had appeared in various spiritualist journals (chiefly his old ally *Light*), and he now tried to interest his publishers. By this stage of his career, the publishers were growing increasingly dubious about the spiritualist works for, unlike Conan Doyle's fiction (and especially the Sherlock Holmes stories), these books did not enjoy good sales in Britain, although they were more popular in America. Eventually Cassells offered to do the book, although they insisted that part of the cost of publication should be met by Conan Doyle himself.

In order to ensure complete accuracy, Conan Doyle commissioned Leslie Curnow, a spiritualist who possessed one of the largest private collections on the subject in Britain, to write many of the chapters. Conan Doyle would have liked both their names to appear on the title page of the book, but the publishers insisted that Conan Doyle must take the credit, for obvious commercial reasons. Eventually Conan Doyle had to bow to pressure. *The History of Spiritualism* was published simultaneously in London and New York in 1926.

Although hardly read today, the monumental two-volume work provides a detailed account of the movement, although from a partisan point of view. Conan Doyle hoped that it would be a book which would be moderate and well-behaved,[27] and it certainly fulfils this criterion, despite some slips by Curnow which make for a number of inaccuracies. Since the history is large in scope, the reader experiences some disappointment that very few of Conan Doyle's own psychic experiences are included, and it has to be admitted that a number of the more controversial figures like Dr Henry Slade, the slate-writing hoaxer, are included without reservation.

Nevertheless, *The History of Spiritualism* was by far the most lively and accessible work on the subject available to its contemporary readers. The section on ectoplasm is particularly interesting to the modern reader, and the assessment of the visionary Swedenborg is well researched. Swedenborg held a special place in Conan Doyle's affections, probably because of his blend of religious fervour and mysticism.

> . . . his name must live eternally as the first of all modern men who has given a description of the process of death, and of the world beyond, which is not founded upon the vague ecstatic and impossible visions of the old churches, but which actually coresponds with the descriptions which we ourselves obtain from those who endeavour to convey back to us some clear idea of their new existence.[28]

Conan Doyle clearly believed that in writing the work with Curnow he was not merely producing a history of the movement but also providing confirmation of the religious message spiritualism offered the world:

> This history has endeavoured to show how special material signs have been granted by the invisible rulers of earth to satisfy the demand for material proofs which come from the increasing mentality of man. It was shown also how these material signs have been accompanied by spiritual messages, and how these messages get back to the great primitive religious forces of the world; the central fire of inspiration which has been ashed over by the dead cinders of what once were burning creeds. Man had lost touch with the vast forces which lie around him, and his knowledge and aspirations had become bounded by the pitiful vibrations which make up his spectrum and the trivial octaves which limit his range of hearing. Spiritualism, the greatest movement for 2,000 years, rescues him from this condition . . .[29]

Throughout 1925 Conan Doyle had also been busy with another major literary work. For some years now he had toyed with the idea of incorporating the spiritualist theme into a work of fiction which would feature one of his most popular creations. Sherlock Holmes was obviously unsuitable since he represented to the mind of the reading public logic, the rational processes, and the visible world. Holmes lived in a materialistic society and the demons he fought were clothed in human form. No, Holmes was out of the question, especially since to Conan Doyle he represented a significant proportion of the author's income and a means of sustaining his continued campaign. However, the old adventurer, dogmatist, and debunker George Edward Challenger would be entirely suitable. Challenger bore something of a resemblance to Joseph McCabe of the Rationalist Association. Like McCabe he was a no-nonsense materialist, a man who would consider the claims of the spiritualists to be patently absurd. Moreover, Challenger, once roused, would do his level best to expose the movement in a thoroughly ruthless manner. In all respects, Challenger provided Conan Doyle with the perfect foil for a book which would bring the message of the spiritualists home to the man in the street.

The title of the new book was originally intended to be 'The Psychic Adventures of Edward Malone' but the publishers persuaded Conan Doyle to change this to *The Land of*

Mist. 'I have for years had a big psychic novel in me which shall deal realistically with every phase of the question, pro and con,' Sir Arthur wrote to the editor of the *Strand Magazine* in October 1924. The *Strand*, which had been eager to print Conan Doyle's psychic observations, was only too happy to oblige with the serialization of the new book in 1925, prior to its publication in 1926.

The Land of Mist reintroduces us to the three stock characters of the Challenger series, Professor Challenger, Lord John Roxton, and Edward Malone. Professor Summerlee has died in Naples and sends Challenger a message at a meeting of spiritualists. Challenger, we learn, now an old and embittered man, has been widowed but is cared for by his daughter, Enid, a journalist who, with her friend Malone, is preparing a series of articles on churches for the *Daily Gazette*. The two colleagues visit a spiritualist service and, having made the acquaintance of some of the leaders of the movement, become converts. Lord John Roxton, a shadow of his former self, assists Malone in his researches into psychic phenomena and becomes convinced of the reality of the spirit world.

From the outset Challenger opposes the new cult, but eventually becomes a convert himself after an extraordinary psychic experience in which two men, Ware and Aldridge, 'come through'. Their names are of great significance to Challenger, for as a young doctor he had given the two patients a drug of the datura family in order to gauge its effects. Both had been later found dead and Challenger had assumed he had inadvertently killed them. However, the spirits confirm that they had died of natural causes. Challenger believes at last that he has been contacted by the dead, for what has happened cannot be explained by either telepathy or subconscious mind action. Moreover, the medium is his own daughter and therefore incapable of trickery.

Although the book differs greatly from its predecessors in the series in that the main characters seem altogether more sombre and humourless, one of the chief features of interest is the factual background to many of the major episodes. The incident concerning Nell Gwynne, for example, mentioned by Lord John Roxton in Chapter 9, was told to Conan Doyle by Colonel Cornwallis West, who experienced the haunting in his own country home, whilst the account of the occupant of the deserted house is based on the experience of Lord St Audries in a house near Torquay. Dr Maupuis is based on Dr Geley, whom Conan Doyle knew and admired, whilst the account of Pitnecanthropus in Chapter 12 of the narrative is taken from the *Bulletin de l'Institut Métaphysique*. The public debate in which Challenger bates his enemies (Chapter 13) is obviously partly based on Conan Doyle's own experience of the Queen's Hall debate when he encountered Joseph McCabe. This mix of fact and fantasy gives the work a documentary flavour which distinguishes it from the other novels in the Challenger series.

There is considerable emphasis in the book on the possible dangers of unseen forces which lie in wait for the inexperienced or uncommitted experimenter, and the emphasis throughout is upon the positive approach. The Rev. Charles Mason, one of the most attractive figures in the story, manages to rid a haunted house of an evil spirit purely by the exercise of prayer. In contrast, the Hammersmith grocer Bolsover, who represents the naïvely curious among dabblers, has held seances at his home for four years. 'It's a disease, this phenomena hunting,' comments one of the investigators. 'I know some of our people, women mostly, who buzz round seance rooms continually, seeing the same things over and over again . . . What the better are they for that as souls or as citizens or any other way?'

Before 1926 came to a close, several issues of psychic interest claimed Conan Doyle's attention. During the months of November and December an international symposium on spiritualism was held at Clark University, Massachusetts. A number of distinguished psychic investigators and leading spiritualists had been asked to participate, including among others Sir Oliver Lodge, Dr Crandon, William McDougall, and Walter Prince. Harry Houdini had been invited, but had died in the interim, the victim of an unexpected attack by a martial arts student which had ruptured his appendix and caused peritonitis. Conan Doyle's contribution (he was unable to attend) consisted of an essay entitled 'The Psychic Question As I See It'. Having traced the history of the movement in Britain and the USA, Conan Doyle had this to say about spiritualism's shortcomings:

The weaker side of spiritualism lies in the fact that its adherents have largely been drawn from the less educated part of the community . . . the result has been to bring about a presentment of the philosophy which has often repelled earnest minds, and in no way represents its true scope and significance. Again, there has been no systematic cultivation of the gift of mediumship–this also being the fault of the community and the law; with the result that it has often fallen into unworthy hands and been exercised for purely utilitarian and worldly motives . . . Again, a retinue of rogues have been attracted to the Movement by the fact that seances have been largely held in the dark when the object has been to produce physical phenomena. This has served as a screen for villainy, and the effect has been increased occasionally by the systematic use of conjurer's apparatus . . .[30]

This note of caution had empirical foundations. By this stage in his career as a spiritualist and psychic investigator, Conan Doyle had encountered a number of fraudulent mediums, and his experiences with the late Harry Houdini and other like-minded opportunists had encouraged him to be wary of zealous detractors also. Above all he had learnt that as a public campaigner he could not rely upon the press to provide an impartial view of the great issues which so concerned him.

If confirmation were needed of this latter point, it was provided when in the spring of 1927 Conan Doyle's *Pheneas Speaks* was published by his own Psychic Press and Bookshop. Conan Doyle believed that these messages received through his wife's mediumship were important for the general public because they confirmed the existence of a complex spiritual design and hierarchy in the afterlife. As he observed in his preface: 'We would beg the most orthodox reader to bear in mind that God is still in touch with mankind, and that there is as much reason that he should send messages and instructions to a suffering and distracted world as ever there was in days of old.'

Pheneas Speaks did not include any messages pertaining to the forthcoming apocalypse. It seems certain that he had intended to publish this material at a later date, but decided that its implications might be misinterpreted by the anti-spiritualist lobby.

In January 1928 H.G Wells wrote a scathing attack in the *Sunday Express*, accusing Conan Doyle of misleading the public. *Pheneas Speaks*, he said, was 'a platitudinous bore',

and as for Pheneas, 'Ever since 1922 he has been promising
wonderful changes for the better in human life and knowledge' but the prophecies had not been fulfilled. Wells went
on:

> This Pheneas, I venture to think, is an imposter, wrought of
> self-deception, as pathetic as a rag doll which some lonely
> child has made for its own comfort . . . We are told of floods
> of spiritual light, and, behold! 'Pheneas Speaks!' Wonderful
> prophecies are spoken of. Where are they?
> For me, the most fatal line of thought for all this stuff lies in
> the steadily changing ideas of modern people about indi-
> viduality. Beneath all these necromancies is an assumption of
> the complete and incurable integrity of the eternal human
> person from the rest of the universe.[31]

Conan Doyle was outraged. Platitudinous Pheneas might
be, but his prophecies had been fulfilled. Since 1923, the
world had been in a state of unrest, especially in Russia,
where the Bolshevist Revolution had manifested itself. Ear-
thquakes and other indications of unrest had also been
witnessed. Pheneas had stated that unless humanity reformed itself, events would culminate in a major trouble. No
precise date had been fixed for such an event, but this did
not mean that the prophecy was invalid.

The Pheneas dispute was typical of the kind of debate in
which Conan Doyle found himself embroiled towards the
end of his life. Increasingly, it appeared to him, he was cast
as an outsider by the camp followers of convention. Orthodox scientific belief remained as entrenched now over the
question of verification as it had been when he was a
medical student, whilst the established Church lacked all
vision. In the last two years of his existence this feeling of
isolation was to intensify so that he was driven back to the
solace offered by his friends and family. Despite this, his
faith in the message that spiritualism had to offer a materialistic world never once faltered.

CHAPTER 10

The Final Phase

In the winter of 1928 Conan Doyle and his family embarked on a tour of southern Africa. Although this expedition was primarily spiritualistic in intention, it is clear from reading his account of the itinerary[1] that failing health had to some extent forced his hand. He particularly wished to see how conditions had changed since his involvement in the Boer War, some 28 years earlier, and therefore devoted a considerable amount of his attention to the study of the economic and political issues confronting the white colonies of Rhodesia, Kenya, Uganda, and Tan-ganyika.

When the Conan Doyles arrived in Cape Town on Monday 12 November 1928, after a somewhat stormy passage, it was perhaps fitting that he should give his first public address to an invisible audience in the form of a prepared radio talk. He told his South African listeners that he believed only a minority of people did not share his view that there was an afterlife. If there was no hereafter, why then should man strive to improve himself? The mass of mankind would argue that if there was only one life, and death ended all, our wisest course was to get as much pleasure as we might. The situation could only be met in one way. That one way was to prove that life existed after death and to demonstrate it scientifically, challenging conventional scientific method and meeting it on its own ground. The proofs he held were, in his opinion, unshakeable.

At the City Hall in Cape Town Conan Doyle addressed an audience of 1,750 and, as he later recalled,[1] 'They listened with indulgence if not aquiescence.' When the speaker asked for questions the results were somewhat amusing. 'If the other world is so pleasant,' asked one, 'why don't you all commit suicide?' and another asked, '*Must* I have the same husband?'

At Stellenborg Conan Doyle met with indifference and hostility. This was the very centre of the Dutch Reformed Church and the spiritualist campaigner was therefore a pariah. This was more than compensated for by an extraordinary seance conducted under the auspices of the Conan Doyles' friends the Ashton Jonsons. The medium, a Mrs Butters, was said to be controlled by the Italian opera singer Sabatini. Conan Doyle and his wife sat in semi-darkness as Mrs Butters sank into a trance. Then suddenly she stood up and began to sing 'Lascio chio panga' in a rich baritone. Conan Doyle recalled:

> She sang for about ten minutes, and Ashton Jonson, who is a musical critic of note and the author of the *Handbook of Chopin's Works*, assured me that the voice was not only undoubtedly male but of exceptional quality . . . then suddenly the song stopped and I heard the singer cry, 'Basta! Basta! (Enough! Enough!) A few minutes later the lady recovered from her trance and complained of pain and discomfort of her larynx, as if it had been unduly stretched.

Conan Doyle was greatly struck by the performance and found himself quite unable to believe that its origins were anything other than psychic.

The Conan Doyles moved on first to Durban and then to Johannesburg, where Sir Arthur lectured before an enormous if not always appreciative audience. Here he found spiritualism very much alive and flourishing and was impressed by a psychic photograph which he was shown. Known as the 'Rustenburg' picture, it showed a spirit face in a tree and was taken by a couple neither of whom believed in the cause.

At Johannesburg Conan Doyle gave no fewer than four lectures, all of them illustrated, the penultimate one dealing specifically with the Cottingley fairies. Even years after the discrediting of the Yorkshire girls, he found it hard to accept the possibility of fraud:

> I took the line in my lecture that I was prepared to consider any explanation of these results, save only one which attacked the character of the children. I am sure that when I had

explained the facts there were few in the Hall who were not prepared to accept the photographs.

In addition to the Cottingley photographs, Conan Doyle also showed his audience several German fairy photographs and a picture of a Devonshire tree spirit. His faith in the invisible world of the fairies remained unshakeable. Throughout his African trip Conan Doyle wrestled in his mind with the question of spiritualism's opponents. Eminently reasonable himself, he could not understand why some of the best minds of his age should adopt such dogmatic positions. A case in point was Bernard Shaw, who argued that since *he* had cheated at the seance table and successfully deceived spiritualists all phenomena were therefore entirely worthless. It seems that Conan Doyle could never understand the more base and devious aspects of human nature and was always dismayed to see these aspects in practice.

After many years spent lecturing, attending seances, investigating psychic phenomena, and supporting the spiritualist movement in a variety of ways, Conan Doyle had come to the conclusion that of all its meanings the religious aspect of his 'new revelation' was not only the most enduring but also offered a possibility of hope for mankind. He had seen many members of his own family struck down by a world war which by the late 1920s had revealed itself to be largely based on materialistic motives; he had watched as science moved further and further away from the spiritual and creative dimensions of mankind. Organized religion remained ossified, a legacy of traditional nineteenth-century values which to Conan Doyle seemed to represent a misinterpretation of Christ's teachings. In Conan Doyle's mind spiritualism needed to grow in both popularity and influence. Once it had gained a world-wide momentum it would lead humanity away from materialism altogether. In *Our African Winter* he wrote:

> I see more clearly that this revelation is the most important which mankind has ever had and that we who are spreading it are doing the most vital work that is done in the world today; . . . I feel a sympathy for those who desire that the movement should be kept quite unconnected with any special creed. It is a broad, noble ideal. But it is not practical and it blocks the way and hinders our advance. If all religions are to be drawn together by this new knowledge there

should be two stages, not one, in the process. The first stage should be that each great religion should separately within its own ranks learn and admit the new revelation. Then the second stage should be that all religions, finding that they have this definite knowledge in common, should draw closer to each other. But the first stage is essential, and that is what our leaders have not seen. In a Christian civilization it is necessary that the personality and ethics of the Christ should be proclaimed in connection with our psychic knowledge, and that the two should be joined together . . . A European Spiritualist should in broad sense be a Christian.

When Conan Doyle talked of Christianity he did not view it in a traditional theological sense. To him Christ was a gifted medium whose example offered humanity a moral code. In essence Jesus Christ was much the same as the other founders of the ancient religions. However, it was Christ's spiritual dimension, his contact with the unseen world, which impressed Conan Doyle. Therefore a man might be a Christian and a spiritualist without any implied contradiction.

Conan Doyle and his family left for England on 13 March 1929. Conan Doyle himself was more than ever convinced that the tour had been a success, despite the indifference and sometimes open hostility shown by some of his audiences. Before the trip he had become weary of the incessant fight which he was forced to wage against the opposition. The sights and sounds of Africa had refreshed him and provided his growing family with a considerable amount of freedom and excitement. 'We come back,' he said, 'each of us, stronger in health, more earnest in our beliefs, more eager to fight once more in the greatest of all causes, the cause of the regeneration of religion and of the restoration of that direct and practical spiritual element which is the one and only antidote to scientific materialism.'

Whilst he was touring Africa Conan Doyle was devoting a considerable proporiton of his time and energy to the solution of a problem. For centuries the Witchcraft Act, placed on the statute books in the reign of King James I, had provided the authorities with a convenient method of prosecuting professional mediums. It was one of Conan Doyle's burning ambitions to get the Act altered and legitimize the mediums. In April 1929, in a letter to *Light*, he suggested that a clause be inserted in the Act to the effect that 'No criminal proceedings shall be instituted or carried on against any person acting or purporting to act as a spiritualist medium'. The spiritualist movement must persuade politicians by acting as a political lobby, for among the 500 registered churches were thousands of people who could persuade the political parties of the necessity of this course of action. If they missed this opportunity before the forthcoming general election, Conan Doyle pointed out, the same routine of secret information from the bigots to the police would continue, the same harassment and imprisonment of honest mediums. He explained:

> We have no desire to uphold cheats or charlatans, but at present the very existence of spiritual powers is in practice denied by the law of England, and the Apostolic circle would have been as liable to criminal arrest as are our mediums. This is an intolerable situation.[2]

Conan Doyle was prepared to stick his neck out over this issue. In August 1929 he wrote to his friend Lodge explaining that the way of achieving freedom from police prosecution would be political. He estimated that the spiritualistic vote was at least 250,000 and announced his intention to vote Labour if the Government refused to act.[3]

In between fighting for the mediums and circulating his *Open Letter to Those of My Generation* (a final appeal to his contemporaries to embrace spiritualism), Conan Doyle was dealing with several matters of psychic interest. In July 1929, on a visit to England, Dr and Mrs Wickland, his friends from California, sat with Conan Doyle and his wife. The company were able to contact Lodge's son Raymond, and Kingsley. Conan Doyle regarded the Wicklands as a most remarkable pair.[4] In August Conan Doyle drove the Wicklands to see the moated manor house Groombridge Place, near Tunbridge Wells. (This was the place he had in mind when he wrote the last of his Sherlock Holmes novels, *The Valley of Fear*.) Shortly after a guided tour of the premises, Mrs Wickland kept glancing back and claimed that she was being followed by a strange, hunched old man dressed in knee-breeches, a striped waistcoat, and a short coat, who had exited form an open door next to the moat. Back at Conan Doyle's home Mrs Wickland became possessed and in an instant revealed the ghost that had pursued her to be an ostler who had been drowned at Groombridge by his master. Dr Wickland reassured 'David' by telling him that he was indeed dead.

> 'You can do anything now by the power of thought, if you know how to use it (he advised the spirit). This hump of yours. Take it off. Take it off, I say. Your back is as straight as mine.' (The bent figure began to straighten up and sit erect in the chair.)[5]

Reunited with his mother, the ostler then disappeared into the hereafter.

A rather more alarming event shook the Conan Doyles in the summer of 1929 when the cottage which they used as a country retreat at Bignell Wood was badly burned by fire. In a letter to Lodge, Conan Doyle revealed the fire's psychic origins. He told Lodge that soon after the incident his wife had received a message explaining that some 200 years ago the house had had a bad psychic aura and that the building must be excoriated so as to render it suitable for high spiritualistic purposes. In the previous week Conan Doyle's friend Ashton Smith had had a sitting with the medium, Mrs Scales where the message had been confirmed. As to the prophecy of Pheneas, the reference to the 'coming events' was connected to a harvest time which was unspecified. It appeared that beings of this order foresaw the future in terms of pictures.[6]

By the autumn of 1929 Conan Doyle must have known that his greatest adventure was shortly to commence. On 11 November he wrote to Lodge explaining that his suspected angina had now been confirmed by his own doctor and that in future he must avoid meetings.[7] Time was growing short and he realized that he must persist if he wished to change the legislation regarding mediums.

Meanwhile he could not fail his fellow spiritualists whatever the state of his health. In October he visited Holland, Denmark, Stockholm, and Oslo on a short lecture tour, despite his doctor's advice, and found the time to produce a well-argued defence of the spiritualist movement in his pamphlet *The Roman Catholic Church – A Rejoinder*. This work was a spirited reply to *Modern Spiritualism*, by his former schoolmate the Jesuit Fr Herbert Thurston, which had been published in 1928. The style of Conan Doyle's writing betrays an angry and embittered man, weary of the prejudice and absurd dogma of the Catholic Church. Yet underlying this is a feeling of immense strength and conviction. Thurston's arguments are dealt with one by one, revealing the essential pettiness and misconception of the priest's reasoning. It was Conan Doyle's last blow in support of the freedom and integrity of the spiritualist movement.

The last major spiritualist work Conan Doyle wrote before his death was published in 1930. All the material in *The Edge of the Unknown* had previously appeared in various newspapers and journals from 1920 onwards, but Conan Doyle had extensively revised much of it, especially the essay on 'The Alleged Posthumous Writings of Known Authors'. In the short preface to the work he penned these telling words:

> We who believe in the psychic revelation, and who appreciate that a perception of these things is of the utmost importance, certainly have hurled ourselves against the obstinacy of our time. Possibly we have allowed some of our lives to be gnawed away in what for the moment seemed a vain and thankless quest. Only the future can show whether the sacrifice was worth it. Personally, I think it was.

Before his demise, Conan Doyle was to fight one final battle against the cynics and sceptics. A book had been published, entitled *Modern Psychic Mysteries*, which gave a detailed account of some remarkable psychic phenomena which had taken place at Millesimo Castle, near Genoa. Conan Doyle had read the account and been convinced of the verifiable nature of the phenomena. The Marquis Scotto, whose son had died, had inaugurated the sittings at which a variety of familiar psychic incidents transpired, including the blowing of aluminium trumpets, sudden inexplicable breezes, and the appearance and disappearance of numerous objects. When the book was subsequently translated into English by G.K. Hack and published in Britain, a scathing review appeared, written by Theodore Besterman, the editor of the *Journal of the Society of Psychical Research*. For Conan Doyle this was the last straw. He had in the past been outraged by the treatment the SPR had allowed Price to mete out to Hope and regarded this present slur upon the Marquis and the author, Professor Bozzano, as unforgivable.

Unable to travel and voice his opinion in person, Conan Doyle penned a long letter announcing his resignation from the Society and explaining his reasons. This he circulated to all the members of the SPR.

Besterman was eager to justify his opinion and circulated a reply. The SPR was concerned not with opinions but with facts, and if Sir Arthur Conan Doyle considered his conclusions to be inaccurate then let him put forward facts and not opinions. Undaunted, Conan Doyle wrote back to the *Journal*:

> The work of the Society is bound to be sterile as long as they are cut off from the raw material of their study, which is their position at present . . . There is a general assumption in many of the Society's papers that the spiritualists are so careless in their methods that their results may be disregarded. In the case of most spiritualists this idea is quite unfounded, but the fact that it should exist naturally predisposes them against the SPR . . . Surely it is evident that there are many phenomena which prove their own truth without any necessity for the constraints of special lights and controls . . . The truth of such phenomena makes it even more incredible than before that large unwieldy objects are concealed in the clothing of the sitters, or that an Italian nobleman is translated from one end of his castle to another, through several locked doors, by complicated method of fraud so cleverly carried out that none of the experienced sitters could detect it, and it requires critics in London to show how it can be done.[8]

Conan Doyle felt fully justified in offering his resignation. He was of the opinion that the Society had done no constructive work of importance since the death of one of its founder members, F.W.H. Myers. The SPR was dominated by a small circle of reactionaries whose influence was entirely negative. They had 'long been not a help but a hindrance to the psychical knowledge of the world', and he believed that a strong protest was called for.

Only a few weeks before he died, Sir Arthur Conan Doyle wrote to the Home Secretary about the Witchcraft Act, and it was agreed that a group of interested representatives should discuss the matter with him. On behalf of the group Conan Doyle suggested that the proposed amendment be embodied in a Private Member's Bill and introduced to Parliament as soon as possible.

It was the last public appearance he was to make. On 7th July 1930 he lapsed into a state of unconsciousness and died on the following morning. Up until the last he had fought the good fight. On the morning of the announcement of his death, for example, the *Daily Herald* published an interview with him on spiritualism which had been conducted only a few days previously.

At Conan Doyle's funeral there were few signs of mourning. Beautiful sunshine flooded the grounds at 'Windlesham' as his body was laid to rest in a flower-lined grave. Standing in a rectangle around the garden grave were 300 guests, many of them literary friends, other spiritualists who had come convinced that they had not heard the last from Sir Arthur. Having offered up a prayer, the Rev. C. Thomas (himself a spiritualist) read out a statement from Lady Conan Doyle which might have been written by the Grand Old Man of spiritualism himself:

> We know that it is only the natural body that we are committing to the ground. The etheric body . . . is the exact duplicate, and lives on, and is able when the psychic conditions are attuned to the spiritual, even to show itself to earthly human eyes. The beloved one here will continue to keep in close touch with the family, although they may not have the power to see his presence. Only those who have that God given extra sight – clairvoyance – will be able actually to see his form . . . Sir Arthur will continue to carry on the work of telling the world the truth.

'He is not dead,' concluded the priest. How apt those words seemed to his family and countless followers. On 13 July a memorial service was held for Arthur Conan Doyle at the Royal Albert Hall, London. Eight thousand people attended. Many of his lifelong friends, including the Rev. Vale Owen, Drayton Thomas, and Hannen Swaffer, the renowned medium, gave speeches and the medium Estelle Roberts claimed to have seen Conan Doyle's figure in evening dress walk to the empty chair which had been set in his memory between Jean and Denis.

It was, of course, inevitable that the mediums should come forward with a variety of claims so soon after Conan Doyle's death. Messages flooded in from New York, Paris, and other parts of Europe. Eventually Lady Conan Doyle was forced to act and issued a statement in which she stressed that, without her own confirmation, communications of this type should be ignored.

A number of these 'official' messages were given credence

by Sir Arthur's widow. A few days after Conan Doyle's funeral, the medium Minesta (alias Mrs Grace Cooke) visited Crowborough, where she was welcomed by Lady Conan Doyle and her family. Through the medium Conan Doyle spoke to his family, providing them with a number of intimate details.[9] Then on 28 July Lady Conan Doyle announced to the British press that she had established communication with her husband through a spirit photograph. The photograph in question had been produced on 14 July by the psychic photographer and friend of Conan Doyle, William Hope. Hope, who had been visited by the Rev. Charles L. Tweedale, the vicar of Weston, offered Tweedale a new unopened packet of plates which Tweedale then signed. Having examined the camera, lens, slide, and background most meticulously, Tweedale put the plates into his pocket after exposure and then developed them himself.[10] Four plates were exposed. On the first were four faces in cloudy banks of ectoplasm, circling Tweedale's head on which one face was partly superimposed. Two of the plates showed the unmistakable face of Conan Doyle, with its drooping moustache and upward-swept hair. Before the second pair of plates was exposed, Tweedale asked the spirit not to show up directly over his own face. When these two plates were developed, Tweedale found the face had left the ring of ectoplasm above him and established itself next to, but not touching, his head. This photograph showed Conan Doyle as a much younger man.

At a subsequent seance with the medium 'B', Tweedale and his wife obtained messages from Conan Doyle, claiming that the afterlife was an exact copy of the world, that spiritualists must commit themselves to fighting the materialism of the churches, and that 'there is no hell except what a man makes for himself, no eternal punishment in fire, as the Churches, especially the Roman, threaten. Later [he concluded] as I gain strength, I shall have much to say about conditions here and surroundings.'[11]

Other revelations were to follow. In January 1931 the first of many messages were received from Conan Doyle through the medium Minesta, in which Conan Doyle set out a full restatement of spiritualism.[12] The following month, Lady Conan Doyle and her younger son, Adrian, attended a seance at the home of H. Dennis Bradley in Kingston Vale, London. Here, through the medium George Valiantine, they talked with Sir Arthur about family matters for nearly an hour and a half. In May another spirit photograph was produced showing Conan Doyle after the ageing Mrs Deane was summoned to the Stead Library. Sadly, Mrs Deane was able to produce only the one photograph.

These messages from Sir Arthur continued on and off for many years. In 1936, for example, when Lady Conan Doyle was ill with cancer, her illness had apparently been diagnosed by Sir Arthur before the medical diagnosis was given. Right up until the time of her death in 1940 Lady Conan Doyle was receiving messages in the form of warnings to her sons about possible accidents and advice on specific business investments. Lady Conan Doyle continued to believe in her husband's spirit existence up until her death.

Conan Doyle's son Denis shared his mother's faith. In February 1931 he told a spiritualist gathering in Portsmouth that three weeks earlier he had received a message which had come from his father.[13] A person whom he had met told him that through a medium he had received the following message: 'Tell the boys that I am very glad they had got the Chitty. Tell them to be careful of her.' Two weeks before this Denis had purchased a racing car called Chitty Chitty Bang Bang and the purchase had been kept a secret. Moreover, the man who had passed on the message to him had no knowledge of the transaction.

With the passing of the decades there have been fewer and fewer communications from Sir Arthur Conan Doyle. How one explains this depends to a large extent on whether one is prepared to accept the claims made for spiritualism. Since the 1930s considerable advances have been made in the field of psychic investigation, and today's experiments are admittedly much more carefully controlled than many of those in which Sir Arthur Conan Doyle participated. After such a passage of time it would be wrong to justify or condemn these experiments, for the evidence we have is second-hand and the experiments themselves are unrepeatable.

It would perhaps be more profitable to address the question *why* Arthur Conan Doyle chose spiritualism as his most deeply felt cause. And it is here that I should like to turn the question around, for it is almost certain that spiritualism found *him*.

Throughout his early life Arthur Conan Doyle had searched for evidence of a pattern or meaning to the universe – one in which humanity played a part. Orthodox religion – and especially Roman Catholicism – based as it was on a narrow misinterpretation of the moral example of Christ, could not sustain such a framework. Scientific theory, concerning itself only with evidential methods and material, likewise failed to provide a satisfactory answer. As a writer, Conan Doyle understood the importance of the psyche. His own imagination and understanding of the creative process led him to regard those irrational and instinctual parts of the mind as worthy of investigation.

And there was one other important part of the jigsaw which led him to spiritualism. Conan Doyle had been trained as a doctor, and under his old mentor, Joe Bell, he knew the importance of analysis and intuitive thought methods. He understood that not only was logical analysis required, but also any believable view of reality had to rely on a model which accounted for both the conscious *and* the subconscious. Rather like Sigmund Freud, his contemporary, he looked around for a framework upon which to hang his training, hopes, and beliefs.

Spiritualism provided the answer. When as a young man he first began his investigations, Conan Doyle was convinced that the truth about psychic phenomena could be established by a purely scientific method. As the years passed he began to realize that the material under examination was inextricably linked with the workings of the psyche. Then he made a breakthrough and grasped the central tenet that the phenomena under consideration could be verified independently of the mind of the medium. Having got this far, he made the final leap into the beyond. Spiritualism was no longer a question of proof: it was a matter of sustainable faith.

How far was Conan Doyle forced along this tortuous path? Certainly he was correct in concluding that spiritualism could not be acceptable as a pseudo-science since it did not fulfil scientific criteria. There is also evidence to suggest that he found the working-class basis of the spiritualist movement irksome with its emphasis on incessant 'proofs' and the limited accomplishments of the seance table. Conan Doyle was far more interested in the bigger achievements of men such as Crawford, Geley, and Schrenck-Notzing. This largely explains his fascination with ectoplasm, which he saw as the living proof being provided by the spirit-world through the agency of the medium.

In order for it to be intellectually acceptable to him, Conan Doyle *had* to believe in spiritualism as a new religion. And as a religion it was both pan-religious and revolutionary in its implications. In his own family circle he had seen at close hand the way in which the belief in a spirit world had revolutionized and reinvigorated the belief of the individual.

The effect of Conan Doyle's conversion to this new religion was certainly profound. As a writer his reputation was damaged; as a public figure he became something of an embarrassment, at least in the eyes of the press. Yet these considerations never once affected or altered his vision.

To some extent fate has indeed played a cruel trick on Arthur Conan Doyle. His sworn opponent was scientific materialism, yet as a religion spiritualism itself was perhaps *the* most materialistic response which the Victorian age produced. The irony is even more acutely felt when one considers that nearly 60 years after the author's death it is not spiritualism for which Arthur Conan Doyle is remembered, but Sherlock Holmes, that product of nineteenth-century rationalism who became a cult hero-figure to the Victorian middle classes. Holmes, who had no time for the supernatural, had provided Conan Doyle with the ladder to success, and, throughout his career as a writer, continued to dog his footsteps, a constant reminder that man's dreams, whether they be verifiable or not, could only exist once the materialistic needs of the individual were satisfied. For this reason, if for no other, it is worth remembering Conan Doyle's adventures among the spirits.

Notes

1 An Unusual Childhood

1 Arthur Conan Doyle, *The Coming of the Fairies* (London: Hodder & Stoughton, 1922), p. 9.
2 *New York World*. Reported in Pierre Nordon, *Conan Doyle* (London: John Murray, 1966), p. 19.
3 Ibid., p. 3.
4 Arthur Conan Doyle, *Memories and Adventures* (London: Hodder & Stoughton, 1924), p. 12.
5 Nordon, *Conan Doyle*, p. 4.
6 Michael Bond, *The Doyle Diary* (London: Paddington Press, 1978).
7 *Memories and Adventures*, p. 16.
8 John Dickson Carr, *The Life of Sir Arthur Conan Doyle* (London: John Murray, 1949), pp. 8–9.
9 *Memories and Adventures*, p. 38.
10 *The Doyle Diary*, p. xxii.
11 Ibid., p. xxviii.
12 Ibid., p. 87.
13 *Memories and Adventures, p. 15.*
14 Owen Dudley Edwards, *The Quest for Sherlock Holmes* (Edinburgh: Mainstream, 1983), p. 34.
15 Adrian M. Conan Doyle, *The True Conan Doyle* (London: John Murray, 1945), p. 10.
16 *Memories and Adventures*, p. 16.
17 Ibid., pp. 19–20.
18 *The Idler*, January 1893.
19 *Memories and Adventures*, p. 22.
20 James Joyce, *Portrait of the Artist as a Young Man* (Penguin Books), p. 111.

21 *Memories and Adventures*, p. 39.
22 Fr Herbert Thurston, *Modern Spiritualism* (London: Sheen & Ward, 1928).
23 Arthur Conan Doyle, *The Roman Catholic Church–A Rejoinder (London: The Psychic Press, 1929)*.
24 *Memories and Adventures*, p. 26.
25 *The Roman Catholic Church–A Rejoinder*, p. 58.
26 Ibid., p. 47.
27 *Memories and Adventures*, p. 24.

2 Dreamland and Ghostland
1 See Edwards, *The Quest for Sherlock Holmes*, pp. 150–1.
2 Ibid., p. 151.
3 Ibid., p. 162.
4 *Memories and Adventures*, p. 31.
5 Edwards, *The Quest for Sherlock Holmes*, pp. 181–2.
6 *Memories and Adventures*, pp. 37–8.
7 Arthur Conan Doyle, *Uncollected Stories*, edited and with an introduction by John Michael Gibson and Richard Lancelyn Green (London: Secker & Warburg, 1982), p. ix.
8 *Memories and Adventures*, p. 40.
9 Ibid., pp. 40–1.
10 Nordon, *Conan Doyle*, pp. 54–5.
11 Arthur Conan Doyle, *The History of Spiritualism* (London: Cassell & Co., 1926), vol. 1, p. 290. Conan Doyle is quoting from the *London World*.
12 'That Little Square Box', *London Society*, Christmas 1881, pp. 52–64.
13 *Memories and Adventures*, p. 75.
14 Edwards, *The Quest for Sherlock Holmes*, p. 280.
15 Arthur Conan Doyle, *The Stark Munro Letters* (London: Longman Green & Co., 1895), p. 45.
16 *Ibid.*, p. 47.
17 *Ibid.*, pp. 100–1.
18 *Ibid.*, p. 62.
19 *Ibid.*, p. 336.
20 William Winwood Reade, *The Martyrdom of Man* (London: Kegan Paul, Trench, Trübner & Co., 1872).
21 Geoffrey Stavert, *A Study in Southsea* (Portsmouth: Milestone Publications, 1987), p. 31.
22 See Ibid., p. 44.

The Survival of Bodily Death

1 'John Barrington Cowles', *Cassell's Saturday Journal*, vol. 1 (12 and 19 April 1884), pp. 433–5 and 461–3. The story was not anthologized by the author.

2 'The Great Keinplatz Experiment', *Belgravia Magazine*, vol. 57 (July 1885), pp. 52–65.

3 Jack Hawkins died at the end of March and was buried at Highland Road Cemetery.

4 Stavert, *A Study in Southsea*, p. 97.

5 An extract from a history of the Ford family compiled by R.A. Parker. See ibid., p. 97.

6 Society for Psychical Research Archives, 4 November 1922. (Hereafter cited as SPR.)

7 *Memories and Adventures*, p. 103.

8 Ibid., p. 104.

9 Arthur Conan Doyle, *The New Revelation* (London: Hodder & Stoughton, 1918), p. 14.

10 *Memories and Adventures*, p. 101.

11 So John Dickson Carr, Doyle's third biographer, informs us. The original seance notebooks are part of the large repository of Conan Doyle papers locked in litigation.

12 *Memories and Adventures*, p. 101.

13 Letter to *Light*, 2 July 1887, p. 303.

14 See Harry Kellehar, 'A Magician's Tour Up and Down and Round About the Earth', *Leisure Hours*, March–May 1892.

15 See Stavert, *A Study in Southsea*, p. 141.

16 See ibid., pp. 145–7.

17 Conan Doyle lunched at Greenwich with a representative of the publishers and the illustrious Oscar Wilde. As a result of this meeting, Wilde penned *The Picture of Dorian Gray*.

4 A Student of Psychic Phenomena

1 Quoted in Pierre Nordon's *Conan Doyle*, p. 150.

2 SPR Archives, no. 401.

3 Nordon, *Conan Doyle*, p. 151.

4 F.W.H. Myers, *Human Personality, and Its Survival of Bodily Death* (New York: Longmans Green & Co., 1903), vol. 1, p. 217.

5 Conan Doyle dates this episode as either 1892 or 1893, but there is evidence to suggest that it occurred later.

6 The room is a symbol of Conan Doyle's own conscious-

ness, a crucible of creativity. It is no coincidence that in the Sherlock Holmes stories the starting point of the adventures is the sitting-room of 221B Baker Street – a powerful and evocative magic.

7 *Memories and Adventures*, pp. 173–6. Pullen-Bury and Felkin were both members of the Golden Dawn. According to Ellic Howe (*The Magicians of the Golden Dawn*, Aquarian Press, 1985), Pullen-Bury was initiated into the Isis-Urania Temple on 27 November 1892 and by 1895 had become one of the Order's most active members. Dr Robert William Felkin joined the Amen-Ra Temple at Edinburgh on 10 March 1894 but transferred to the Isis-Urania group in London and by the end of 1896 was a member of the second Order of the Dawn.

8 See my monograph, *The Mythology of the Hound of the Baskervilles* (privately printed, Rochester, 1986; available from the author).

9 Charles Richet, *Thirty Years of Psychical Research* (London: Collins, 1923), vol. 2, p. 505.

10 See Charles Higham, *The Adventures of Conan Doyle* (London: Hamish Hamilton, 1976), p. 196.

5 The Vital Message

1 Reported by Charles Higham in *The Adventures of Conan Doyle*, pp. 232–3.

2 Hubert Stansbury, *In Quest of Truth* (London: Watts & Co., 1913, 268 pp.).

3 Conan Doyle provided a detailed account of this affair in a lecture he gave in Australia. This was reported in the *Sydney Morning Herald* in 1920. See Higham, *The Adventures of Conan Doyle* p. 256.

4 He was no doubt thinking of Flammarion, Richet, Geley, and his close friend Lodge.

5 SPR Archives, no. 405, 2 December 1916.

6 SPR Archives, no. 406, 11 March 1917.

7 Estelle Stead, the famous medium.

8 SPR Archives, no. 408, 3 April 1917.

9 See the *Journal of the Society for Psychical Research*, vol. 19 (January 1919), pp. 10–12.

10 *Two Worlds*, 18 January 1918, p. 19.

11 Reported in the *Hampshire Telegraph and Post*, Friday 20 September 1918.

A Spiritual Breakthrough

1 Introduction to Sydney A. Moseley *An Amazing Seance and an Exposure* (London: Sampson Low, Maston & Co., 1919), pp. ix–x.
2 *Sunday Express*, 9 March 1919, p. 2.
3 Moseley *An Amazing Seance and an Exposure*, pp. 104–11.
4 Introduction to ibid.
5 J.M. Wilson, *Life After Death: Two Lectures on Christianity and Spiritualism* (London: Hodder & Stoughton, 1920).
6 Reported in the *Two Worlds Christmas Supplement*, 19 December 1919, p. 10.
7 SPR Archives, no. 422.
8 See Joseph McCabe, *Verbatim Report of a Public Debate on the Truth of Spiritualism* (London: Watts & Co., 1920).
9 Arthur Conan Doyle, *The Vital Message* (London: Hodder & Stoughton, 1919), p. 82.
10 In 1848 America was astounded by the manifestations at Hydesville, NY. The episode marks a cornerstone in psychic history.
11 *Two Worlds*, Friday 5 September 1919.
12 W.J. Crawford, *The Reality of Psychic Phenomena* (London: Watkins, 1917).
13 *History of Spiritualism*, vol. 2, p. 116.
14 Gustave Geley, *Clairvoyance and Materialization* (London: T. Fisher Unwin, 1927).
15 Ibid., pp. 10–11.

7 A Missionary Zeal

1 Baron von Schrenck-Notzing, *Phenomena of Materialization* (London: Kegan Paul, Trench, Trübner & Co., 1920).
2 *Two Worlds*, vol. 33 (6 August 1920), p. 451.
3 Arthur Conan Doyle, *The Wanderings of a Spiritualist* (London: Hodder & Stoughton, 1921).
4 Ibid., p. 102.
5 *The Coming of the Fairies*.
6 SPR Archives, Doyle/Lodge Correspondence, no. 423.
7 *Sunday Chronicle*, 10 September 1922.
8 *The Wanderings of a Spiritualist*, p. 317.
9 See the *Hampshire Telegraph and Post*, 10 June 1921.
10 See *Two Worlds*, 21 October 1921.
11 See Higham, *The Adventures of Conan Doyle*, p. 272.
12 *Sunday Express*, 11 December 1921.
13 An early psychic photographer who was exposed in the USA.

14 *Saturday Review*, 21 January 1922.

8 Photographs and Fairies
 1 *Two Worlds*, vol. 35 (20 January 1922), p. 29.
 2 Arthur Conan Doyle, *The Case for Spirit Photography* (London: Hutchinson & Co., 1922), p. 41.
 3 Ibid., p. 43.
 4 SPR Archives, Doyle/Lodge Correspondence, no. 434.
 5 SPR Archives, Doyle/Lodge Correspondence, no. 440.
 6 SPR Archives, Doyle/Lodge Correspondence, no. 446.
 7 SPR Archives, Doyle/Lodge Correspondence, no. 455.
 8 *The Coming of the Fairies*, p. 88.
 9 Quoted in Charles Higham's *The Adventures of Conan Doyle*, p. 266. The issue of the Cottingley fairies has never been satisfactorily resolved. In recent times Elsie has claimed them to be false and has expressed pride in maintaining the hoax over so long a period. On the other hand Frances was keen to avoid stating her complicity in the matter and her daughter Christine continues to believe in the genuineness of the phenomena. Most commentators now believe that the photographs were fakes, but whether the girls did actually witness fairies remains open to dispute. For a fuller treatment of the issue see Janet Bord, 'Cottingley Unmasked', *Fortean Times*, no. 43 (Spring 1985), and Leslie Shepard, 'The Fairies Were Real', *Fortean Times*, no. 44 (Summer 1985).
10 Arthur Conan Doyle, *Our American Adventure* (London: Hodder & Stoughton, 1923), p. 10.
11 Reported in *Two Worlds*, vol. 35 (1922), p. 206.
12 Reported in Higham, *The Adventures of Conan Doyle*, p. 278.
13 Reported in *Two Worlds*, vol. 35, p. 218.
14 *Our American Adventure*, p. 81.
15 Ibid., p. 82.
16 *Two Worlds*, vol. 35, pp. 1–3.
17 Quoted in Bernard M.L. Ernst and Hereward Carrington, *Houdini and Conan Doyle: The Story of a Strange Friendship* (London: Hutchinson, 1933), pp. 51–2.
18 Ibid., p. 67.
19 Ibid., p. 70.
20 Ibid., p. 88.
21 Ibid., p. 144.
22 In *Our American Adventure*, however, Doyle records that

he himself asked Houdini to participate.
23 Ibid., pp. 180–1.
24 Ernst and Carrington, *Houdini and Conan Doyle*, p. 165.
25 Ibid., p. 172.
26 Higham, *The Adventures of Conan Doyle*, p. 290.
27 *Two Worlds*, vol. 35, pp. 557, 592.
28 Ibid., p. 365.
29 Ibid., p. 592.
30 Arthur Conan Doyle, *Pheneas Speaks* (London: The Psychic Press, 1927), p. 42.
31 F.W. Warrick, *Experiments in Psychics* (London: Rider & Co., 1938), p. 275.
32 SPR Archives, Doyle/Lodge Correspondence, no. 455.
33 *Two Worlds*, vol. 36, p. 144.

Another American Adventure
1 Arthur Conan Doyle, *Our Second American Adventure* (London: Hodder & Stoughton, 1924), p. 57.
2 Ibid., pp. 111–12.
3 Ibid., pp. 113–14.
4 Carl August Wickland, *Thirty Years Among the Dead* (London: The Spiritualist Press, 1924).
5 *Our Second American Adventure*, pp. 186–7.
6 Ibid., p. 227.
7 *Two Worlds*, vol. 36, p. 446.
8 Ibid., p. 308.
9 Quoted by Ernst and Carrington, *Houdini and Conan Doyle*, p. 193.
10 Quoted by Doyle in SPR Archives, Doyle/Lodge Correspondence, no. 476.
11 Quoted in 'The Margery Mediumship', in C. Murchison (ed.), *The Case For and Against Psychical Belief* (Massachusetts: Clark University, 1927), p. 80.
12 SPR Archives, Doyle/Lodge Correspondence, no. 463.
13 SPR Archives, Doyle/Lodge Correspondence, no. 483.
14 SPR Archives, Doyle/Lodge Correspondence, no. 539.
15 Ibid.
16 SPR Archives, Doyle/Lodge Correspondence, no. 490.
17 *Two Worlds*, vol. 37, pp. 104, 157, 237, 278–9, and 657.
18 SPR Archives, Doyle/Lodge Correspondence, newscutting (undated).
19 SPR Archives, Doyle/Lodge Correspondence, no. 494.
20 *Morning Post*, 15–22, June 1925.

21 SPR Archives, Doyle/Lodge Correspondence, nos. 503 and 505.
22 SPR Archives, Doyle/Lodge Correspondence, no. 544.
23 Letter to *Light*, 24 January 1925, p. 41.
24 Letter to *Light*, 5 July 1930.
25 Higham, *The Adventures of Conan Doyle*, p. 320.
26 SPR Archives, Doyle/Lodge Correspondence, no. 515.
27 SPR Archives, Doyle/Lodge Correspondence, no. 523.
28 *The History of Spiritualism*, vol. 1.
29 Ibid., vol. 2.
30 In Murchison (ed.), *The Case For and Against Psychical Belief*, p. 19.
31 H.G. Wells, 'What Is Immortality?', *Sunday Express*, 8 January 1928.

The Final Phase

1 Arthur Conan Doyle, *Our African Winter* (London: John Murray, 1929).
2 Letter to *Light*, 20 April 1929.
3 SPR Archives, Doyle/Lodge Correspondence, no. 560, 8 August 1929.
4 SPR, Doyle/Lodge Correspondence, no. 574.
5 Arthur Conan Doyle, 'The Ghost of the Moat' from *The Edge of the Unknown* (London: John Murray, 1930).
6 SPR, Archives, Doyle/Lodge Correspondence, no. 563.
7 SPR, Archives, Doyle/Lodge Correspondence, no. 564.
8 Letter to the SPR which Conan Doyle himself issued, 25 February 1930, SPR Archives, no. 569.
9 See Ivan Cooke (ed.), *The Return Of Sir Arthur Conan Doyle* (Hampshire: The White Eagle Publishing Trust, 1963), pp. 29–30.
10 *Two Worlds*, vol. 43, p. 478.
11 Account in ibid., p. 598.
12 See Cooke (ed.), *The Return Of Sir Arthur Conan Doyle*, for a full account.
13 *Hampshire Telegraph*, 27 February 1931.

Chronology

22 May 1859	Birth of Arthur Ignatius Conan Doyle at 11 Picardy Place, Edinburgh. Arthur was the second of 10 children born to Charles and Mary Doyle.
1865–7	Arthur Conan Doyle attends a day school in Edinburgh. Later (1869–9) he transfers to Hodder Preparatory School, Lancashire.
1870–5	Arthur Conan Doyle is enrolled at Stonyhurst Jesuit College, Lancashire, and later (1875–6) he transfers to Stonyhurst Branch School, Feldkirch, Austria. Whilst with the Jesuits the young Arthur becomes dismayed by their zealotry. Later in his career he is to react violently to their teachings.
October 1876	Conan Doyle enters Edinburgh Medical School and two years later becomes Student Assistant to Dr Richardson, Sheffield, Dr Elliot, Shropshire, and Dr Hoare, Birmingham (summer 1879).
September 1879	Conan Doyle published his first short story, 'The Mystery of the Sasassa Valley'.
	Conan Doyle's first medical publication describes his self-experimentation with the sedative gelsemium.
August 1881	Conan Doyle graduates as Batchelor of Medicine and Master of Surgery.

237

July 1882	Conan Doyle begins his own medical practice in Southsea, Portsmouth.
6 August 1885	Conan Doyle marries Louise Hawkins, youngest daughter of the late Jeremiah Hawkins at Thornton-in-Lonsdale parish church, Westmorland.
1885	Conan Doyle makes the acquaintance of Douglas Morey Ford, a solicitor. Douglas's wife, Honor, holds table-turning sessions in their home at Grand Parade, Portsmouth, where Conan Doyle participates as an interested party.
1886	'About this time,' Conan Doyle records in his memoirs, '. . . the family of a General whom I attended professionally became interested in table turning and asked me to come and check their results.' This was Major-General Alfred Drayson, a fellow member of the Portsmouth Literary and Scientific Society.
24 January 1887	Conan Doyle takes part in a number of seances with an acquaintance, Henry Ball. The seances, at which an experienced medium named Horstead was present, carried on until July.
2 July 1887	Conan Doyle sends a letter to the weekly periodical *Light*, in which he describes the results of a seance he has attended.
27 August 1887	Conan Doyle writes a second letter to *Light*, in which he calls himself a spiritualist.
November 1887	Conan Doyle publishes his first Sherlock Holmes story, *A Study in Scarlet*.
1889	Conan Doyle publishes his first historical novel, *Micah Clarke*.
7 May 1889	Mr John Beaumont of Bournemouth delivers a scathing attack on spiritualism at the Yorke Rooms, St Paul's Road, Portsmouth. In the *Portsmouth Evening News* two days later Conan Doyle responds to the challenge, sign-

ing himself 'Spiritualist'.

6 April 1891   Conan Doyle sets up as an eye specialist at 2 Devonshire Place, London. He receives few patients.

June 1891   Conan Doyle gives up his medical practice and devotes himself full-time to writing.

10 October 1893   Charles Doyle dies in the Crighton Royal Institution, Dumfries. Cause of death is given as epilepsy 'of many years' standing'.

November 1893   Conan Doyle joins the British Society for Psychical Research, just three weeks after the death of his father, Charles. Through the Society he mets such celebrated men as Sir Oliver Lodge, Arthur Balfour, and F.W.H. Myers.

January 1894   Shortly after receiving *The Transactions of the Society for Psychical Research*, which contains a lengthy address from Balfour on mesmerism, Conan Doyle begins his novella *The Parasite*, also about mesmerism and sexual obsession.
sexual obsession.

1906   Conan Doyle's first wife dies.

18 September 1907   Conan Doyle marries Jean Leckie, his second wife, at St Margaret's Church, Westminster. Jean's mediumistic powers will later prove to be of considerable interest to Sir Arthur. At first, however, Jean does not believe in spiritualism.

Winter 1907   Conan Doyle becomes fascinated by the extraordinary case of the medium 'Eva C.' through the reports made of her by Dr Charles Richet.

1914   Lily Loder-Symonds, Lady Conan Doyle's closest friend, comes to stay at 'Windlesham' (She had been a bridesmaid at Conan Doyle's second wedding.) Employed initially as a nanny to the Doyle children, she suffers from bronchial trouble and is bedridden most of the time. She develops the art of automatic writing and Conan Doyle becomes impressed by her powers.

Autumn 1916   Lily Loder-Symonds's condition worsens.

She produces startling messages from her brothers, all of whom have been killed at Ypres in April 1915. Conan Doyle quizzes Lily about a conversation he had had with Jean's brother Malcolm some years before. The accuracy of reply astonishes him, and from then on he becomes a committed believer in the afterlife.

4 November 1916   Conan Doyle publicly declares his belief in spiritualism in an article published in *Light*.

25 October 1917   Conan Doyle gives an address to the London Spiritualist Alliance at the Salon of the Royal Society of British Artists in Suffolk Street. The address is entitled 'The New Revelation'.

1918   Conan Doyle publishes *The New Revelation*, a book which was to represent his official view of spiritualism and its relevance to mankind.

1919   Conan Doyle publishes *The Vital Message*, a companion book to *The New Revelation*. The book, like its earlier counterpart, enjoys wide sales in Britain.

13 August 1920   Conan Doyle sails to Australia with his family on a missionary tour of the Antipodes. He arrives at Fremantle on 17 September and subsequently visits Adelaide, Melbourne, and Sydney. After a detailed excursion to New Zealand Conan Doyle is reunited with his family and the party sail home on 1 February 1921.

1920   Harry Houdini tours Britain. Learning that he is to perform at Portsmouth,

Conan Doyle takes his family to see the show. A firm friendship is cemented between the two men.

Conan Doyle publishes *Spiritualism and Rationalism*, his reply to Joseph McCabe's *Is Spiritualism Based On Fraud?* which had appeared earlier that year.

1921   Conan Doyle publishes *The Wanderings of a Spiritualist*, a geographical and discursive account of his tour of Australia and New Zealand.

1922   Conan Doyle writes his defence of the medium William Hope, entitled *The Case for Spirit Photography*. Hope had been accused of malpractice by Harry Price, who had attended a meeting of the Crewe circle in January. Conan Doyle maintained Hope to be a true psychic.

Conan Doyle publishes his controversial work about the Cottingley fairy photographs, entitled *The Coming of the Fairies*. The author had first heard of the business in May 1920.

9 April 1922   Conan Doyle and his family arrive in the USA ready for their lecture tour. In March 1922 he was advised by his spirit guide that he would leave his mark 'for ever upon America'. Conan Doyle draws large audiences in Boston, Washington, Philadelphia, New Haven, Buffalo, Toronto, Detroit, Toledo, and Chicago. He leaves for England on 24 June.

17 June 1922   Houdini stays with the Conan Doyles whilst they are in Atlantic City. On the Sunday following, Lady Conan Doyle invites Houdini to a private mediumistic sitting in her suite at the Ambassador Hotel. During the seance, Houdini contacts his dead mother. Later, in December 1922, Houdini refutes the evidence.

10 December 1922	Pheneas, Conan Doyle's spirit guide, comes through for the first time while Lady Conan Doyle is in semi-trance. Conan Doyle keeps a detailed record of the messages that follow.
3 April 1923	Conan Doyle arrives in New York, ready for his second tour of America and in response to the many spiritualists who had clamoured for his return. He travels via Rochester to Hydesville, Cleveland, Pittsburgh, Cincinnati, Indianapolis, Columbus, Chicago, St Louis, Kansas City, Denver, Salt Lake City, and thence to Los Angeles, where he meets Douglas Fairbanks and Mary Pickford. From San Francisco he journeys north to Portland, Seattle, Vancouver, then back through Edmonton, Calgary, Winnipeg, and Montreal. He leaves for England on 4 August.
1923	Conan Doyle publishes his account of his American lecture tour, which he entitles *Our American Adventure*.
1924	Conan Doyle publishes his account of his return visit to the USA in the volume *Our Second American Adventure*. Conan Doyle publishes his memoirs, entitled *Memories and Adventures*, in which he gives a full account of his conversion to spiritualism.
1925	His essay *Psychic Experiences* is printed as a separate volume. Conan Doyle publishes a defence of the spiritualist movement in his tract entitled *The Early Christian Church and Modern Spiritualism*.
29 August 1925	Conan Doyle opens his Psychic Bookshop, Library, and Museum on the gound floor and basement of Abbey House, 2 Victoria Street, Westminster. There he exhibits numerous books, apports, and psychic photographs.
5 September 1925	Conan Doyle arrives in Paris as acting

president of the International Spiritualist Congress. There he delivers two lectures on the topic of spiritualism.

1926 Conan Doyle's monumental work entitled *The History of Spiritualism* is published simultaneously in London and New York. Parts of the work were written by Conan Doyle and other parts by Leslie Curnow, a spiritualist who possessed one of the largest private libraries on the subject in England. Conan Doyle's contributions had already appeared as a series of disconnected articles in a number of spiritualist journals.

Conan Doyle publishes his Professor Challenger story *The Land of Mist*. The title was originally 'The Psychic Adventures of Edward Malone' and the MS was completed on 24 February 1925. In October 1924, Conan Doyle wrote to the editor of the *Strand*: 'I have for years had a big psychic novel in me which shall deal realistically with every phase of the question, pro and con.'

11 November 1926 Conan Doyle addresses 5,000 people on Armistice Day at the Albert Hal. Leading spiritualists Vale Owen and Estelle Stead join him in prayer.

21 March 1927 Conan Doyle publishes a collection of spirit communications received by Lady Conan Doyle between 21 July 1921 and 26 November 1926, under the title *Pheneas Speaks: Direct Spirit Communications in the Family Circle Reported by Arthur Conan Doyle, M.D., LL.D.* Pheneas was an Arabian spirit guide who was contacted through the mediumship of Conan Doyle's second wife.

Winter 1928–9 Conan Doyle tours southern Africa with his family. He visits parts of the Union, North and South Rhodesia,

Kenya, Uganda, and Tanganyika. He reaches Cape Town on 12 November and leaves for home on 13 March. Although his tour is primarily spiritualistic in intention, he comments widely on economic and political questions in the book he compiles during this tour.

1929   Conan Doyle publishes his account of his African tour, *Our African Winter*.

Conan Doyle tours Scandinavia and Holland, where he gives spiritualist lectures.

Conan Doyle publishes another defence of the spiritualist movement in his pamphlet *The Roman Catholic Church–A Rejoinder*. This work is a reply to the Jesuit Fr Herbert Thurston's *Modern Spiritualism*, published in 1928. Father Thurston, who had been at Stonyhurst with Conan Doyle, was an avowed opponent of the movement.

August 1929   Dr and Mrs Carl A. Wickland, friends of the Doyles from California, visit them at 'Windlesham'. Conan Doyle takes them to the moated manor house Groombridge Place where Mrs Wickland psychically identifies herself with the spirit of a murdered ostler.

1930   Conan Doyle publishes his collection of essays on spiritualism, *The Edge of the Unknown*. Most of the material in the book had appeared previously in newspapers and journals from 1920 onwards, but Conan Doyle had extensively revised many of them, especially the essay on 'The Alleged Posthumous Writings of Known Authors'.

January 1930   *The Journal of the Society for Psychical Research* publishes an attack on the seances held at Millesimo Castle, Italy, by the Marquis Scotto. Conan Doyle, a friend of the Marquis, resigns from the

Society and circulates a letter among fellow members, attacking the review. He maintains that, since the death of F.W.H. Myers, the Society has done no constructive work of any kind.

7 July 1930   In the early hours, Conan Doyle dies at his home, 'Windlesham', surrounded by his family. The funeral that follows is simple, Conan Doyle's body being burried in a grave by the summerhouse where he used to work.

13 July 1930   Eight thousand people fill the Albert Hall for Doyle's memorial service. The medium Estelle Roberts, a friend of the family, claims to have seen Conan Doyle's figure in evening dress walk to the empty chair between Jean and Denis.

28 July 1930   Lady Conan Doyle announces to the press that she has established communication with her husband through a spirit photograph.

February 1931   Lady Conan Doyle and Adrian–Lady Conan Doyle's younger son–attend a seance at the home of H. Dennis Bradley in Kingston Vale, London. Through the medium George Valiantine, they discuss family matters with Doyle for an hour and a half.

1940   Lady Conan Doyle dies, having been ill with cancer for a number of years. She continues to believe in her husband's spirit existence until the day of her death. In her last moments she cries out joyfully that she has seen those on the other side.

Bibliography

A The Spiritualist Writings of Arthur Conan Doyle

The New Revelation. London: Hodder & Stoughton, 1918 (88 pp.). New York: George H. Doran Co. (64 pp.).

Life After Death, 1918 (reprinted by the author from the *Daily Chronicle* of 5 November 1918), (2 pp.).

The Vital Message. London: Hodder & Stoughton, 1919 (116 pp.). New York: George H. Doran Co. (80 pp.).

Our Reply to the Cleric. London: Spiritualists' National Union, 1920 (8 pp.).

Spiritualism and Rationalism (with a Drastic Examination of Mr. Joseph McCabe). Hodder & Stoughton, 1920 (16 pp.).

The Wanderings of a Spiritualist. London: Hodder & Stoughton, 1921 (160 pp.). New York: George H. Doran Co. (152 pp.).

The Coming of the Fairies. London: Hodder & Stoughton, 1922 (72 pp.). New York: George H. Doran Co. (98 pp.).

Spiritualism–Some Straight Questions and Direct Answers. London: Two World Publishing Co., 1922 (2 pp.).

The Case for Spirit Photography. London: Hutchinson & Co., 1922 (56 pp.). New York: George H. Doran Co. (68 pp.).

Our American Adventure. London: Hodder & Stoughton, 1923 (104 pp.). New York: George H. Doran Co. (96 pp.).

Our Second American Adventure. London: Hodder & Stoughton, 1924 (128 pp.). Boston: Little, Brown & Co. (120 pp.).

Memories and Adventures. London: Hodder & Stoughton, 1924 (208 pp.). Boston: Little, Brown & Co. (212 pp.).

The Early Christian Church and Modern Spiritualism. London: Psychic Bookshop and Library, 1925 (6 pp.).

Psychic Experiences. New York: G.P. Putnam's Sons, 1925 (14 pp.).

The History of Spiritualism. London: Cassell & Co., 1926 (2 vols.: vol 1 180 pp., vol 2 176 pp.). New York: George H. Doran Co. (as above).

Pheneas Speaks–Direct Communications in the Family Circle Reported by Arthur Conan Doyle, M.D., LL.D. London: The Psychic Press and Bookshop, 1927 (112 pp.). New York: George H. Doran Co. (100 pp.).

Spiritualism. London: The Psychic Bookshop, c.1927 (1 p.).

What Does Spiritualism Actually Teach and Stand For? London: The Psychic Bookshop, 1928 (8 pp.).

A Word of Warning. London: The Psychic Press, 1928 (10 pp.).

An Open Letter to Those of My Generation. London: The Psychic Press, 1929 (6 pp.).

Our African Winter. London: John Murray, 1929 (152 pp.). Toronto: The Ryerson Press.

The Roman Catholic Church–A Rejoinder. London: The Psychic Press, 1929 (36 pp.).

The Edge of the Unknown. London: John Murray, 1930 (170 pp.). New York: G.P. Putnam's Sons (169 pp.).

B A Checklist of the Supernatural Stories of Arthur Conan Doyle

'The Ghosts of Goresthorpe Grange', *London Society*, vol. 44, 1883.

'The Captain of The Polestar', *Temple Bar*, January 1883.

'John Barrington Cowles', *Cassell's Saturday Journal*, April 1884.

'The Great Keinplatz Experiment', *Belgravia Magazine*, July 1885

'A Literary Mosaic', *Boys' Own Paper*, Christmas 1886.

'Uncle Jeremy's Household', *Boys' Own Paper*, January–March 1887.

The Mystery of Cloomber. London: Ward & Downey, 1888.

'The Ring of Thoth', *Cornhill Magazine*, January 1890.

'De Profundis', *The Idler*, March 1892.

'Lot No. 249', *Harper's Magazine*, September 1892.

The Parasite. London: Constable & Co., 1894.

'The Fiend of the Cooperage', *Manchester Weekly Times*, 1 October 1897.

'The Sealed Room', *Strand Magazine*, September 1898.

'The Japanned Box', *Strand Magazine*, January 1899.

'The Brown Hand', *Strand Magazine*, May 1899.

'Playing With Fire', *Strand Magazine*, March 1900.

The Hound of the Baskervilles. London: George Newnes, 1902.

'The Leather Funnel', *Strand Magazine*, June 1903.

'The Silver Mirror', *Strand Magazine*, August 1908.

'The Terror of Blue John Gap', *Strand Magazine*, August 1910.

'Through the Veil', published in *The Last Galley*. London: Smith, Elder & Co., 1911.

'How It Happened', *Strand Magazine*, September 1913.

'The Horror of the Heights', *Strand Magazine*, November 1913.

The Land of Mist. London: Hutchinson & Co., 1926.

C Arthur Conan Doyle: Works of Biographical and Related Interest

Bond, Michael, *The Doyle Diary*. London: Paddington Press, 1978.

Carr, John Dickson, *The Life of Sir Arthur Conan Doyle*. London: John Murray, 1949.

Cooke, Ivan (ed.), *The Return of Sir Arthur Conan Doyle*. Hampshire: The White Eagle Publishing Trust, 1956. Reprinted 1963.

Doyle, Adrian M. Conan, *The True Conan Doyle*. London: John Murray, 1945.

Doyle, Richard, *In Fairyland: A Series of Pictures from the Elf-World*. London: Michael Joseph Webb & Bower, 1979.

—, *Richard Doyle's Journal* (1840), ed. C. Wheeler. London: Bartholomew, 1980.

Drayson, Alfred Wilkes, *The Earth We Inhabit, Its Past, Present and Possible Future*. London, 1859.

Edwards, Owen Dudley, *The Quest for Sherlock Holmes*. Edinburgh: Mainstream, 1983.

Ernst, Bernard M.L., and Carrington, Hereward, *Houdini and Conan Doyle: The Story of a Strange Friendship*. London: Hutchinson, 1933.

Forster, Lieut.-Col D., *The Vital Choice: End or Calvary? A Reply to Sir A. Conan Doyle's 'The New Revelation'*. London: Morgan & Scott, 1919.

Gardner, Edward Lewis. *Fairies: The Cottingley Photos and Their Sequel*. London: Theosophical Publishing House, 1945.

Green, Richard Lancelyn, and Gibson, John Michael, *A*

Bibliography of A. Conan Doyle. Oxford University Press, 1983.

Higham, Charles, *The Adventures of Conan Doyle.* London: Hamish Hamilton, 1976.

Lamond, J., *Arthur Conan Doyle, A Memoir (with an Epilogue by Lady Conan Doyle).* London: John Murray, 1931.

Moseley, Sidney A., *An Amazing Seance and an Exposure.* London: Sampson Low, Maston & Co., 1919.

—, *The Mysterious Medium.* London: Stanley, Paul & Co., 1924.

Nordon, Pierre, *Conan Doyle.* London: John Murray, 1966.

Pearson, Hesketh, *Conan Doyle, His Life and Art.* London: Methuen, 1943.

Stavert, Geoffrey, *A Study in Southsea.* Portsmouth: Milestone Publications, 1987.

Wilson, J.M., *Life After Death: Two Lectures on Christianity and Spiritualism with replies by Sir A. Conan Doyle.* London: Hodder & Stoughton, 1920.

D Works Relating to Spiritualism

Barrett, William, *On the Threshold of the Unseen.* London: Kegan Paul, Trench, Trübner & Co., 1918.

Bayley, Harold (ed.), *The Undiscovered Country, 1874-1918.* London: Cassell, 1918.

Blunsdon, Norman, *A Popular Dictionary of Spiritualism.* London: Arco, 1961.

Brath, Stanley de, *The Physical Phenomena of Spiritualism.* London: LSA Publications, 1947.

Carrington, Hereward, *The Invisible World.* London: Rider & Co., 1947.

Coates, J., *Photographing the Invisible.* London, 1921.

Crawford, Dr W.J., *The Reality of Psychic Phenomena.* London: Watkins, 1917.

—, *Experiments in Psychical Science.* London: Watkins, 1919.

—, *Psychic Structures at the Goligher Circle.* London: Watkins, 1921.

Crookes, William, *Researches in the Phenomena of Spiritualism.* London: Two Worlds Publishing Co./Psychic Bookshop, 1926.

Edmunds, Simeon, *Spiritualism: A General Survey.* London, 1966.

Geley, Gustave, *Clairvoyance and Materialization. A Record of Experiments.* London: T. Fisher Unwin, 1927.

Gurney, Edmund, Myers, F.W.H., and Podmore, Frank, *Phantasms of the Living*, 2 vols. London: Rooms of the Society for Psychical Research, 1886.

Hall, Trevor, *The Spiritualists*. London: Duckworth, 1962.

—, *New Light on Old Ghosts*. London: Duckworth, 1965.

Henslow, Rev. Prof. G., *The Proofs of the Truths of Spiritualism*. London: Kegan Paul, Trench, Trübner & Co., 1919.

Hill, J. Arthur, *Spiritualism, Its History, Phenomena and Doctrine*. London: Cassell, 1918.

Houdini, Harry, *A Magician Among the Spirits*. London and New York: Harper & Bros., 1924.

Kellock, Harold, *Houdini, His Life Story*. London: Heinemann, 1928.

Kernahan, Coulson, *'Black Objects': Plain Speaking and Painful Facts About Spiritualism*. London: Religious Tract Society, 1920.

Lodge, Sir Oliver, *Demonstrated Survival*. London: London Spiritualist Alliance, 1930.

—, *Raymond, Or Life After Death*. Methuen & Co., 1916.

—, *The Reality of a Spiritual World*. London: Benn, 1930.

Lombroso, Cesare, *After Death, What? (Spiritistic Phenomena and Their Interpretation* London: T.Fisher Unwin, 1909.

McCabe, Joseph, *Is Spiritualism Based on Fraud?* London: Watts & Co., 1920.

Milbourne, Christopher, *Houdini: The Untold Story*. London: Cassell, 1969.

Moses, William Stainton, *More Spirit Teachings*. London: The Spiritualist Press, 1952.

Murchison, C. (ed.), *The Case For and Against Psychical Belief*. Massachusetts: Clark University, 1927.

Myers, F.W.H., *Human Personality and Its Survival of Bodily Death*, 2 vols. New York: Longmans, Green & Co., 1903.

Owen, George Vale, *The Life Beyond the Veil*. London: Butterworth, 1919.

Patrick, C. Vincent, and Smith, W. Whateley, *The Case Against Spirit Photography*. London: Kegan Paul, Trench, Trübner & Co., 1921.

Pearsall, Ronald, *The Table Rappers*. London: Michael Joseph, 1972.

Price, Harry, *Fifty Years of Psychical Research*. London and New York: Longman Green & Co., 1939.

—, and Dingwall, Eric J. (eds.), *Revelations of a Spirit Medium*. London: Kegan Paul, Trench, Trübner & Co., 1922.

Richet, Charles, *Thirty Years of Psychical Research*. London: Collins, 1923.

Schrenck-Notzing, Baron von, *Phenomena of Materialization*. London: Kegan Paul, Trench, Trübner & Co., 1920.

Stoddart, Jane T., *The Case Against Spiritualism*. London: Hodder & Stoughton, 1919.

Thurston, Fr Herbert, *Modern Spiritualism*. London: Sheen & Ward, 1928.

Truedell, John W., *The Bottom Facts Concerning the Science of Spiritualism Derived from Careful Investigation, Covering a Period of 25 years*. New York: G.W. Dillingham, 1892.

Vesme, Count Caesar B. de, *A History of Experimental Spiritualism*, 2 vols. London: Rider & Co., 1931.

Warrick, F.W., *Experiments in Psychics*. London: Rider & Co., 1939.

Whitehead, George, *Spiritualism Explained*. London: Watts & Co., 1928.

Wickland, Carl August, *Thirty Years Among the Dead*. London: The Spiritualist Press, 1924.

Index

Stavert, Geoffrey, 49, 59
Stonyhurst, 20-21

Thomas brothers, 124-6
Thurston, Herbert, 25, 221-2

Valiantine, George, 225-6

Waller, Bryan Charles, 30
Wells, H. G., 214-15
Wilson, Canon James, 132
Witchcraft Act, 219-20, 223
Wright, Elsie, 158

Young, Filson, 167-8